Small Wonders

Nature Education for Young Children

by
Linda Garrett and Hannah Thomas

Illustrated by
Hilary Elmer

Published by
Vermont Institute of Natural Science
Woodstock, Vermont

Distributed by
University Press of New England
Hanover and London

Published by Vermont Institute of Natural Science, Woodstock, Vermont

Printed in the United States

Library of Congress Cataloging-in-Publication Data
Garrett, Linda
    Small wonders : nature education for young children / Linda Garrett and Hannah Thomas ; illustrated by Hilary Elmer.
        p. cm.
Includes bibliographical reference and index.
ISBN-13: 978-1-58465-574-9 (pbk. : alk. paper)
ISBN-10: 1-58465-574-7 (pbk. : alk.paper)
1. Science–Study and teaching (Preschool) 2. Nature study. 3. Education, Preschool–Activity programs. 1. Thomas, Hannah. II. Title.
    LB1140.5.S35G37 2005
    372.3'5–dc22
                    2005030643

Credits:

p.131, Chipmunk Beds in Chipmunks and Their Cousins was adapted from *Mother Goose Meets Mother Nature* by Linda Garrett and Pat Straughan, the Vermont Center for the Book, 2000.

p. 141 Language Activity/Song in Life Underground is by Bascom Lamar Lunsford.

p. 154 Snowmen activity in The Snow's My Home was contributed by Sandra Drown.

p. 166 Owl Puppets activity in Owls: Nighttime Hunters was adapted from *Mother Goose Meets Mother Nature* by Linda Garrett and Pat Straughan, Vermont Center for the Book, 1997.

p. 170 *Small Wonders* at Home activity in Owls: Nighttime Hunters was adapted from *Mother Goose Meets Mother Nature* by Linda Garrett and Pat Straughan, Vermont Center for the Book, 1997.

p. 231 Water Can Float Things activity in Wild about Water was adapted from *Mother Goose Asks Why? Program Leader Manual,* Vermont Center for the Book, 1998.

Illustrator: Hilary Elmer
Photographers: Linda Garrett, Steve Faccio, Sharon Plumb, Cathy Glass, Dan Lambert, Corbis, and Brenda Hillier

Produced by RavenMark, Inc., Montpelier, Vermont
info@ravenmark.com

Printed on recycled paper.

Small Wonders is the product of more than thirty years' experience in environmental education at the Vermont Institute of Natural Science (VINS). VINS is a non-profit membership organization whose mission is *to protect Vermont's natural heritage through education and research designed to engage individuals and communities in the active care of their environment.* In addition to *Small Wonders*, the Vermont Institute of Natural Science publishes *Hands-On Nature*, an environmental education resource for elementary school-aged children.

Additional information on VINS' publications, programs, and research may be found at www.vinsweb.org

TABLE OF CONTENTS

PREFACE

For more than 30 years, the Vermont Institute of Natural Science (VINS) has offered nature-related presentations, curricula, and other learning opportunities for elementary-school age children, adolescents, and adults. The Environmental Learning for the Future (ELF) program at VINS reaches thousands of elementary-aged children every month and was the basis of the award-winning VINS publication, *Hands-On Nature*. As its environmental education programs continued to develop, VINS became eager to touch the hearts and minds of our youngest learners through lessons that address their unique developmental abilities and interests. In 1997, the Vermont Institute of Natural Science launched its Small Wonders educational program for children ages 3 to 5 and their adult caregivers. *Small Wonders: Nature Education for Young Children* provides a collection of activities and experiences that have grown out of the hands-on, multi-disciplinary approach of VINS Small Wonders program.

With Gratitude

Like a tiny seed transformed into a vibrantly mature tree, this book has grown and blossomed with the loving care of many.

Financial contributions have allowed the seed of a mere idea – a nature study program designed especially for young children – preschool and kindergarten age – to sprout into a reality. At the onset, the Henderson Family Foundation helped VINS to develop the first Small Wonders teaching units and to launch a first-class series for teachers and child care providers. Subsequent grants from the Fieldstone Foundation, the Vermont Community Fund, Chittenden Bank's "Card for Kids" program, and the New Hampshire Charitable Foundation's Wellborn Ecology Fund have allowed Small Wonders to grow and extend its roots into every region of our small state of Vermont and beyond. Finally, thanks to the generous support of the Canaday Foundation, Small Wonders was given a chance to expand in both content and audience, and, ultimately, to be transformed into the book you now hold in your hands.

We also extend our sincere thanks to the hundreds of Vermont and New Hampshire preschool and kindergarten teachers, child care providers, children's librarians, and other early childhood educators who've participated in our Small Wonders courses over the years. Your reflections, questions, and suggestions inspired us to keep revising in an effort to make this book a useful tool for adults and young children eager to learn about nature. Your enthusiasm, creativity, and unwavering dedication to the young children in your care are truly heartwarming.

To transplant the already thriving Small Wonders curriculum and courses into a written book form was a task both daunting and, ultimately, extremely fulfilling. My greatest pleasure was working with Hannah Thomas and Heather Behrens (with myself, the Small Wonders revision team) to pilot test activities with eager young children and teachers, to search our brains for effective and creative ideas, and, finally, to put our thoughts to paper. When my own life circumstances changed, Hannah Thomas stepped forward to assume the role of revision team leader. Her keen eye, gentle prodding, and organizational talents kept this project moving forward. Words can only convey so much, though, and I'm immensely grateful for the artistic talents and untiring work of our project illustrator, Hilary Elmer. Also deserving great thanks are several other VINS staff members who've added their wonderful contributions to the Small Wonders soup: Marlys Eddy, Lisa Greene, Win Johnson, Sharon Plumb, Lisa Purcell, Susan Sawyer, and Marcia Whitney. It's been my great pleasure to work with each and every one of you.

Beyond VINS, a project such as this book requires the professional expertise of people deeply engaged in the magic of transforming an idea into a text. In particular, I would like to thank Linda Mirabile, Rebecca Davison, and the team at RavenMark for their excellent design, editorial, and marketing work, their generosity of their time and expertise as they guided us throughout the process. This project reflects a wonderful blend of their creativity and ours.

Last but not least, sincere thanks and admiration must be given to the audience without whom this book would have no purpose – the children. Their eager faces, probing questions, boundless curiosity, and joyful exuberance informed this project more than any adult editor could ever do.

Gratefully,

Linda Garrett, *Small Wonders Founder*

HOW TO USE THIS BOOK

A child's world is fresh and new and beautiful, full of wonder and excitement.
~ Rachel Carson

Biologist and author Rachel Carson, who awakened the American conservation movement in the 1960s with her book, *Silent Spring,* had a soft spot in her heart for young children. It is no wonder why. Although it's all too often fleeting, the young child's sense of wonder is both inspiring and deeply heartening.

You can see it in the way their eyes widen and their tiny fingers reach to gently touch a robin's egg, in the way they blow kisses to a monarch butterfly before it continues on its long migration to Mexico, as they skip through a field of dandelions collecting blossoms for a flower crown. Young children teach us a valuable lesson about making the most of the moment at hand. When they pretend – with all their hearts – to be mice running from hungry owls, we adults can't help but admire their enormous capacity for empathy.

Given opportunities to discover nature, preschool age children not only experience the natural world to its fullest extent, they use those experiences to form important and lasting attitudes toward nature. From the seeds of nature awareness and experience, come the fruits of appreciation, understanding, and, ultimately, responsibility.

THE SMALL WONDERS APPROACH

Small Wonders represents a desire to reach young learners through a nature education program that is rooted in imagination and experience, yet also rich in science content. The approach is multidisciplinary, with attention to language arts, movement, music, and visual arts in addition to science. Lessons have been designed to include activities that develop a variety of developmentally appropriate skills, including observing, noting similarities and differences, sorting, and classifying. School readiness skills, such as listening, color/shape/letter/ number recognition, following directions, and cooperative learning, are also incorporated throughout. Within any unit, caregivers can find activities that engage children's diverse learning styles through visual, oral, and kinesthetic methods, as well as opportunities for inquiry-based learning that provide open avenues for child-directed creativity and decision making.

At the heart of the *Small Wonders* approach is the desire to have children experience the topics they are learning about. Rather than telling children about the habits of mice, *Small Wonders* activities encourage leaders to ask the children to pretend to be mice scurrying away from danger or searching for food in a dark room, and then to reflect upon the experience. Children who participate in *Small Wonders* lessons role play, imitate, imagine, question, experiment, and create – all the while learning a great deal of specific information about animals, plants, and the entire world of nature. By participating in the outdoor activities included in each unit, young learners are given the opportunity to connect the lessons and projects they engage in within the classroom to the natural communities that surround them. Critical to the outdoor experience is the modeling of appropriate behavior and gentle guidance that the adults provide. The ultimate goal of the units within *Small Wonders* is to provide an access point through which young children, their caregivers, and families begin noticing, spending time in, and wanting to learn more about the fascinating world of nature.

GENERAL ORGANIZATION

The activities within *Small Wonders* are divided into three themes: Growth and Change, Animal Homes, and Connections to Nature. Within each theme are eight units, each addressing a focused topic in nature and science directly related to the theme. (For example, "Beautiful Butterflies" in the Growth and Change theme introduces the transformation a caterpillar experiences during its life cycle.) Each group of eight units is arranged in a general autumn to summer seasonal progression.

Every *Small Wonders* unit begins with a "Digging In" section that provides background information to help leaders become comfortable with and build enthusiasm for the topic at hand. This information is not specifically intended to be shared with the children but can be extremely helpful in creating teachable moments that add depth to a lesson or when answering the many questions young learners are bound to come up with. The activities that follow the "Digging In" section are grouped into specific categories: indoor activities, outdoor activities, crafts and projects, snack ideas, and a language activity. Each indoor activity includes a "Talk about. . ." section that provides background and discussion questions specific to the activity. The information and questions you use from the "Talk about. . ." section will vary depending on the interests and abilities of the children you are working with. Bold words that appear throughout the book are defined in the glossary.

Every unit also suggests ideas for independent play and has a reproducible "Small Wonders at Home" page that can be used as a home-school link. The "We Care about. . ." section presents simple environmental stewardship information and/or activities that you can do with the children. Finally, each unit provides a list of fiction and nonfiction books for children as well as reference books for adults that relate to the theme of the unit.

MATERIALS AND EQUIPMENT

Every activity includes a list of needed materials before the activity description. Nearly all of the activities outlined in *Small Wonders* may be completed using materials that are readily available in the classroom and/or community. Reproducible illustrations are provided throughout each unit for activities that require specific illustrations. Appendix A, "Equipping the Classroom for Small Wonders Nature Studies," provides information on materials you may wish to gather in advance, simple materials that you can create to augment your outdoor explorations, as well as information on where to find additional books and materials for those who wish to expand their nature exploration collections.

CUSTOMIZING *SMALL WONDERS* ACTIVITIES TO YOUR NEEDS

As a user of the information contained within this book, you may choose to focus on a theme to be taught throughout the year, or on a series of units or activities chosen from throughout the book. *Small Wonders* has been designed to present a balance of indoor and outdoor activities as well as crafts and projects. A wide range of activity options is presented within each lesson. Not all of the activities may be appropriate for the age you are teaching, but you should be able to find an array of options that will appeal to – and suit the abilities of – three, four, and five-year olds within each unit. To present children with a well-rounded program, we suggest selecting a variety of activities from each category as you plan your explorations.

GROWTH AND CHANGE

GROWTH AND CHANGE

Nature is constantly growing and changing. The seasons progress from winter to spring to summer to fall to winter again. Butterflies lay eggs, caterpillars hatch, grow, and turn into butterflies. Even the rocks around us are slowly changing: weathering and eroding, going from rocks to sand. In nature, such changes are cyclical: seasons come and go, butterflies lay eggs, die, and are born, rocks turn to sand and back into stone.

Young children are just beginning to develop an awareness of the changes occurring around them. They watch in amazement as leaves fall to the ground in autumn and then reappear again in the spring. Their families exclaim over how much their children have grown in a year, and the children watch the growth marks moving up a door frame. Every day brings new abilities, accomplishments, and understandings, whether they be stringing words into sentences, successfully writing a name, or correctly identifying a winter bird at a feeder.

The Growth and Change theme provides opportunities to peek into a bird's nest, to pretend to be animals preparing for winter, and to learn about a wide variety of life cycles. As they experience activities in this theme, young children will discover that nature is growing and changing right along with them.

Growing Grasshoppers

Focus: Grasshoppers are easily caught and observed by children and adults alike. Studying grasshopper life cycles, behaviors, and physical features provides general knowledge about insects and insight into the lives of these common creatures.

Objective: To teach children about the life cycles of grasshoppers, as well as the food they eat and their adaptations, and to spend time outdoors helping children to learn how to handle live insects and develop observation skills.

Extra Information for Adult Leaders

Grasshoppers appear in late spring and early summer, when their **nymphs** hatch from eggs laid by females the previous fall. Some insects (like butterflies and ladybugs) have larvae that look completely different than the adults and must undergo a **complete metamorphosis**, or change, before maturing. Grasshopper nymphs, however, resemble miniature adults with the exception that they lack wings and are smaller in size. The nymphs go through an **incomplete metamorphosis** as they grow into adults.

Like all insects, grasshoppers have three body parts: the head, **thorax**, and **abdomen**. A single pair of **antennae** sprout from the head, and the grasshopper's six legs and wings are attached at the thorax. **Spiracles**, tiny holes through which grasshoppers breathe, are found on the abdomen.

While our bodies are supported by bones, a grasshopper's is supported and protected by its **exoskeleton**, a hard outer covering made out of **chitin** (a substance comparable to our fingernails). Because their hardness prevents them from increasing in size, exoskeletons must be shed, or **molted**, as the grasshopper grows. Just prior to a molt, glands secrete a new, flexible skin below the old one. Growth begins as soon as the grasshopper splits and climbs out of its old skin and continues until the new skin is completely hardened. A nymph matures in about sixty days, over which it will molt five times, increasing in size and developing wings.

Grasshoppers are built for jumping. Hind legs that are almost three times longer than the front legs give the insect spring. The upper leg joint is enlarged to house jumping muscles, and spines at the

DIGGING IN...

bottom of the back leg provide traction. Many **species** also use their wings as a parachute to increase their time in the air.

The legs of some grasshoppers also house the equivalent of an ear, which is used to locate other grasshoppers through their calls.

Short-horned grasshoppers (those with antennae shorter than the length of their bodies) call by rubbing raised veins on their wing covers with a scraper on their hind legs. Grasshoppers with antennae longer than their bodies, the **long-horned grasshoppers**, make sound by rubbing their wings together. Additional sounds may be produced by grinding **mandibles** (mouth parts), drumming with the hind legs or abdomen, or beating wings in flight. All are displays to attract females or discourage opponents.

As grasshoppers mature throughout the summer, their chorus becomes stronger and stronger, until it climaxes in late summer and early fall. As the days become cooler and shorter, the females pierce the earth using their **ovipositors** (often visible at the hind end of the abdomen) and lay their eggs in the soil. Finally, as frosts approach, the grasshoppers cease calling and the adults die off, leaving eggs to lay dormant within the earth until the days warm again and nymphs appear.

adult red-legged grasshopper

Indoor Activities

HAPPY HOPPERS

Objective: To take a close look at some real, live grasshoppers.

Materials:
- live grasshoppers
- large plastic or glass jar with nylon stocking stretched over top, or other suitable collecting container with air holes
- bug boxes with magnifier tops (see Appendix A)
- paper or chalkboard to record children's observations and questions

Activity:
1. Display the grasshoppers so all can see.
2. Allow the children to make observations and ask questions.
3. Record what they say as "things we notice about the grasshoppers" or "questions we have about the grasshoppers." Tell the children you'll help them to find answers to their questions either during the activities or later in some books about grasshoppers.

Talk about the parts of a grasshopper's body: head, thorax, abdomen, four wings, antennae, and mouth with its sharp mandibles for cutting grass and short **palps** for manipulating small pieces of food. Talk about how the grasshopper's color helps it **camouflage** itself in its grassy home.

• •

"NYMPH GROWS UP" PUPPET SHOW

Objective: To introduce basic physical features of grasshoppers and to introduce the word "metamorphosis."

Materials:
- puppet show script (see end of unit)
- puppets: nymph and adult grasshopper (see end of unit)
- collection of live grasshoppers
- another (2nd) grasshopper container
- butterfly metamorphosis illustration (see "Butterflies: Flying Flowers" unit in Growth and Change) (optional)
- color photo of an adult grasshopper (optional)

Activity:
1. Present the puppet show for the children. Afterwards, talk about the grasshopper's physical adaptations and metamorphosis.
2. Compare the metamorphosis of a grasshopper (egg to nymph to adult) to that of a butterfly (egg to **caterpillar** to **chrysalis** to adult).
3. If available, show a color photo of a grasshopper to the children. Ask them, "Is this a baby (nymph) or a grownup (adult) grasshopper?" An adult can be identified by its wings. Notice other features of the grasshopper as well.
4. Return to your live grasshopper collection. Help the children to sort the nymphs from the adults using the second collection container. How many do you have of each?

Talk about how the grasshopper's body changes through incomplete metamorphosis. The grasshopper changes from an egg to a small nymph, then to successively larger nymphs, and finally to an adult grasshopper. The grasshopper nymph looks just like a small adult, except it lacks wings.

GROWING GRASSHOPPERS

Objective: *To practice sequencing grasshoppers from smallest to largest.*

Materials: • grasshopper nymph and adult illustrations

Activity:

1. To prepare, copy the grasshopper illustrations into progressively larger sizes (the smaller ones should be nymphs, the largest should be the adult)
2. In a small group, give each child one grasshopper illustration card.
3. Holding the cards in front of them, have the children order the illustrations (and themselves) from smallest to largest. Notice the point where the wingless nymph changes to the winged adult.

Talk about the grasshopper's growth. As grasshoppers grow bigger, they get too big for their "skins" (actually their exoskeletons or outside shells), so they must shed them. First, a little split or rip appears on the grasshopper's back, then the grasshopper slips out of its old skin. A new, bigger one is underneath. After a few hours, that larger, soft skin grows hard, like a shell. This process is called molting. Usually, a grasshopper molts about six times in its life.

Ask the children to imagine what would happen if they tried to wear the same clothes they wore when they were just two years old. They would be too small! The seams would tear and split! It's the same with grasshoppers (and other insects), but luckily they have another "set of clothes" under the old ones.

• •

I'M A GROWING GRASSHOPPER

Objective: *To imagine what it might feel like to be a grasshopper molting.*

Materials: • newspaper
• masking tape

Activity:

1. Tape together a couple of sheets of newspaper.
2. Ask for a volunteer to be a growing grasshopper.
3. Securely tape the newspaper around that person's body (arms inside). The grasshopper then pretends to grow larger, finally splitting open his/her newspaper "exoskeleton."

Talk about how insects often swell themselves with air to split open their old skeletons. Sometimes it is possible to find these old exoskeletons on the ground, attached to vegetation, or in other natural places.

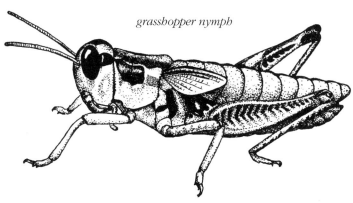

grasshopper nymph

WHAT'S FOR DINNER?

Objective: *To notice one way grasshoppers and people are alike – we both eat grasses.*

Materials:
- a complete grass plant with roots, stem, and leaves
- several dinner plates
- a variety of grass plant-origin foods for people (flour, crackers, sugar, corn, oatmeal, cereal, rice)
- a variety of non-grass plant foods for people (fruit, vegetables)

Activity:
1. Show the grass plant to the children. Very briefly describe the characteristics that help you know this plant is a grass plant:
   - overall tall skinny shape of plant
   - thick mat of roots
   - division of the stem into sections
   - way the leaves wrap around the stem before spreading open
   - long, narrow shape of the leaves
   - cluster(s) of flowers or seeds
2. Ask the children, "What do grasshoppers eat?" (They eat grass, as well as other leafy plants.) Now ask, "Do people eat grass?" (Yes. We eat many foods that come from grass plants.)
3. Display all the foods together on a table, along with the plates.
4. Ask the children to examine the foods on the table. These are all foods people eat.
5. Ask them to put on the plates any foods they think might come from plants. Explain they all actually come from plants. Within the group, point out the ones that come from grass plants.

Talk about the surprising number and variety of foods we eat that come from grasses. Unlike grasshoppers, however, people must process the plants somehow (cooking, separating the grain from the remainder of the plant, grinding it into flour, etc.) in order to eat them. Grasshoppers, of course, don't do that. They just eat the plant as it is. As an extension, encourage the children to try grinding some grass seeds (wheat berries or corn) into flour. Is it hard work?

· ·

GRASSHOPPER EGGS

Objective: *To practice counting and to recognize that grasshopper eggs are laid in the ground.*

Materials:
- several small jars, each wrapped with brown paper to simulate dirt
- mini marshmallows
- cards with numbering from 1 to 10 or so

Activity:
1. Ask the children, "Do you remember what grasshopper nymphs come from?" They come from eggs. After mating, the mother grasshopper lays her eggs in soft soil. She may lay anywhere between three and 100 eggs at a time, depending on the grasshopper species, as well as environmental conditions.
2. Place a number card and a handful of mini marshmallows next to each jar.
3. Challenge the children to count the correct number of marshmallows into each jar.

Talk about how a female grasshopper, after mating, uses a needle-like "ovipositor" located in the rear of her body to place her eggs into the soft ground. If the eggs are laid early in the summer, the eggs can hatch in just a few weeks. But if the eggs are laid later in the season, they'll remain as eggs all fall, winter, and spring; they'll hatch the following summer when food is again available.

GRASSHOPPER EYES

Objective: *To learn about typical insect eyes.*

Materials:
- several live grasshoppers in containers with air holes or in magnifying bug boxes (1 per 2 or so children)
- grasshopper head illustrations shown here
- crayons (optional)

Activity:
1. Help the children to look for eyes on the grasshopper's head.
2. How many eyes do they count? What do they look like? Use the grasshopper head drawing to illustrate their comments, coloring it in or adding detail as necessary.
3. Share with the children that grasshoppers have two large eyes (**compound eyes**), and the three black dots in a triangle that are called **simple eyes**. Describe the purpose of each type of eye.

Talk about the different roles of a grasshopper's eyes. The compound eyes are made of thousands of separate facets, or lenses, which focus light rays. Each lens receives a small bit of light from a section of the total scene that the insect sees. In other words, each lens "sees" just one small part of the entire scene. The separate images are combined to form the whole picture. (Note: Unlike what common toy store variety "insect eye" toys seem to suggest, the insect does not see many duplications of the same scene; instead, it sees one scene broken into many separate images or sections.) Compound eyes do not focus between near and far like ours do. They are probably best at seeing images that are close to the insect, and they excel at detecting motion. The three simple eyes can detect the difference between light and dark but cannot see images.

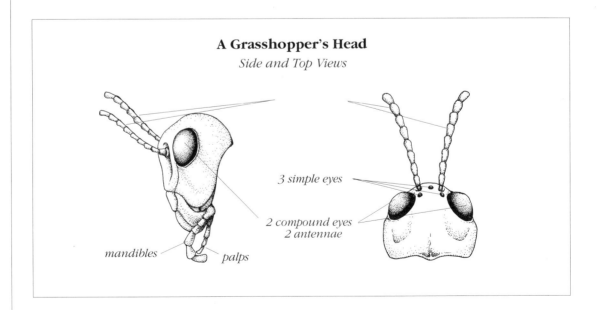

A Grasshopper's Head
Side and Top Views

3 simple eyes

2 compound eyes
2 antennae

mandibles   palps

I HAVE SIMPLE EYES!

Objective:	*To compare our eyes to a grasshopper's simple eyes.*
Materials:	• bright light source, either a window, lamp, or movable light, such as a large camp flashlight or battery lantern
Activity:	1. Have the children sit in a group in the room.
	2. Tell them to close their eyes.
	3. Turn off the lights in the room. Open the window shades or turn on the bright lamp.
	4. Encourage the children to keep their eyes closed and look up and down, left and right.
	5. Ask them to point to the light, then open their eyes.
	6. How did the children know where the light was?
	7. Play the game again, only move the light around the room and have the children point toward the light source. (Optional)

Talk about what the children saw. Where was the light coming from? How did they know? How do the children think a grasshopper uses its simple eyes?

Outdoor Activities

HOPPER CATCHING

What You Need
- sweep nets (see Appendix A)
- bug boxes
- secure collecting container

What to Do

Use a sweep net or just your hands to (carefully) catch some grasshoppers. You can collect them temporarily in a jar or container with sufficient air holes. Can you find some nymphs, as well as some adults?

Note: In defense, grasshoppers will sometimes poop in the hands of catchers. They also may regurgitate a drop of brown liquid into the hand of any handlers that squeeze them (the liquid is recently eaten plant material). You might want to warn the children of these possibilities.

• •

CLEAN LIKE A GRASSHOPPER

What You Need
- jars with grasshoppers for observation (1 per 2 or 3 children)

What to Do

Divide children into groups of two or three. Encourage them to observe the grasshoppers in the jar for a few moments. What do the children think they are doing? Eating? Sleeping? Fighting? One behavior that the children may notice is cleaning. Grasshoppers spend a tremendous amount of time keeping their bodies clean.

Many species of grasshoppers pull their antennae through their mouths to clean them. The body is cleaned with the legs and feet; and the face is washed by using the legs to moistening it with saliva or wiping it on the ground.

Have the children pretend to be grasshoppers cleaning themselves. Have them grab imaginary antennae and run them through their mouths. Encourage them to try to use their legs to clean their bodies. Show the children how to *pretend* to lick their hands and rub their faces or run their faces on the ground. (The children shouldn't actually do this.)

A DAY AT THE GRASSHOPPER RACES

What You Need
- an old sheet
- permanent marker

What to Do

To prepare, use a permanent marker to draw two concentric circles on the sheet, one small one in the center and another larger circle toward the edge. At race time, the children carefully release their grasshoppers into the center circle and cheer them on until the winner reaches the outer circle first.

I'M CALLING YOU!

What You Need
- blindfolds – 1 per child
- noisemakers (2 of each different sound) – 1 per child

What to Do

Remind the children that grasshoppers do not have voices. So, if they don't have voices, how can one grasshopper (say, a male) call to another grasshopper (say, a female)? Grasshoppers produce their "song," or **stridulation**, by rubbing their wings and/or legs. (Usually, it's the males who sing like this.) Ask the children to imitate this motion by rubbing their elbows against their legs.

Now blindfold the children and distribute the noisemakers (two of each). Encourage the children to find their partners. (If the children don't want to use blindfolds, they can shake their noisemakers behind their backs instead.)

We Care about... Grasshoppers

Teach children to be gentle when handling live grasshoppers and other creatures. They should always cup their hands around the insect's whole body and hold it close to the ground. This way, if the insect falls to the ground, there is less chance of internal or external injury. If walking with a grasshopper, step carefully and keep hands closed.

Remember: Grasshoppers may occasionally poop or spit up in the hands of their catchers. This is one way for such a tiny creature to defend or protect itself. Handling the grasshoppers very gently can help you avoid this sometimes unpleasant occurrence. Be sure to wash your hands after handling live animals.

Language Activity / Song

(To the tune of "Five Little Ducks")

Five little hoppers went out one day
Through the fields and far away
Mother hopper said, . . .
And four of the little hoppers came back.

Poor mama hopper went out one day,
Through the fields and far away
Poor mama hopper said, . . .
And all of the little hoppers came back!

[hold up five fingers]
[snaking hand, point far away]
[scrape plastic comb and knife together four times]
[hold up four fingers]
[keep counting down until you reach zero]

Crafts and Projects

GRASSHOPPER GROWS UP WHEEL

What You Need
- paper plates or cardboard pizza rounds (1 per child)
- rice, which will represent the egg
- glue
- scissors
- markers and crayons
- paint brushes (1 per child)
- plastic lids
- grasshopper nymph illustration (1 per child)
- grasshopper adult illustrations (1 per child)

What to Do
First ask the children to color the grasshopper nymph and adult illustrations. Then, using the glue and brushes, attach the pictures to the bottom half of the plate. Glue the rice to the top half. Draw colored arrows to show the direction of the grasshopper's growth (from rice/egg to nymph to adult).

• •

GRASS SEED PICTURE

What You Need
- paper (optional: copy an enlarged picture of a grasshopper onto the sheet)
- seeds from grass (corn, rice, grass seed, wheat berries, oatmeal, etc.)
- glue
- markers or crayons

What to Do
Encourage children to use glue to make their own designs on the paper, then sprinkle seeds over the glue. Or, if you choose, use pages with an outline of a grasshopper copied on them and have children trace the lines or fill in the picture with glue and seeds.

Snacks

CORN COBBERS

What You Need
- frozen or fresh corn on the cob (1 piece per child)

What to Do

Now that many grocery stores carry frozen corn on the cob year round, it's easy to have this tasty treat any time of year – and it's a fun way to eat a favorite grass plant. Cook the corn according to the package directions, and enjoy with a little butter, if desired.

• •

GRASS PICNIC

What You Need
- variety of grass plant foods (wheat crackers, popcorn, rice cakes, oatmeal, etc.)

What to Do

Be grasshoppers! Enjoy a grassy snack made up of many grass plant foods such as wheat crackers, popcorn, rice cakes, and even oatmeal – preferably eaten in a field of tall grass!

Independent Play Ideas

1. Practice counting marshmallow "eggs" into jars.
2. Leave out a collecting container of live grasshoppers for the children to observe (without removing the hoppers!). If the hoppers will be observed in a jar, add some plant material and/or sticks for climbing and hiding and a damp cotton ball as a water source.

Book Ideas

CHILDREN'S FICTION

Grasshopper to the Rescue, a Georgian Story, translated by Bonny Carey, William Morrow, 1979 – an amusing folk tale about friendship.

CHILDREN'S NONFICTION

Bugs, by Nancy Winslow Parker and Joan Richards Wright, Greenwillow Books, 1987 – superbly illustrated, with possibilities for quick skimming or more in-depth reading to young children.

Chirping Crickets, by Melvin Berger, HarperCollins, 1998 – a very nice overview of a close relative of the grasshopper.

Grasshoppers, by Graham Coleman, Gareth Stevens, 1997 – a nice introduction, good pictures.

Grasshoppers and Crickets, by Theresa Greenaway, Raintree, 1999 – full of facts and pictures in an easy-to-read format, describes how to keep insects as pets.

Have You Seen Bugs, by Joanne Oppenheim, Scholastic, 1996 – a uniquely illustrated book introducing bugs – their habitats, unique features, and life cycles.

RESOURCE BOOKS FOR ADULTS AND CHILDREN

Facts about Insects, by Elizabeth Cooper, Steck-Vaughn Library, 1990 – a fine introduction to insects, their bodies and adaptations, filled with lots of great photos.

Grasshoppers, by Janet Halfmann, Smart Apple Media, 1999 – very informative, easy to read, and well laid-out, gives information about habitat, songs, life cycle, and more.

A Guide to Observing Insect Lives, by Donald W. Stokes, Little, Brown, 1983 – great information on why insects behave the way they do.

Insects, by Ellen Doris, Thames and Hudson, 1996 – a full resource book about many insects, geared toward helping kids learn.

Insects Under the Microscope, by Tamara Greene, Grolier Educational, 2000 – a series of excellent resource books, large in size with many pictures, that explains insects in depth, including such titles as "Lifecycles."

Insects and Spiders, by Janice VanCleave, Scholastic, 1998 – a teacher resource, filled with ideas for science fair-type experiments, many appropriate for younger children.

Joyful Noise, by Paul Fleischman, Harper Trophy, 1998 – an unusual collection of insect-inspired poems written for two voices (simultaneously reading).

PUPPET SHOW SCRIPT

"Nymph Grows Up"

Nymph – *[Off stage]* I think I can . . . RRrrrgh! . . . ummph . . . AARGH! Get . . . out . . . of . . . this egg *[popping noise]* HATCH!"

[On stage] I've Hatched! I'm so happy to be free of that egg and the dirt that I was laid in! There's more room out here! *[Breathe deeply and look around.]* Now. Down to business: What am I!?

Grasshopper – *[Leaps onto stage behind Nymph]* You're a Grasshopper!

Nymph – A grasshopper!?

Grasshopper – Well . . . a grasshopper nymph, to be exact. You've got some growing up yet to do, little one!

Nymph – *[Grumpy]* I don't know why I have to be a nymph. I'm not in an egg anymore. I'm not a baby. I'm ready to go.

Grasshopper – Well . . . you aren't as big as I am.

Nymph – But, look! I've got six legs, just like you! *[Nodding at grasshopper's legs.]* One, Two, Three, Four, Five, Six!

Grasshopper – Yes, but . . . .

Nymph – And look! I've got five eyes, just like you – three on top, two below *[looks on top of Grasshopper's head, then in front].*

Grasshopper – *[Quickly]* But do you have wings!?

Nymph – *[Reluctantly]* No . . . . . . But I have three body parts: Look! One, Two, Three!!!!

Grasshopper – *[Slightly exasperated]* Yes, Nymph, you have a head, a thorax, and an abdomen – you look like me (except for the growing, and the wings) . . . but you also have some learning to do!

Nymph – What do you mean!?

Grasshopper – Well, Nymph, What do you eat!?

Nymph – Ummmmm . . . .cheeseburgers!?

Grasshopper – *[Laughing, now, and hopping over to a plant with Nymph]* – Noooo, Nymph, I can see I have some teaching to do! We eat plants! Our strong mandibles – our mouthparts – grind up the plants and then we can digest them.

Nymph – *[Munching on a leaf]* Mmmmmph! Good!

Grasshopper – Oh, and – the more you eat, the more you'll grow, and as you grow, you will have to molt.

Nymph – *[Doubtful]* Molt!?

Grasshopper – Yup. You'll split your old skin and shed it for a new, larger one.

Nymph – Yeeeaach!

Grasshopper – *[Trying to cheer Nymph up]* Oh, it's not so bad – the new skin feels great – all roomy and comfy. Say, check this out! We breathe through holes in our abdomen. Spiracles, they call them.

Nymph – Wow! You're a good teacher! I thought I had to use my mouth to breathe!

Grasshopper – The last thing you have to learn about is your wings.

Nymph – My wings! *[Hopping around, trying to look over shoulder]* Wait! You said I don't have wings!

Grasshopper – You will grow them someday, though. The changes in our bodies – growing wings, getting larger, we call that metamorphosis. When your metamorphosis is complete, you will have wings, and they will help you hop as far as I can *[hops off stage, and back]* See!?

Nymph – Oh! I can't wait! I've got to start growing! *[Looking at Grasshopper].* Thanks for all the help, Grasshopper! *[Nymph hops off stage muttering]* Gotta eat to grow. Gotta leap to get strong. Gotta molt to grow. Gotta grow some wings . . . .

Grasshopper – *[Hopping off stage]* It's a pleasure to help you Nymph!

The End

NYMPH PUPPET

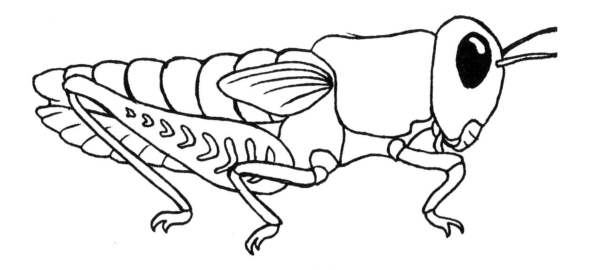

GRASSHOPPER PUPPET

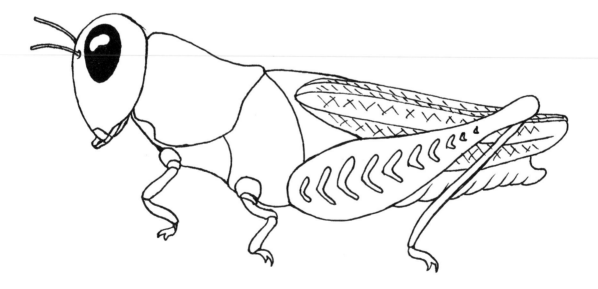

GROWING GRASSHOPPERS

We have been learning about grasshoppers' bodies, life cycles, eating habits, and ways to communicate.

Continue the Learning at Home

Grasshoppers, like all cold-blooded animals, vary their level of activity with temperature. Cool mornings and evenings result in sluggish insects that are slow to move and slow to call. Warm days and nights result in greater activity: quicker movements and louder, more frequent calls. Mornings, when grasshoppers are sluggish from the cold are a good time to try to catch them, while warm evenings result in some of the loudest insect choruses.

Listen to the Hoppers!

Go out for an evening of insect song. Bring a comb. How many different voices do you hear? Can you hear more than one type of grasshopper song? Sit close together in the darkness and listen in silence. When your explorer becomes restless, take out the comb and "sing" back to the grasshoppers by scraping your thumb across the teeth. Finish your evening with a cracker or two (foods made from grass) eaten in the darkness or in the comfort of your kitchen. If possible, sleep with the windows open and allow the chorus to lull you to sleep.

Produced and copyrighted by Vermont Institute of Natural Science, 2005.

Spiders: Weavers and Hunters

Focus: Spiders have many fascinating features and behaviors which enable them to survive and to perform important roles in nature.

Objective: To help children learn to overcome their fear of spiders by learning about their lives, pretending to be spiders, and finding and observing them.

Extra Information for Adult Leaders

DIGGING IN...

Spiders! Just the thought of them makes some people jump in fright or recoil in disgust. Spiders may look scary, but most of them don't hurt us at all. In fact, spiders help us. They play an important role by eating many insects that are harmful to crops and people. Scientists have discovered that spider webs contain a fever-reducing drug and are incredibly strong and durable. Spiders can be fascinating to watch, especially the ways in which they catch and consume their food.

There are many styles of spider webs – tangled, funnel, triangle, orb, bell-shaped, underwater, sheet webs, and more – and each design is ideally matched to its purpose. For example, the **web weavers** spin webs to catch **prey**. Other spiders are **wanderers** who do not use webs to catch food. Some hide in burrows or beneath rocks and stones. When the spider sees an insect, it quickly runs out and grabs it. Another type of spider digs a vertical tunnel and lines it with **silk**. To protect itself, it covers the tunnel entrance with a hinged trapdoor created from dirt and silk. When an unwary insect ventures nearby, the hungry spider throws open the door and dashes out to catch the insect. Another type of spider, a spitting spider, hides motionless under piles of leaves or dead grass. When an insect passes by, the spider fires a sticky, toxic substance from its fangs over the victim's body. Then the spider rushes at the struggling insect and pierces it with sharp fangs.

A spider's strong silk is extremely versatile. Besides building webs, it is used in many other ways. Some spiders spin a special escape thread, called a **dragline**. If an enemy comes, the spider can quickly drop down the dragline and skitter away. Because it's three times stronger than steel of the same thickness (plus much more elastic), silk is an important tool in capturing prey that is bigger and stronger than the spider itself. The silk also protects a spider's eggs from wasps and birds. Humans have used spider silk in nets, weapons, baskets, doormats, traps, and optical devices. (Not for fabric, though – that silk is spun by silk worms or moths.)

Life is very dangerous for a spider. It is constantly wary of predators and must seek shelter from severe weather. Most spiders have a **life span** of about one year. Some species (particularly the larger varieties) live much longer – up to 25 years, if they are not preyed upon by a hungry toad, frog, bird, small mammal, fish, insect, or even another spider.

Next time the children encounter a spider in an unlikely place, crouch down and make some observations. Share some of the fascinating aspects of a spider's life. Remind them of all the pesky insects that the spider is likely to eat! Over time when the children see a spider they may see it as fascinating rather than frightening.

Spider Anatomy

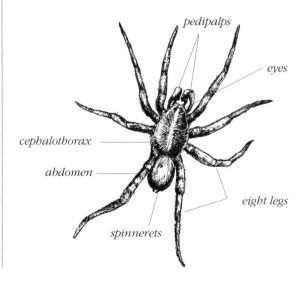

pedipalps

eyes

cephalothorax

abdomen

eight legs

spinnerets

Indoor Activities

SPIDER WORD WEB

Objective: *To discuss children's feelings and attitudes toward spiders.*

Materials:
- large spider web drawing (bulletin board size)
- spider drawing, 1 per child
- light colored crayons
- dark marker
- tape

Activity:
1. Distribute the spider drawings and have the children color them.
2. When the children are finished coloring, ask each child to suggest a word that somehow describes spiders.
3. Write these words on the spider drawings and post them on the large spider web drawing on the wall.
4. When everyone has completed their spiders, review the words and accompanying feelings/attitudes.
5. Extension – Recite the "Little Miss Muffet" poem. Compare her feelings about spiders with the feelings the children expressed.

Talk about the fact that although many people are frightened of spiders, the great majority of spiders are harmless to people. Still, both to avoid the pain of a bee sting-like bite and to protect the spiders, we should not handle them.

LITTLE CRAB SPIDER

Objective: *To consider a familiar rhyme from a child's point of view.*

Materials:
- large sheet of paper
- marker

Activity:
1. Review the rhyme:
   Little Miss Muffet sat on her tuffet,
   Eating her curds and whey,
   Along came a spider,
   Who sat down beside her,
   And frightened Miss Muffet away.
2. Discuss any unfamiliar words. In pairs, practice acting out the rhyme.
3. Then imagine a similar poem the spider might have written...
   Little Crab Spider sat on her _____ ,
   Eating her _____ and _____ ,
   Along came a big child,
   Who sat down beside her,
   And frightened Crab Spider away.
4. Let the children fill in the blanks and act out that rhyme, too.

Talk about how the poem changes when written from the spider's perspective.

LOOK! WE'RE SPIDERS!

Objective:	*To pretend to be giant spiders, crawling on the floor.*
Materials:	• rope or fabric strips, each about 6 feet long (1 for every 2 children)
Activity:	1. Help the children to form pairs.
	2. Standing side by side, use the fabric strips or rope to *loosely* tie two children together at the waist.
	3. Ask the children to get down on the floor, side by side. With their hands and legs forming the eight legs of a spider, have the children pretend to be spiders crawling across the floor.
	4. Help the children to notice that they're probably moving sideways for a spider (that is, forward for them). That's how a Crab Spider moves. To move like most spiders, though, they need to move differently. Can they figure out how?

Talk about different types of spider legs. Some spiders have very long and thin legs, while others have short and stout legs. Usually, the longer legged spiders are those that use a web to catch their prey, while the shorter (stronger) legged spiders chase and kill their prey without the help of a web. Also, all spiders have several joints (or "knees") on each of their legs. That's why they seem to creep so quickly!

BUILD A SPIDER

Objective:	*To learn the names of several spider body parts.*
Materials:	• illustration of spider anatomy
	• black permanent marker
	• felt, paper or fleece pieces, cut to provide a set of spider legs, a **cephalothorax**, and an abdomen to each pair of children
Activity:	1. Prepare the spider body parts, cutting them from felt, paper or fleece. Make enough sets for one spider for every two children.
	2. Gather the children in a circle, surrounding a sample spider that you've already assembled. Point out the various body parts and their functions.
	3. Provide one set of spider body parts for each pair of children and ask them to duplicate the sample spider you've made. Again, discuss the body parts.

Talk about the fact that spiders are **arthropods**, animals with jointed legs and exoskeletons covering their bodies. Other arthropods include lobsters, insects, mites, and centipedes. Further, spiders are members of the **arachnid** class; they have jointed legs, exoskeletons, eight legs, and two body sections.

Spiders are not insects. Insects have six legs and three body parts; spiders have eight legs and two body parts (**abdomen** and cephalothorax). Insects have compound eyes and antennae; spiders have up to eight simple eyes and **pedipalps** for sensing their environments. In addition, all spiders are equipped with **spinnerets**, enabling them to produce varying qualities of silk.

TRAPPED!

Objective: *To simulate how flies and other insects might get caught in a spider's web.*

Materials:
- hula hoop with fuzzy yarn tied across it in a spider web fashion
- several "flies" made from ping pong balls with pieces of hook-and-loop tape fastened to them (hook side out). (Add paper wings, if you like.)
- piece of rope or yarn (about 6 feet long)

Activity:
1. Show the children the hula hoop spider web. Discuss how spiders spin silk and build nearly invisible webs to trap insects.
2. Ask for two volunteers to hold the web vertically.
3. Spread a rope line a few feet away from the hoop. This is the fly toss line. Have the children take turns stepping up to the fly toss line and gently tossing one (or more) of the flies into the yarn spider web. The children holding the web should, at first, hold it still. The child tossing the fly tries to toss it (that is, the ping pong ball) through the web without getting caught. Then, the children holding the web can move it slightly, so they can "catch" the flies.

Talk about the fact that all spiders are able to manufacture silk, a fiber-like protein. Spider silk is produced by glands inside the spider's abdomen and then expelled through the spinnerets. Initially, the silk is liquid, but it hardens when it hits the air. Spiders are able to produce varying qualities of silk, depending on the task to be done. For instance, a spider might produce different silks ideal for wrapping prey, attaching safety draglines, forming egg sacs, or building a sticky web.

SPIDER JUICE

Objective: *To understand what spiders eat and how they drink their food.*

Materials:
- straws (1 per child)
- juice
- cups (1 per child)
- tiny plastic flies – optional (taped to straws or cups)

Activity:
1. First, ask the children to suggest some foods that spiders might like. (Spiders are **carnivores**, eating only other animals, no plant materials. They eat flies, crickets, bees, grasshoppers, beetles, mosquitoes, and other insects.)
2. Now explain that spiders don't actually EAT their foods, they DRINK them. (See the "Talk about" below. Try to put the information into your own words.)
3. Serve "fly juice" to the children, having them drink it with straws.

Talk about the way a spider eats (or drinks) its food. When a spider catches a fly in its web, for instance, it first wraps it up in silk (spun from the spinnerets located in the back of its abdomen). The silk wrapping will hold the fly still – but still alive – while the spider consumes it. The spider then bites into the fly's hard shell (exoskeleton) with its sharp fangs (**chelicerae**). Then, through those fangs, the spider injects a kind of **venom** that quickly turns the inside of the fly's body to liquid. Finally, the spider uses its straw-like mouth to suck up the food.

THE SPIDER AND THE FLY

Objective: *To pretend to be giant spiders capturing flies in their webs.*

Materials:
- roll of masking tape
- crackers
- blindfold or winter hat

Activity:
1. Preferably on a carpeted area (though bare floor works, too), use the masking tape to construct a giant spider web (ten or so feet across). Make it simple, like a pie cut into wedges.
2. Gather the children around the outside of the web (a step or two back).
3. Choose one child to be the spider. Blindfold or pull the hat down over that child's eyes. Have him get down on hands and knees at the edge of the web.
4. Quietly place the cracker somewhere on the web.
5. Now, using his hands to feel and follow along the strands of the web, challenge the spider child to crawl along the web until he finds the fly (cracker).
6. Everybody cheers for the successful spider. Then choose a new spider.

Talk about the importance of the sense of touch for a spider. Many spiders barely use their eyesight. Instead, they feel movements in their web when the fly hits; then they crawl to it using their sense of touch.

• •

FLOATING SPIDERLINGS

Objective: *To understand the first stages of a spider's life cycle.*

Materials:
- 2-inch paper circles (1 for each child)
- pencils
- clear tape
- thread (light color)
- toilet paper tubes (may be decorated by the children)

Activity:
1. Begin by explaining that like butterflies, for instance, spiders begin their lives as tiny eggs.
2. On the small paper circles, ask the children to draw spiders.
3. Help each child to tape a length of thread to her paper spider.
4. Now go outdoors, gently floating the spiders on their "gossamer" lines – or even letting the breeze carry them.
5. Then, while singing the familiar "Itsy Bitsy Spider" song, encourage the children to feed the thread through the toilet paper tubes (water spouts) and dramatize the song.

Talk about how a mother spider may lay between one and several hundred eggs at a time (depending on the spider's species). The tiny eggs are wrapped securely in a silk egg sac that protects them from rain, cold, predators, and other dangers. When they're ready, tiny baby spiders (called **spiderlings**) hatch from the eggs. Spiderlings look just like adult spiders, except they're much smaller. To avoid having to compete for food and shelter with their many siblings and mother, the spiderling must soon travel to a new home. To do this, the spiderling lets out a very light strand of silk (dragline or gossamer), and then floats away (called "ballooning"). Spiderlings may travel many, many miles this way.

Outdoor Activities

SEARCHING FOR SPIDER WEBS

What You Need
- old socks, filled with cornstarch and then tied closed – one for every two children
- digital camera to photograph webs (optional)

What to Do
Go for a walk outside, searching for spider webs. Assign the children to pairs. If they find a web, one child holds the cornstarch-filled sock above the web, while the other child taps the sock so the cornstarch makes the web more visible. Compare the webs you discover. If possible, photograph the webs and post the photos in the room.

ADOPT A SPIDER

What You Need
- pencil and paper for notes and sketches

What to Do
Find and observe the same spider every day for as long as possible. Take down notes of the children's observations.

FEEDING SPIDERS

What You Need
- live fly, cricket, grasshopper, or other small insect

What to Do
Find a spider web with a spider waiting in or near it. Have the children find a fly or cricket or other small insect. Gently toss the fly into the spider's web and watch what happens!

We Care about . . . Spiders
When you discover a spider inside, show the children how to gently place a cup over the spider then slide an index card or piece of paper under the cup. You can then safely carry the spider outdoors, without touching it or harming it.

Language Activity / Song

First, have the children make simple spider puppets for their hands. (See "Crafts and Projects" section.) Then, sing the following song while moving the spider puppet to the appropriate place. Have the children take turns suggesting new locations.

(To the tune of "The Farmer in the Dell")

The spider's on my _____, *(head, arm, leg, food, etc.)*
The spider's on my _____ ,
Hi-ho the derry-o,
The spider's on my _____ .

Crafts and Projects

SPIDER PUPPETS

What You Need
- simple outline of a spider's body without legs, about 3 x 6 inches (adapt drawing used in the "Spider Word Web" activity)
- toilet paper rolls (cut into 3 ring sections)
- half-inch wide paper strips, folded accordian style
- glue and crayons

What to Do
Help the children to cut simple spiders from paper. Add eight accordian-folded legs, as well as eyes and any other features you like. Glue the spiders to the cardboard rings to make simple puppets.

• •

GOLF BALL SPIDER WEB PAINTINGS

What You Need
- black construction paper
- boxes or box lids (slightly larger than paper)
- white paint
- golf balls (or marbles)

What to Do
Place a piece of black construction paper inside the box lid. Put a small glob of white paint in the center of the paper. Then put a golf ball inside the box lid, and have a child roll the ball by tipping the box lid this way and that, until an attractive web has formed. (Marbles can be used instead of golf balls, if you like.)

SPAGHETTI SPIDER WEB

What You Need
- cooked spaghetti
- black construction paper
- string, liquid starch or glitter glue, gel pens (optional)

What to Do
Cook a small amount of spaghetti till soft. Do not rinse. While still warm, have the children lay the wet spaghetti on black construction paper, forming a web. Let dry. (You can also use string dipped in liquid starch, or glitter glue, or gel pens to make your web.)

• •

PAPER PLATE WEB

What You Need
- paper plates – 1 per child
- scissors
- hole punches
- colored yarn – cut into one 3-foot-long piece per child
- Styrofoam meat trays and knife (optional)

What to Do
Prepare one paper plate for each child by cutting out the center, leaving the rim intact (save the centers for another day). Then use a hole punch to make ten or so holes around the inside edge of the plate rim. Give each child a length of colored yarn and have them sew the web by connecting the holes with yarn.

For younger children, use a craft tray or a foam meat tray that has been bleached. Make notches around the perimeter, then invite the children to wrap yarn from notch to notch until a "web" is created.

Independent Play Ideas
1. Provide a variety of materials (like egg cartons, yarns, glue, paper, crayons, etc.) for children to craft into spiders, webs, or other related things.
2. Prepare four to six copies of a spider illustration in progressively larger sizes. (Use a photocopy machine and thick cardstock paper.) Have the children practice putting the sketches in order from the smallest to the largest spider.

Snack

FRUIT FLIES

What You Need
- liquid-filled fruit snacks

What to Do
Purchase some liquid-filled fruit snacks at the grocery store. Have the children eat the gooey snacks, pretending to be spiders biting into flies and sucking out their insides!

Book Ideas

CHILDREN'S FICTION

Dream Weaver, by Jonathan London, Silver Whistle of Harcourt Brace, 1998 – a story based on factual information about spiders. A boy gains new insights and respect for spiders after observing one while out walking on a mountain path.

The Roly-Poly Spider, by Jill Sardegna, Scholastic, 1994 – a fun picture book about the many insects that a spider ingests in a single day.

Sophie's Masterpiece, by Eileen Spinelli, Simon & Schuster, 2001 – lovely and imaginative, this book inspires kindness and gratitude for spiders.

The Very Busy Spider, by Eric Carle, Philomel, 1984 – a fun story about a spider's activities.

CHILDREN'S NONFICTION

Do All Spiders Spin Webs?, by Melvin and Gilda Berger, Scholastic, 2000 – how spiders see at night, the different types of spider webs, and what makes spider silk so strong, a question-and-answer format.

Eight Legs, by D.M. Souza, Carolrhoda Books, 1991 – excellent quality photographs and nuggets of information about spiders and their lives.

A House Spider's Life, by John Himmelman, Children's Press, Grolier, 1999 – a peek at the actual life of a house spider, one of the most common species encountered.

Outside & Inside Spiders, by Sandra Markle, Scholastic, 2000 – an excellent nonfiction book, with plenty of top-notch photographs.

Spiders and Their Web Sites, by Margery Facklam, Little, Brown, 2001 – describes the physical characteristics and habits of 12 different spiders and daddy longlegs.

Spiders Spin Webs, by Yvonne Winer, Scholastic, 1996 – a beautiful book of poetry and careful illustrations, encourages new admiration for spiders.

Where's That Spider?, by Barbara Brenner and Bernice Chardiet, Scholastic, 1999 – rhymes and fine illustrations, a hide-and-seek book that encourages readers to discover many facts about spiders.

RESOURCE BOOKS FOR ADULTS AND CHILDREN

Spiders Near and Far, by Jennifer Owings Dewey, Dutton Children's Books, 1993 – excellent identification and natural history information about spiders all over the world.

Web Weavers and Other Spiders, by Bobbie Kalman, Crabtree, 1997 – contains good spider photos, labeled diagrams, and background information on spiders.

SPIDERS

We've been learning about the various parts of spiders' bodies and their functions. We've learned about spider silk and how it not only helps a spider to catch its insect food, but also to care for its eggs and protect itself from dangerous falls.

Continue the Learning at Home

To make hard-to-see spider webs suddenly visible, fill an old sock with ordinary cornstarch, taking care to tie the open end in a knot afterwards. Take a walk with your child to a spot where you might discover spider webs. A neighborhood park, a grassy field, or even alongside your house or other buildings are all fine spots to check. When you find a web, dangle the cornstarch-filled sock just above the web while your child gently pats the sock. The cornstarch released from the sock will dust the web and make it instantly visible!

The process of discovering these webs is almost like magic for children. Examine the various designs of the webs nearby your home. Notice how some are mostly round, while others are funnel-shaped. Look for other web designs, too.

More Fun with Spiders

Start with a nice clean table or a large plate. With your child's help, cook up a small batch of spaghetti. After it's cooked, rinse with warm water and place in a bowl on the table. Together, you and your child can use the cooked spaghetti to create spider web designs right on your kitchen table! Eat up when you're finished.

Produced and copyrighted by Vermont Institute of Natural Science, 2005.

From Rocks to Soil

Focus: Although every rock is unique in its shape, size, color, texture, and character, certain rocks do have features in common. All rocks, subjected to the forces of weathering, become soil.

Objective: To explore the variety in rocks and learn some rock vocabulary and to learn how rocks, like all else in nature, change over time.

Extra Information for Adult Leaders

Geology is the study of rocks and soil, but it is also the study of the changes that take place on the earth's surface and below it, as well as what happened to the earth in the past. **Geologists** (or geoscientists, as some prefer to call themselves) study a variety of topics, including the evolution of landscapes, the chemistry of earth materials, earthquakes and the interior of the earth, the dynamics of groundwater, and rocks and their formation. Rocks hold a nearly universal fascination for young children, and collecting rocks is where many a young geologist gets their start.

Rocks are divided into three groups based on their formation: igneous, sedimentary, and metamorphic. **Sedimentary** rocks can be formed from physical processes (such as the transportation and deposition of sand to form sandstone) or chemical processes (such as the crystallization of salt as water evaporates). Sedimentary rock formation occurs at or within the earth's surface. **Igneous** rocks are formed from lava or magma that once was molten rock but solidified as it cooled at or near the earth's surface. **Metamorphic** rocks are igneous and sedimentary rocks (and can even be other metamorphic rocks) that have been changed by heat and/or pressure.

DIGGING IN...

It is easy to think of rocks as constants, but they are continually being created and destroyed – often on such a slow time scale that humans barely notice. As soon as a rock is exposed at the earth's surface, it begins the process of **chemical weathering**: breaking apart into smaller particles. **Physical weathering** can happen when a plant root or ice wedges into a crack in the rock's surface, expands, and splits the rock. It can also be chemical: water or weak acids dissolve minerals in the rock. **Erosion** is the process where these particles or **solutes** are moved from one place to another, perhaps by a drop of rain, a gust of wind, or an ocean wave.

As with everything in nature, the earth's geology also has its cycle. The rocks composing mountains will eventually be weathered and transported away by erosive forces. Over time, however, some of those particles will be cemented into new sedimentary rocks, or buried deep within the earth and melted, reappearing at the earth's surface as igneous rocks. These rocks, in turn may be eroded and transported, or perhaps buried again and melted, or even metamorphosed. The cycle goes on and on. Rock is created and destroyed, then created again. Mountain ranges rise, fall, and rise again.

Indoor Activities

LET'S MAKE A ROCK

Objective: *To have some fun making a rock.*

Materials:
- bucket or coffee can of plaster of paris (with a small amount of dry black tempera paint added)
- bucket or coffee can of sand
- 3 coffee scoops
- cup of gold glitter, with small measuring spoon
- bucket or source of water
- small (3-ounce) size paper cups – 1 per child (You might label these with the children's names beforehand.)
- wooden craft sticks – 1 per child
- waxed paper (to shape the rocks on)
- (optional – small shells to put inside rocks)

Activity:
1. Give each child a cup and craft stick.
2. To each cup, add two scoops each of plaster and sand.
3. Add a small spoonful of glitter.
4. Finally, add one scoop of water.
5. Have the children use their craft sticks to mix the ingredients. (If you're concerned that children might inhale the plaster powder while stirring, you might either add the water yourself first, then have the children complete the mixing; or you might provide disposable face masks [available at hardware stores].)
6. If desired, children can place a small shell inside the rock. (Later when the rock is dry, it can be cracked to reveal a fossil-like imprint.)
7. Leave the mixture and cups in a warm, sunny spot to dry and harden a bit. If you're careful, you can catch the rocks when they're hard enough to shape but not yet "rock hard" and shape them into round stones. Providing a piece of waxed paper for each child will cut down on messy hands and floors.
8. Remember, when cleaning up, never wash plaster of paris down the drain.

Talk about how sedimentary rocks like sandstone are really made. Sediments (rock, animal, and plant bits) accumulate over time, burying the oldest sediments far beneath the youngest layers. The deepest layers of sediment experience high quantities of pressure that squeeze particles together until they are tightly packed. Over time, the particles become cemented by minerals carried into the forming rock by groundwater. Rock formation can be an incredibly long process.

ROCK SORTING

Objective: *To closely observe the characteristics of several different rocks.*

Materials:
- a variety of rocks – at least 1 per child
- spritzer bottle filled with water (labeled)
- spritzer bottle filled with vinegar (labeled)
- a penny
- construction paper – dark and light colors – several sheets per child
- a balance scale
- a tray

Activity:
1. Encourage the children to carefully observe the collected rocks.
2. What colors do they see? How do the rocks feel? What shapes do they notice?
3. Use the spritzer to spray water on a rock or two. How does the rock's appearance change when you spritz it with water? Challenge the children to dry the rock without touching it.
4. Use a penny to make scratch marks on the rocks. (Notice that some leave marks, while others are too hard – harder than the penny.)
5. Choose a couple of rocks to spray with vinegar. (Limestone or sandstone work best.) What happens? (Some might bubble, as the vinegar acid interacts with the calcium in some rocks.)
6. Have the children try to draw on the paper with their rocks. Now wet the rocks and try again.
7. Use a balance scale to weigh and compare the rocks.
8. After the children have spent some time exploring the rocks, ask them to help you sort them. Suggest: colors – brown, gray, black; textures – smooth, bumpy; other – bubbles with vinegar, doesn't bubble.
9. Finally, have everyone select a favorite rock and describe why to the others.

Note: Many educational suppliers of science materials sell reasonably-priced sets of rocks that are ideal for this type of exploration (see Appendix A).

Talk about the different characteristics of the rocks and that geologists use these characteristics (hardness, color, whether or not it fizzes, and weight) to learn about rocks.

"ROCKS AREN'T FOREVER" PUPPET SHOW

Objective: *To describe some of the many physical forces that can change a rock to soil.*

Materials:
- puppet show script (see end of unit)
- puppets: old boulder, squirrel, and oak tree (see end of unit)
- split rock samples from "Let's Make a Rock" activity (split with a hammer and nail)

Activity:
1. Prepare the puppet stage by putting the tree on the left side and the old boulder on the right side.
2. Present the puppet show for the children.
3. Afterwards, leave the puppet show materials out, so the children can re-create the play.
4. Show the children the split rocks. What happened?

Talk about how water expands when it turns to ice. Where have they seen water change to ice? Other than ice, can they think of something that might cause a rock to break into pieces? Here are some examples: plant roots (think of weeds in a sidewalk), machines (think about bulldozers and jack hammers), water (think about ocean waves or a river).

The process by which rocks break down to soil is called "weathering," and rocks of all sizes are subject to erosion (the movement of rocks or rock particles from place to place). Even the highest mountains, over millions of years, will be worn down to mere remnants of their former size.

• •

ERODE THAT BOULDER!

Objective: *To understand erosion, the movement of weathered particles from one place to another.*

Activity:
1. First, discuss the words that describe rocks of different sizes. The biggest is usually called a "boulder," then "rock," then "stone," then "pebble," and finally "sand grain."

2. Tell the children they are going to create a human boulder, which will shrink in size until it becomes a sand grain.

3. Have one child sit in the middle of the circle.

4. Four other children then kneel around the child in the center and put their hands on each other's shoulders.

5. Keep making larger and larger kneeling (or standing) circles around the center child.

6. Remind the children that boulders are rocks, so they don't move on their own. All children should be "stone still."

7. Now ask the students to use their imaginations. Imagine that a tree is growing on top of the boulder. Its roots wedge themselves into the cracks and split the boulder . . . but still, the pieces cling to each other. (Children can wiggle a bit farther apart, still holding on to each other.) Winter comes and goes. Water dribbles into the cracks in the boulder, freezes and splits the boulder into smaller, separate rock pieces. (Children remain frozen still, but put their arms down by their sides).

8. Now the teacher becomes the eroding forces of wind and rain. You come up to the children, drum your fingers on their backs (rain), and lightly rub their backs while making "swooshing" sounds (wind). When the children feel this, they become pebbles and roll away from the boulder. Finally, with more wind and rain sounds, the children shrink down as small as they can, becoming grains of sand.

Talk about some possible forces of erosion: wind, rain, ice, flowing water (streams or rivers). Also describe how plant roots, rocks, and other materials can be useful in slowing erosion.

LET'S MAKE SOME SAND

Objective: *To witness and participate in the formation of soil (sand, in this case).*

Materials:
- several (preferably cracked) sea shells
- a sturdy zip-lock plastic bag
- rubber mallet or hammer
- colored chalk (several large pieces)
- rock salt
- sugar cubes

Activity:
1. Place the shells inside the baggie and close it carefully.
2. Have the children take turns using the mallet (carefully) to break the shells inside the bag. Continue until the shells turn to fine grains of sand.
3. Repeat with the rock salt, chalk and sugar cubes – pounding each until they form tiny grains instead of big chunks.
4. Mix the powdered sand, salt, sugar and chalk together. (Save this for a craft.)

Talk about the forces that might turn shells into sand at a beach – primarily waves. Have you ever watched as waves pour over and turn up shells at the beach? Do shells turn to sand quickly or over a long period of time?

Chalk is made from limestone, a type of rock formed from the skeletons of tiny sea animals that have been deposited on the floor of the ocean.

Sun, rain, wind, snow, ice expanding and contracting, and the grinding caused by glaciers, rivers, or wind also break down rocks.

• •

SOIL SAMPLES

Objective: *To observe a variety of soil types and notice their characteristics.*

Materials:
- four basins/pans
- sand
- gravel
- clay
- humus or peat
- pitcher of water
- large spoon
- large plastic tarp

Activity:
1. To prepare, fill one basin each with sand, gravel, clay, and humus/peat. Place the plastic tarp under the children's work area.
2. Have the children look at and feel each of the soil samples (dry). What do they notice?
3. Mix some water into each basin, and compare the soils again.
4. Which soil is best for making a mud pie? For making drip castles? For putting on an icy walkway?

Talk about possible best uses for each of the soils (planting, driveway, creating pots, etc.) Soil, in its many forms, is a very important material for people and animals alike. Of course, good rich soil, high in organic material, is essential to successful gardening and agriculture. Other soil types are used for other purposes. Clay is an excellent building material, from pots to bricks. Gravel is great for driveways, fish tanks, and many other uses. Sand is mixed with other materials to form concrete, and is, of course, the stuff that sandcastles are made of.

Outdoor Activities

FAVORITE ROCKS: HARD CHOICES

What You Need
- egg cartons – cut in half crosswise (1 half per child)

What to Do
Take the children for a walk in a place where they're likely to find loose, small rocks. After giving each of the children a six-compartment egg carton, explain to them that they can now collect their favorite rocks. The rules, however, are that only rocks small enough to fit in the egg cups can be collected, and there can be only one rock in each cup. So, if a child already has six rocks but wants to pick up another, she must choose one rock to come out.

• •

ROCK WASH

What You Need
- variety of rocks (preferably dirty), collected by the children outdoors
- used plastic grocery bags for carrying the rocks
- basin(s) of warm soapy water
- toothbrushes, cloths, and/or vegetable scrubbers

What to Do
Have the children bring their rock collections inside. Provide brushes, etc. so they can clean up the rocks and "make them pretty." Notice how the appearance of the rocks changes when they're wet and/or clean.

FIND YOUR ROCK

What You Need
- a collection of egg-size rocks – 1 per child
- nail polish

What to Do
Use the nail polish to mark each child's initials on his rock. Be sure to let the nail polish dry thoroughly.

Gather the children in a circle facing outward. One at a time, pass the rocks around the circle. Encourage the children to use only their sense of touch to explore the rocks (no peeking). When a child thinks they have found their special rock, the child should exclaim, "I've got my rock!" Check to see if the child is right. Continue until all the rocks have been matched with their owners.

MUD RELAY RACE

What You Need
- 2 or more large buckets of wet, oozing mud
- 2 or more small size yogurt cups
- plastic spoons – 1 for each child
- robin's nest illustration

What to Do
Divide the children into two or more teams (not so much to compete, as to spread out a bit). Show the children the drawing of the robin's nest, and talk about how robins build their nests from mud, grass, and sticks. Robins may make several hundred trips back and forth, from mud puddle to nest, until their nests are finally complete.

The children are going to pretend to be robins building their nests. Instead of carrying mud in their beaks as robins do, they'll carry it in spoons. Give each child a spoon. Practice chanting the following together:

> Fly, robin, fly,
> Build your nest,
> Carry the mud,
> Like you do best.

Now the children dip their spoons into the mud bucket, scoop up some mud, and run (or fly) a distance to add the mud to their robin family's nest (the yogurt cup). The children may chant the above verse as they do. Continue until both yogurt cup nests are full. End with the following:

> Stop, robin, stop,
> Rest your wings,
> Now's the time,
> To do other things.

> ### We Care about . . . Rocks and Soil
> Go on a walk around your block or the play area. Show the children eroded areas – where the plants have been worn away and the soil exposed. If possible, show them how the soil washes away. This is a good activity to do during or just after a heavy rainstorm. Plant roots help prevent erosion but can be weakened if frequently walked on. Make an extra effort to stay on the path on this and future walks.

Language Activity/ Guided Imagery

You are a small rock lying in a streambed. *(Children curl themselves up on the floor.)* It is winter, and the water above you is frozen. Slowly, slowly, the temperature begins to warm, the snow melts, and the stream begins to flow. *(Spread a blanket out and pull it over each of the children.)* As more snow melts, and the stream grows stronger, the water begins to rock you back and forth in your spot on the streambed. A rainstorm hits! *(Teacher pats legs.)* The stream becomes a raging torrent. The stream picks you and the other rocks up and rolls you around. The water moves along the streambed. *(Children roll around in their spots.)* Slowly, the stream's strength decreases, and it sets you down. *(Children stop rolling.)* You settle into your new spot, and once again, the water flows over you. *(Pull the blanket over the children again.)*

Crafts and Projects

ROCK JARS

What You Need
- plastic mayonnaise or similar size jars – 1 per child
- bowls or other containers with small rocks, pebbles, and sand
- aquarium gravel (optional)
- several tablespoons

What to Do
Let the children create layered rock jars, using the rocks, pebbles, and sand. You may want to add aquarium gravel for color.

• •

SHAKE JARS

What You Need
- plastic mayonnaise or similar size jars with screw-on lids
- bowls or other containers with small rocks, pebbles, and sand
- several tablespoons
- water
- packing or duct tape

What to Do
Place a spoonful or two each of sand, pebbles, and small rocks into a jar. Add water almost to the top of the container, screw on the lid, and tape the lid to the jar to avoid accidents. Shake the jar, then let it settle. What happens to the sand, pebbles, and rocks?

Independent Play Ideas

1. Provide lots of rocks to explore, weigh, decorate, paint, glue together, etc.
2. Create several Shake Jars (see "Crafts and Projects" section) containing a variety of combinations of sand, gravel, and rock. You might even want to add color with aquarium gravel. Let the children explore the various effects as the jars are shaken and settle.

SENSATIONAL SAND

What You Need
- clean sand, mixed with dry tempera paint (1 tablespoon paint to each half-cup sand) – a variety of colors OR the powdered salt/sugar/sand mixture from an earlier activity
- salt shakers or baby food jars with holes poked in their lids – 1 for each color
- cardboard or sturdy paper
- thinned glue or paste
- small paintbrushes

What to Do
Instruct the children to make glue designs on their papers – squiggles, dots, etc. Then have them sprinkle the different colored sands over their designs. When the glue is dry, shake off the excess sand.

Snacks

BAG O' MUD

What You Need
- zip-top baggies – 1 per child
- chocolate pudding
- Oreo cookies – pounded into crumbs by the children beforehand
- gummy worms or insects
- large and small spoons

What to Do
Give each child a baggie with some chocolate pudding inside. Using the spoons, the children can then add cookie crumbs (pebbles) and gummy worms. Finally, they can use the spoons to eat their bag o' mud.

• •

ROCK BISCUITS

What You Need
- baking sheet (greased or ungreased, according to recipe)
- at least 2 mixing bowls
- measuring cups
- biscuit baking mix and water or milk to add to mix (according to recipe instructions)
- add-ins (food coloring, colored sprinkles, cinnamon, shredded cheese, dill, paprika, etc.)
- fork or spoon

What to Do
Following the recipe, select an amount of baking mix that will produce the desired number of biscuits. Divide the mix between two bowls (at least). Put add-ins into the different bowls, for example, sprinkles and cinnamon for sweet biscuits, dill and cheese for herbed biscuits. Follow the recipe to form a dough the consistency of craft dough. You may need to knead in some extra flour to make the dough workable.

Give each child a lump of each kind of dough, or let the children select their own! Have the children roll and press the two doughs together (each should still retain their individuality!). This illustrates PRESSURE!

Bake biscuits according to package directions. HEAT!

Enjoy snacking on your rocks with a bit of honey or butter.

Book Ideas

CHILDREN'S FICTION

If You Are a Hunter of Fossils, by Byrd Baylor, Charles Scribner's Sons, 1980 – portray geologic time with a nice reverent tone and excellent drawings.

Matthew Wheelock's Wall, by Frances Ward Weller, MacMillan, 1992 – a beautiful, simple story of a farmer who creates a stone wall.

Sylvester and the Magic Pebble, by William Steig, Simon & Schuster, 1969 – a funny, imaginative story; contains animals dressed in clothes.

Rocks in His Head, by Carol Hurst, Greenwillow Books, 2001 – a touching, true story of a rock collector's life, illustrated with watercolor and pen and ink.

CHILDREN'S NONFICTION

The Amazing Dirt Book, by Paulette Bourgeois, Addison-Wesley, 1991 – examines the wonders of dirt, where it appears, what life it contains, and how it can be used.

If You Find a Rock, by Peggy Christian, Harcourt Children's Books, 2000 – describes how people might interact with rocks of various shapes and sizes – a wishing rock, for example.

Salt, by Melinda Lilly, Rourke, 2002 – all about salt and its historical significance.

RESOURCE BOOKS FOR ADULTS AND CHILDREN

Geology Crafts for Kids, by Alan Anderson, Gwen Diehn, and Terry Krautwurst, Sterling, 1996 – contains lots of ideas for geology themed art.

Rocks and Minerals, by John Farndon, Marshall Cavendish, 2003 – includes information, activities, and experiments for adults and children.

Rocks and Minerals, by Dr. R.F. Symes, Alfred A. Knopf, 1988 – background information on many aspects of rocks for older children and adults.

PUPPET SHOW SCRIPT

"Rocks Aren't Forever"

Narrator – Once there was an old tree. His branches were broken and his trunk was split. But he still had lots and lots of beautiful green leaves. One sunny morning, a squirrel was playing near Old Mr. Tree's roots.

Squirrel – Hello, Mr. Tree. You have such beautiful leaves. Are there some nice, fat acorns up there too!? I bet they'll grow into oak trees just like you when they fall! But, hey, there's not much soil down here – just a bunch of rocks. That's not good! What will your acorns grow in!?

Tree – Oh, they'll be all right. Just be patient. There's soil down there, and over time there will be more.

Squirrel – What do you mean, we'll get more soil? *[jumping around]* Is someone bringing a dump truck load of soil here? I love dump trucks! I wanna see the dump truck!

Tree – No, no. No dump trucks are coming here. Let me explain it to you. See that big rock over there?

Squirrel – *[squirrel runs over to the boulder and stands on it]* This great big boulder here? The one I'm standing on!?

Tree – Yes. Well, years and years ago, that boulder used to be big. REALLY BIG. HUGE. HUMUNGOUS. IMMENSE. TREMENDOUS. COLLOSAL . . .

Squirrel – Okay, I get it. It was BIG. So what happened to it? Did some hungry child take bites out of it?

Tree – No, Squirrel. Children don't eat rocks! The big rock just sort of crumbled. Little by little, cold, snow, ice, heat, rain, even my roots – they all broke off pieces of the big rock. See all the pebbles on the ground?

Squirrel – *[looking at the ground.]* Sure, there are lots of them. OOOHHHHH ... the big boulder is crumbling into small pebbles. But what does that have to do with getting enough soil for your acorns to sprout!?

Tree – Well, if the big rock breaks down into smaller pebbles, what is going to happen to the little pebbles as they break down?

Squirrel – Wait – wait! I've got it! They'll get smaller and smaller, until they become *soil!*

Tree – That's absolutely right. The pebbles will become sand or clay, and they'll mix with my fallen leaves, which are also breaking down into tiny pieces. Small rock pieces plus small leaf pieces: VOILA! Soil! Soil for my acorns to grow in!

Squirrel – Will it happen *today?* Will the rocks and leaves change into soil *today? [running back and forth.]* Should I get the watering can, so I can help the acorns grow with a nice, big drink?

Tree – No, no, Squirrel it takes a long, long, LONG time for rocks to change into soil. And, besides, you won't be needing a watering can today. It looks like rain any minute now. Hey, why don't you come close, and take shelter in my cozy branches.

Squirrel – Well, thanks, Mr. Tree. I think I'll do just that. I am feeling a little bit sleepy... *[snoring begins].*

The End

TREE PUPPET

BOULDER PUPPET

SQUIRREL PUPPET

FROM ROCKS TO SOIL

We've been focusing on the ground beneath our feet to learn about the sizes and shapes of rocks, their colors and textures, and how rocks turn to soil.

Continue the Learning at Home

Take a rock walk with your child. Search for interesting rocks. Can you find . . .

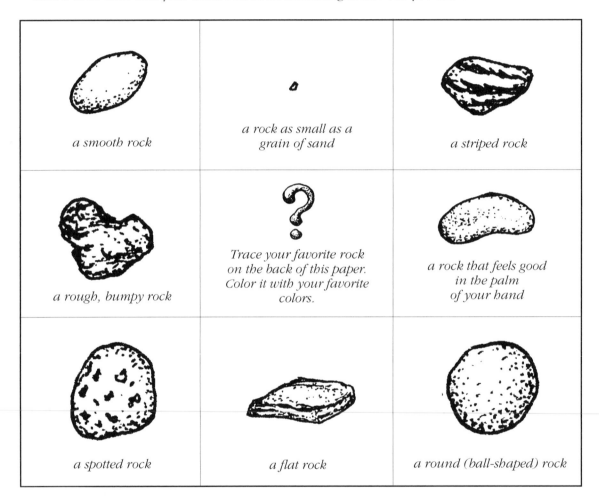

a smooth rock	*a rock as small as a grain of sand*	*a striped rock*
a rough, bumpy rock	*Trace your favorite rock on the back of this paper. Color it with your favorite colors.*	*a rock that feels good in the palm of your hand*
a spotted rock	*a flat rock*	*a round (ball-shaped) rock*

More Fun with Rocks

Bake a tasty sedimentary (layered) rock. Divide a batch of biscuit dough into two halves. Color or season each half differently. Press or roll the two dough types first separately, then together (one on top of the other). Cut the biscuits using a cup edge. Then bake as directed on the biscuit package.

Produced and copyrighted by Vermont Institute of Natural Science, 2005.

The Year of a Tree

Focus: There are many different types (species) of trees. Each tree species is specially designed for survival in its particular location.

Objective: To become aware of the parts of a tree, to learn their functions, to understand how trees change through the seasons, and to recognize the importance of trees to people and wildlife.

Extra Information for Adult Leaders

DIGGING IN...

A tree is made up of many parts, all working together to help it grow. Botanically speaking, trees are woody plants with stems – trunks and branches. The job of the trunk and branches is to get the leaves as high as possible, so they can maximize the amount of sunlight available to the leaves. (Being tall also keeps tree leaves out of reach of hungry animals, such as deer and goats.) The **leaves** use sunlight and gases in the air to produce sugars to feed the tree – a process termed **photosynthesis**. Gathering water and minerals from the soil, a tree's **roots** help the tree grow (while also anchoring the tree in the ground). On a warm day, a large tree can take in several hundred gallons of water (most of which is later **transpired** through the leaves and into the air). Working together, the various parts of a tree help to ensure its survival.

There are two main types of trees – **coniferous** and **deciduous**. **Conifers** have leaves that resemble needles or tiny **scales**. Deciduous trees have leaves that are broad and flat. Coniferous trees have leaves (**needles**) year round, while deciduous trees drop their leaves usually once a year and are bare for a period of time. Also, **cones** are found on coniferous trees. Cones do the same job as flowers do on other trees – they produce and capture **pollen**. When pollen from male cones lands on female cones, seeds begin to grow. The cone scales harden and close to protect the seeds.

Most conifers are tough trees that can cope with extreme weather conditions. Their hard, needlelike leaves do not dry out as easily as the leaves of deciduous trees, so conifers survive in hot and dry climates, as well as cold and snowy ones. Thanks in part to the special adaptations of these two types of trees (coniferous and deciduous), virtually every **habitat** can grow trees. Deserts, extremely cold places, and very high mountain peaks are the only places in the world where trees do not grow.

Deciduous trees sometimes have colorful, sweet-smelling flowers to attract bees and other insects. When these animals visit the flowers and drink their nectar, they also transfer pollen from male flowers to female flowers. Once this happens, female flowers make seeds that may grow into new trees. Other trees have flowers that are far less conspicuous; many of these are wind-pollinated.

Trees are important in so many ways. A single tree may be home to hundreds of living things. A variety of animals (like mice and insects, even moose) and **fungi** feed on the tree itself. Other animals live in the tree, and they may help the tree by eating other organisms that may be harmful to the tree's health – this relationship is termed **mutualism**. A woodpecker, for example, might find shelter inside a hollow portion of a tree. In exchange, the woodpecker consumes insects that might harm the tree. Trees provide people with many useful things such as wood, paper, maple syrup, rubber, and cork. Perhaps the best thing trees provide is something we cannot see – **oxygen**! Every growing tree pumps life-saving oxygen into the air and removes carbon dioxide gas from people, cars, and smoke.

Indoor Activities

WHAT SEASON IS IT?

Objective: *To guess the time of year by observing trees in various stages of their life cycles.*

Materials:
- illustrations of a tree at various times of the year – copied onto cardstock, then cut into separate cards (1 per season)
- children's book, *Fall Is Not Easy,* by Marty Kelley

Activity:
1. Review the four seasons. Then, showing one tree card at a time, ask the children to guess the season shown in each sketch. What clues did they use to know the season? How did the tree change?

2. Read *Fall Is Not Easy* (see "Children's Nonfiction"). Then review the challenges of each season for the tree.

Talk about how trees have to adapt to the changing seasons the best they can. Some lose all their leaves in the winter (or in the dry season), while others shed just some of their leaves. In the spring, a deciduous tree in the northern half of the world produces new leaves. The leaves are curled up inside the buds. They expand quickly and immediately begin making food for the tree. During the summer, the leaves grow darker and tougher to keep hungry, leaf-eating insects away. Before the leaves fall in autumn, they lose their green color. Some leaves experience chemical changes that make them turn red or yellow or other colors. The tree is inactive until spring, so no matter how cold and icy the winter, its leaves cannot be damaged. They are safely packed away inside winter buds.

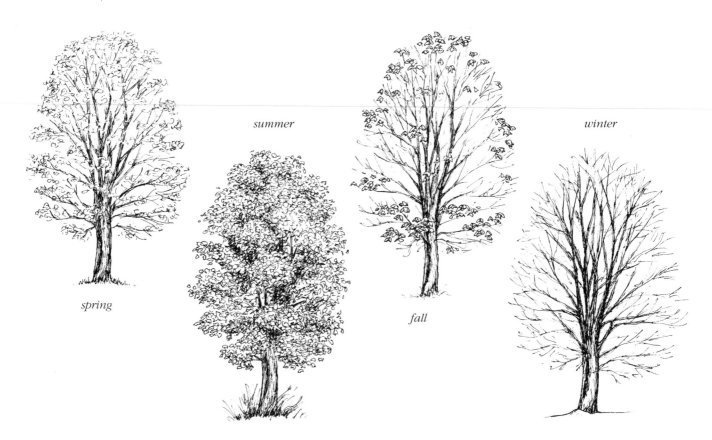

spring   summer   fall   winter

GROWING UP

Objective: *To determine a tree's approximate age by observing a tree slice.*

Materials:
- illustration of a tree slice
- illustrations of a tree of varying ages
- illustrations of a person at different stages of life
- thin half-inch slices from a tree branch (optional)

Activity:
1. Show the children the sketches of people at different life stages. Ask them to guess the approximate age of each person shown. What clues do they use to determine age?
(The children might also put the sketches in a line, from youngest to oldest; then they can guess ages.)

2. Now do the same with the tree illustrations. What clues might the children use to determine age in trees?

3. Explain that tree scientists often determine a tree's age by counting its rings. Give a tree slice or copies of the tree slice illustration to each pair of children. Ask the children to observe their tree slice or sketch and to count the rings to estimate its age.

Talk about how you can tell how old a tree is by counting its rings after it has been cut down or after a core sample has been taken from a living tree. The pale ring is the spring growth, the narrower, darker ring is the summer growth. Each pair marks one year.

The oldest trees in the world are the Bristlecone Pine trees of the Rocky Mountains. Some of these twisted little trees may be 6,000 years old. That makes them some of the oldest living things on earth.

TWO TYPES OF TREES

Objective: *To notice that there are two main types of trees – deciduous and coniferous.*

Materials:
- a branch, with leaves, from a deciduous tree (like a maple or oak)
- a branch, with needles, from a coniferous tree (like a pine or spruce)
- deciduous tree illustration (such as a maple)
- coniferous tree illustration (such as an evergreen)
- blindfolds (optional)

Activity:
1. Gather the children into a circle, placing the two branches in the center. Ask the children to describe the differences between the two. Introduce terms like "needles," "branches," and "twigs" – as well as "deciduous" (or "broad leaf") and "coniferous" (or "evergreen").
2. Pass the branches around the circle, inviting the children to compare the two branches using their sense of touch. Which one is prickly?
3. Now, with their eyes closed or blindfolded, ask the children to pass one branch around the circle BEHIND their backs. (You might want to have the children rotate around, so their backs are toward the center of the circle.) Once the branch has come full circle, ask the children to decide if the branch was from the deciduous or coniferous tree. Repeat.
4. Finally, show the children the illustrations of the deciduous and coniferous trees. Notice their shapes.

Talk about how coniferous tree branches are built for shedding excess snow. The woody part of the branch is flexible, so they bend under the weight of the snow, and the snow slides off. The needles are thin and waxy, so the snow doesn't easily collect on them.

BRANCH MATCHING

Objective: *To look closely at the branches and needles/leaves of several local conifer trees.*

Materials:
- two matching sets of small branches from 4 to 6 coniferous trees found nearby
- photocopies of the same 4 to 6 branches

Activity:
1. Seat the children in a circle. Display both sets of branches in the center of the circle.
2. Ask the children to match the branches. What is special about each branch pair? (For example: They have needles in bundles of five.)
3. Afterwards, place the four to six (or more) branches spread about the room. Give each child a photocopy of one of the branches. The children should then walk around the room, visiting the branches, until they find their matching branch.

Talk about some of the language used to describe tree features – branch, twig, needle. Highlight the various lengths of the needles. Suggest some ways you might measure needle lengths – as long as my fingernail, as long as my thumb, etc.

CONE MATCHING

Objective: *To match several cones to their branches.*

Materials:
- illustrations of cones from local trees
- actual cones from the same trees
- magnifying lenses
- one fully opened cone (preferably from a white pine)
- bowl of warm water

Activity:
1. Sitting in a circle, display the cones and sketches for the children. Ask the children to match the cones to the sketches. What clues do they use?
2. See if the children can find the seeds inside the cones. Use the magnifying lenses to see the small "resting place" for the seed on top of each scale.
3. Look closely at the fully opened cone. Show the children how, once the seeds were ripe, the cone would be held upside down on the tree's branch. Are there any seeds left inside? Why not?
4. Now place the opened cone into the warm water. Notice (over time – perhaps hours) how the cone's scales close.

Talk about how conifer (evergreen) trees produce their seeds in cones (versus berries, fruit, or nuts). The purpose of the cone is to hold the seeds until they become mature. Then the cone opens its scales to release the seeds, so they can blow on the wind. If it's going to rain soon, however, it's best for the cone to wait to release its seeds. That's why the cone's scales often close in humid, pre-rainstorm weather.

WHO CALLS A TREE HOME?

Objective: *To understand that a tree provides all that is needed as a home for many creatures.*

Materials:
- large simple picture of a tree with leaves (about 2 feet tall)
- cicada illustration
- bird illustration (see "From Rocks to Soil" unit in Growth and Change)
- squirrel illustration (see "Chipmunks and Their Cousins" unit in Animal Homes)
- spring peeper illustration (see "Friends with Frogs" unit in Growth and Change)
- owl illustration (see "Owls: Nighttime Hunters" unit in Animal Homes)
- scotch tape
- 4 large index cards with each card having one of the following words written clearly: EAT, RAISE A FAMILY, SLEEP, PLAY

Activity:
1. Beforehand, prepare the tree and the animal illustrations. Color and laminate both. Prepare the index cards, too. Post the tree sketch securely to the wall.
2. Gathering around the tree, ask the children to tell you some animals they know who spend time in trees. Discuss some ways a tree might be a perfect place for an animal to eat, sleep, play, and raise a family.
3. Give one of the laminated animal pictures to one child. When you hold up the "eat" card, ask that child to place the animal in a spot in the tree where it might find something to eat (say, the branches for a bird looking for insects).

4. The child then passes the same picture to the next child, who places the picture where the animal might "play." Continue through all four cards for each animal.

Talk about how a tree provides needed resources for animals during all or just part of their lives. The chickadee is one of the tree's best friends. In exchange for a place to raise its family in a **cavity nest** inside a branch or trunk, it eats many of the caterpillars, aphids, and other insects that like to nibble the tree's leaves or suck its sap. Earthworms are important to trees too. In exchange for the shelter and food they find amidst a tree's roots, worms drag fallen leaves underground to rot and release nutrients.

• •

USEFUL TREES

Objective: *To become aware of the many things trees give us.*

Materials: • Post-It pad pages – 5 or so for each child

Activity:
1. Have the children give examples of some of the things trees provide for people (furniture, paper, chewing gum, toys, etc.)
2. Then give each child several sticky pages. Have the children place them on items in the classroom that come from trees.
3. What else, beyond the classroom, comes from trees? (building materials, shade, oxygen, play set, etc.)
4. Say thank you to those hardworking trees!

Talk about the usefulness of wood. Some of the first tools made by the earliest people were probably wooden sticks for digging up edible roots. Many years later we still use wood in dozens of different ways. Beyond the things we build with wood like boats, toys, and tables, eucalyptus oil is used in some medicines and comes from the leaves of the eucalyptus tree. Chewing gum is made from the sap of the sapodilla tree. Rubber is made from the latex of the rubber tree. Most cork is the bark of the cork oak tree. Other barks are used for food flavoring, medicines, and for tanning leather.

> **We Care about . . .**
> **Trees**
> Before the grass is mowed for the first time in spring (or in a nearby woodland), look for small, bright green tree shoots. Dig one up, taking care to keep the roots intact. Put the **seedling** into a pot with some soil and tend it carefully over the summer. Plant it in the ground in the fall.

Outdoor Activities

STAY IN TOUCH: ADOPT A TREE

What You Need
- various colors of ribbon
- simple "meet a tree" journal for each child

What to Do

Encourage the children to adopt their own tree by choosing an accessible tree in the schoolyard or in their yard at home. Have them tie a colored ribbon onto a branch of their tree. Each child should have her own tree and ribbon color to mark it. Have the children visit their trees in different seasons and notice how they change. Once a month, visit the trees to notice the trees' leaves, buds, flowers, fruit, animal inhabitants, and any other changes.

• •

BARK RUBBING

What You Need
- newsprint
- crayons with paper removed

What to Do

Working in pairs, have one child hold the paper over the bark of the tree. Have another child use the broad side of a crayon and rub the crayon over the paper. You might also take back a sample leaf or twig to do a rubbing later.

• •

WHO'S HERE NOW?

What You Need
- magnifying lenses

What to Do

In pairs, have children visit their adopted trees (or other trees) to look for signs of wildlife activity such as animal holes, insect holes in bark, or nibbled leaves. Remind them to look for life under the bark, on the leaves, at its base, or in the branches. Look for signs of very small creatures, as well as large ones.

TOGETHER AGAIN

What You Need
- cones and/or nuts from nearby trees (within walking distance)

What to Do
Give each child a cone or nut. Then take a walk around the neighborhood, searching for the trees from which the nuts and cones came.

Language Activity / Poem

You are a tree, standing tall. *[stand tall with arms outstretched]*
The wind bends your branches. *[sway your arms]*
Imagine a woodpecker tapping and tickling your trunk. *[wiggle and giggle]*
Brrrrr . . . feel the cold ground around your roots. *[wiggle toes]*
Snowflakes flutter down onto your branches and trunk.

Discuss other types of weather the tree might experience. Have the children describe what that weather might feel like. Write down their answers. Repeat the exercise incorporating the children's imagery.

Crafts and Projects

FROM BUD TO LEAF

What You Need
- jars
- forsythia, magnolia, serviceberry or other branches

What to Do
In the late winter, make buds open early by cutting some twigs and bringing them indoors. Put them in a jar of water, and you can watch how they burst into life.

• •

PAINT A TREE

What You Need
- variety of branches, leaves, and/or twigs
- tempera paint
- large paper
- brayer (paint roller), brushes, and/or sponges

What to Do
Help the children to use the branches, paint, and tools to create colorful paintings.

CHEERIOS FOR THE BIRDS

What You Need
- cheerios or fruit loops
- blunt darning needles (1 per child)
- thread or thin yarn

What to Do
Help the children to make long strands of cheerios. Drape them over the branches of nearby trees. Then watch to see which birds eat the foods you've provided.

Snacks

TASTY TREES

What You Need
- large and small pretzel sticks
- peanut butter and/or marshmallow spread
- paper plates or plain paper
- plastic or other small, safe knives

What to Do
Using the large pretzels as trunks and the small ones as branches, encourage the children to create edible trees.

Independent Play Idea
Provide twigs, nuts, bark, cones, weighing scales, boxes, and other materials for free play.

WHITE PINE TREE TEA

What You Need
- fresh white pine needles
- clear plastic or glass pitcher
- plastic wrap
- sugar and stirring spoon
- cups

What to Do
Gather a large bunch of fresh white pine needles. Place them in water in a large pitcher. Cover the pitcher with plastic wrap. Place the pitcher in a sunny spot, and wait a day or two. Remove the needles, stir in a bit of sugar, and serve the children cups of white pine tea (very high in vitamin C!).

Book Ideas

CHILDREN'S FICTION

A Tree for Me, by Nancy Van Laan, Alfred A. Knopf, 2000 – the story of a boy who is looking for the perfect tree to climb and who meets all kinds of animals inhabiting trees.

Are You Spring?, by Caroline Pitcher and Cliff Wright, Dorling Kindersley Publishing, 2000 – a bear named Una, who was told she cannot leave her winter den until spring, finally gets to explore the world as spring arrives.

When Will the Snow Trees Grow?, by Ben Shecter, HarperCollins Children's Books Group, 1993 – a boy who cannot wait for the arrival of winter learns from his bear friend about how all the seasons must arrive in their own time.

CHILDREN'S NONFICTION

A Walk in the Boreal Forest, by Rebecca Johnson, Carolrhoda Books, 2001 – describes the climate, seasons, plants, animals, and soil of the boreal forest, great pictures and factual information, as well as an excellent reference list for further information.

Fall Is Not Easy, by Marty Kelley, Zino Press, 1998 – describes a tree's experiences in all four seasons.

Have You Seen Trees?, by Joanne Oppenheim, Scholastic, 1967 – explore and experience a variety of trees throughout the seasons in this wonderful, poetic book, includes a section on tree identification.

RESOURCE BOOKS FOR CHILDREN AND ADULTS

A Tree Is Growing, by Arthur Dorros, Scholastic, 1997 – covers many aspects of the natural history of trees and forests.

Meeting Trees, by Scott Sanders, National Geographic, 1997 – on a walk through the woods, a father shares his knowledge about trees and forest life with his son.

Mighty Tree, by Dick Gackenbach, Gulliver Books, 1992 – follows the fate of three seeds as they grow into trees, then used by humans and animals as food, products, and shelters.

Peterson First Guide: Trees, by George Petrides, Houghton Mifflin, 1998 – a condensed guide to the most common North American trees, useful for adults and children.

Sky Tree: Seeing Science through Art, by Thomas Locker, HarperCollins, 1995 – a tree changes through the seasons and with the sky that serves as a backdrop behind it.

Tell Me, Tree: All about Trees for Kids, by Gail Gibbons, Little, Brown, 2002 – includes information on how to identify trees by shape, leaves, and bark. Also includes general information about trees and tree activities.

Trees, by Linda Gamlin, Dorling Kindersley, 1993 – full-color illustrations with information and experiments on trees and their parts.

THE YEAR OF A TREE

We've been learning about trees – their parts and functions, how they grow and change through the seasons, and their importance to people and wildlife.

Continue the Learning at Home

Create a "thanksgiving" tree. Cut several large twigs to place in a clay pot (or decorated coffee can) full of rocks or marbles. Cut ten or so three-inch leaf shapes from colored construction paper or cardstock paper. Punch a hole in each. Ask your child to tell you some reasons we should thank a tree (ways that trees are useful to people). Write these ideas on the paper leaves. Help your child to tie a piece of string or yarn to each leaf card, then attach it to your "thanksgiving" tree. You might use this as a table centerpiece.

More Fun with Trees

Find a tiny tree seedling in your yard, nearby woods, or at a garden center. Carefully transplant the seedling into your yard, so you and your child can watch it grow!

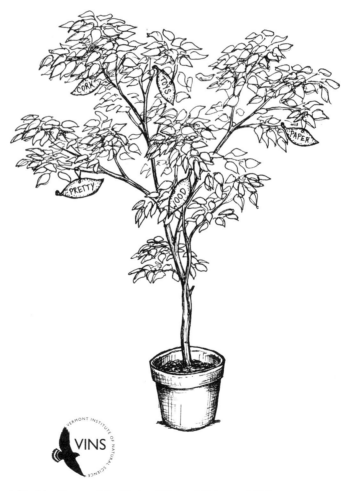

Produced and copyrighted by Vermont Institute of Natural Science, 2005.

Butterflies: Flying Flowers

Focus: Butterflies are a wonderfully diverse group of insects, yet with several observable similarities (wing symmetry, body parts, plant diet). The beauty and variety of butterflies makes them attractive to children and adults alike.

Objective: To become familiar with the life cycle of butterflies and to learn about butterflies' body parts and food preferences.

Extra Information for Adult Leaders

Butterflies are an incredibly diverse and colorful group of insects. Their life cycle involves a series of complete transformations from a tiny egg to a growing **larva (caterpillar)** to a **pupa (chrysalis)** and, finally, to an adult butterfly.

This process of change, or **metamorphosis**, begins when the mother butterfly, having already mated with another butterfly of her species, prepares to lay her eggs. (The adult butterflies find their mates using scents or **pheromones**.) The mother butterfly is careful to find just the right spot to place her tiny eggs, often on the underside of a plant's leaf (where it will be protected from rain, sun, and hungry birds). It is no coincidence that the mother butterfly chooses a plant that will later serve as a food source for the hungry caterpillars.

Inside the egg, the body of the butterfly is transforming – from egg to caterpillar. Once it emerges, the caterpillar launches into its mission in life – to eat and grow, eat and grow. As the caterpillar grows larger, its skin actually becomes too small. The skin must split and then **molt** (fall off), revealing a new, loose skin layer underneath. Some caterpillars do this four or more times before they're fully grown. Finally, after the caterpillar has grown several times larger, its skin changes again, this time into the exterior cover of the pupa or chrysalis. The chrysalis hardens to protect the creature inside. After perhaps several weeks or even months (depending on the kind of butterfly), the chrysalis splits open and a butterfly emerges with wings, legs, and **antennae**!

All adult butterflies have similar body parts. Their bodies are divided into three sections: **abdomen**, **thorax**, and head. On their heads, they have two eyes, two antennae and a long tongue, called a **proboscis**. Attached to the thorax (or mid) section, butterflies have six legs and two pairs of wings (**forewings** and **hindwings**). The wings look smooth, but their surfaces are actually covered by tiny, overlapping scales, each pigmented or structured to lend color and pattern to the wing. Often, the brightest coloration is seen when the wings are outstretched. When folded above the body, the wings usually display colors and patterns that help butterflies blend with their surroundings. Wing coloration may serve any combination of the following: absorbing heat, attracting mates, camouflaging, and/or startling predators.

Butterflies are very closely related to moths, and distinguishing the two can be challenging. While butterflies are generally active during the day, and moths at night, there is some overlap (notably the Sphinx moth, which can sometimes be found hovering like a hummingbird in front of summer blossoms). A general way to tell them apart is by their antennae. Butterfly antennae are smooth, with a slightly wide, or clubbed, tip. The antennae of moths appear feathery. Observing butterflies and moths provides an opportunity to watch delicate, but also very tough, insects navigate through life.

DIGGING IN...

The Body of a Butterfly

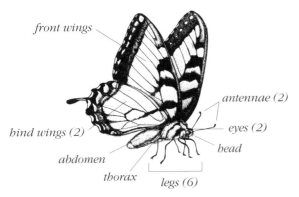

front wings

hind wings (2)

abdomen

thorax

legs (6)

head

eyes (2)

antennae (2)

Indoor Activities

BUTTERFLY DRESS UP

Objective: *To pretend to be butterflies flying about on colorful wings.*

Materials:
- colorful scarves (wings) – or paper or cloth streamers
- party blowers (proboscis)
- aluminum foil (antennae)
- tape player and music for "butterfly dancing"

Activity:
1. Help the children to shape the aluminum foil into antennae. First, twist a section long enough to wrap around the child's head. Then add two antennae with more foil.
2. Provide party blowers for the children to use as their mouth parts (proboscis).
3. Help the children to tie the scarves or streamers to their wrists.
4. Finally, turn on the music and have the children dance and move like flying butterflies. (Include movements for both flapping and gliding butterflies.)

Talk about how butterflies flap their wings behind (or above) their bodies. Can we do that? Can we pull our wings back far enough so that they nearly touch behind our backs? Sometimes, as warm air rises off the earth's surface (thermal currents), butterflies simply hold their wings out still, rise up on the warm thermal currents, then gently glide downward.

GROWING UP

Objective: *To become aware of butterfly metamorphosis.*

Materials:
- illustrations of butterfly growth (egg, caterpillar, chrysalis, adult butterfly)

Activity:
1. Using the pictures as your guide, describe for the children the stages of a butterfly's metamorphosis.

Talk about the various stages of growth and, especially, the job of each life stage. The egg is the beginning; the caterpillar must eat and grow; the chrysalis is the resting and rearranging stage; and the adult is the flying and mating stage.

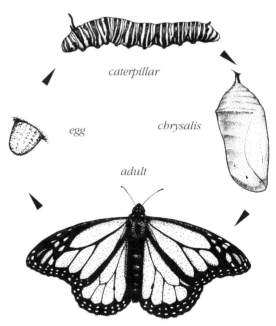

caterpillar

egg

chrysalis

adult

DO YOU STILL KNOW ME?

Objective: *To practice changing appearance, much like the way a butterfly changes its appearance as it grows.*

Materials:
- illustrations of butterfly growth (egg, caterpillar, chrysalis, adult butterfly)
- curtain or sheet (behind which children can change clothes)
- hats, scarves, glasses, wigs, and other dress up clothes

Activity:
1. Show the children the egg and adult pictures. Ask them, "Do these two creatures look alike or different?" They look very different. In fact, it would be difficult to guess that the tiny, one-color egg would eventually change into a colorful adult butterfly.
2. Now explain that we're going to take turns changing our appearances, too.
3. Ask for three volunteers to step behind the changing curtain.
4. Select one of those children to put on a wig, hat, glasses, shirt, etc. (The other two children can help.)
5. Then the child steps out so the other children can see him/her, and they try to guess who is hiding beneath all the dress up clothes!
6. Repeat until every child has had a chance to dress up.

Talk about how butterflies and people are similar in that they both must grow and change from babies (eggs) to adults. However, unlike people, butterflies completely change their appearance along the way. This is accomplished in a rather complex way, with the cells of the butterfly's body actually changing, growing, and rearranging.

IT ALL STARTS WITH AN EGG

Objective: *To appreciate the special care a mother butterfly must take when choosing where to place her eggs.*

Materials:
- white rice – some of it cooked and sticky, some of it raw
- plants with sturdy leaves (could be tree branches brought indoors)

Activity:
1. Ask the children to recall the very first stage of the butterfly (the egg).
2. Explain that butterfly eggs are almost always very small, similar in size to a grain of rice. (Let the children hold a grain of raw rice.)
3. Also explain that most butterfly eggs are a bit sticky, like a cooked grain of rice. (Let the children feel the sticky cooked rice now.) That's because the eggs are placed on the underside of a leaf. If the eggs were not sticky, they would immediately fall from the leaf.
4. Have the children compare the holding abilities of raw and cooked rice grains by trying to press the rice grains to the bottom of the leaves provided.

Talk about the fact that a mother butterfly may lay hundreds of eggs, depositing each on its own plant leaf. The mother specially selects these leaves because they will be the right food for the growing caterpillars to eat after they've hatched from their eggs. Also, by placing the eggs on the underside of the leaf, the mother butterfly helps to protect her eggs from harsh sunlight, hungry birds, and strong rains. (On rainy days, adult butterflies also hide under leaves and along the trunks of trees to get out of the rain.)

THE CATERPILLAR STRETCH

Objective:	*To have fun making paper caterpillars "stretch."*
Materials:	• straws with paper wrappers
Activity:	1. Show the children how you can scrunch the straw wrapper up tightly, then slide it off the straw. Pretend the paper is a tiny caterpillar.
	2. Ask for a volunteer to add one small drop of water to the scrunched wrapper. Notice how the water makes the caterpillar grow!
	3. Repeat as desired.

Talk about what real caterpillars need to grow – lots of appropriate plant food. Different kinds (species) of caterpillars need different kinds of plants. For example, monarch butterfly caterpillars need milkweed plants, while black swallowtail butterfly caterpillars need parsley family plants (like carrots and Queen Anne's Lace).

• •

GROWING CATERPILLARS

Objective:	*To feel what it might be like to discard your old skin as you grow bigger.*
Materials:	• several pairs of knee socks or tights – cut into 10-inch lengths
	• green paper leaves
	• stickers for eyes (optional)
	• pipe cleaners for antennae (optional)
Activity:	1. Introduce the concept of caterpillar molting.
	2. Choose a volunteer. Help that child to put several layers of socks or tights over his arm (like layers of caterpillar skin).
	3. If desired, you might also apply sticker eyes and antennae to the child's hand, which is the "head" of the caterpillar.
	4. The child should then help the pretend caterpillar to eat some of the leaves available (making suitable munching noises, of course).
	5. Pause and help the caterpillar (arm) to shed a layer of skin (sock). Then continue eating.

Talk about caterpillar molting. Molting is when a caterpillar splits and discards its outer skin layer as it grows larger. The fresh skin layer underneath is stretchy and slightly larger than the discarded layer. Depending on how large they might grow, caterpillars may molt several times. Monarch caterpillars, for example, usually molt five times. Towards the end of its final molt, the caterpillar finds a twig from which to hang, forming a "J" shape with its body. This signals that the chrysalis or pupa stage will be coming soon.

BEAUTIFUL BUTTERFLIES

Objective: *To witness some of the many beautiful varieties of butterflies.*

Materials:
- field guide to butterflies
- diagram of a butterfly body
- magnifying lenses (optional)

Activity:
1. Seat the children in a small circle, and then together look at the photos of the many beautiful butterflies.
2. Let the children notice colors, patterns, spots, and sizes.
3. Show them the butterfly body diagram, asking them to notice the body parts (head, thorax, abdomen), eyes, antennae, four wings, and six legs.

Talk about how some butterflies have **eye spots** – large spots on their wings (especially their **underwings**). These spots are designed to flash when the butterfly opens its wings in imitation of the large eyes of a predatory animal.

• •

BUTTERFLY BUDDIES

Objective: *To notice the symmetry of butterfly wings.*

Materials:
- pairs of butterfly wings (Prepare these by cutting wing shapes from large paper. Paint a design on one wing, then press a second wing to the wet paint. Repeat with new colors and designs, so that each wing pair is unique.)
- large mirror

Activity:
1. Show the children one pair of wings. Point out how one wing is the "mirror" match of the other. (Hold one wing up to the mirror to show what you mean.)
2. Give each child a single wing.
3. Have the children move about, comparing wings, until the correct matches are found.

Talk about the special word to describe the "matches" found in butterfly wings, for example – symmetry. Notice how the wings would fit together in a real butterfly; that is, the colorful sides would face each other and be on the top side.

A FLASH OF COLOR

Objective: *To notice a detail of some butterflies: the top and bottom sides of their wings are often quite different.*

Materials:
- sample set of large butterfly wings (Prepare these four wings by making the top sides bright and colorful, while the bottom sides are dull and camouflaged.)
- colorful scarves – one or two per child

Activity:
1. Gather the children in a circle, and show them the top side of the wings. (Display the wings butterfly fashion.) Notice how the top sides of the wings are colorful, patterned, and symmetrical.
2. Now flip over the wings to reveal the bottom sides. Notice the wings are now dully colored and could be quite well camouflaged against, say, tree bark.
3. Explain to the children that those two sides have a special purpose. When the butterfly is in flight, the colors of the upper wings flash – and attract the attention of potential butterfly mates. When the butterfly needs to hide (say, while resting in the evening and trying to avoid detection by bird predators), the wings are closed, held behind the butterfly's back, and the dull wing side now shows.
4. Now have the children hold their scarves in their hands, flapping them at their sides – those are the colorful upper wings showing.
5. You, the adult, pretend to be a hungry bird. One at a time, call a child's name, saying something like, "Nora, I see you and your beautiful butterfly wings. I'm coming to eat you!" Then Nora brings her arms together in front of her. The closed butterfly wings are no longer easy to see. And you reply, "Oh, no, the colorful butterfly disappeared!"
6. Repeat for the other children.

Talk about other animals that use camouflage coloring to hide themselves in their habitats. Moths, which come out at night, are masters of camouflage because they rest (and must remain hidden) during the daylight hours.

Outdoor Activities

METAMORPHOSIS ROLE PLAY

What You Need
- large burlap bags
- brightly colored cloth scarves

What to Do

Have the children pretend to be butterflies in their various life stages. As eggs, they will curl up small and hold still. As caterpillars, they will stretch out and wiggle across the ground in search of food. As chrysalides, they will climb inside the burlap bag and wait a moment. As adults, they will don their colorful scarf wings and fly!

FOLLOW THE LEADER BUTTERFLY

What You Need
- colorful scarves for wings

What to Do

After providing wings for everyone, challenge the children to follow your movements, while you fly in circles, under branches, up over rocks, etc.

• •

BUTTERFLY SEARCH

What You Need
- field guide to local butterflies

What to Do

To prepare and not overwhelm and confuse the children, it's best if you can make enlarged, color copies of four or so of your area's most common butterfly pictures from the guide. (Contact your local nature center or state conservation department for information on butterflies common to your area.)

Equipped with the color pictures, take the children outside to search for these (and other) butterflies nearby. If possible, observe which plants the butterflies seem to land on most. Might the adult be preparing to lay eggs?

• •

IF I COULD FLY . . .

What to Do

Find a nice, comfortable, shady spot to sit with your group. Talk with the children about how special and important it is that butterflies can fly. Flight not only helps them to get away from dangers and move quickly toward food and mates, but it makes them look beautiful as they flit delicately through the air. Now ask the children to imagine that they, too, could fly like butterflies. If they could fly, what would they most like to do? Have them complete this sentence: "If I could fly, I would . . . ."

We Care about . . . Butterflies

Take the children for a walk in the autumn, when the wooly bear caterpillars are abundant. Practice gently lifting the fuzzy caterpillars and moving them to safe spots along the trail or sidewalk. (Wooly bears overwinter as caterpillars, then spin their cocoons in the spring, and metamorphose into an Isabella moth. Although wooly bears are not butterfly caterpillars, they are very child-friendly: cute, fuzzy, and easily handled). Do mention that wooly bears turn into moths rather than butterflies.

In the spring, ask for donations of or purchase several **perennial** plants chosen to attract butterflies. Milkweed, butterfly bush, and bee balm are good choices. The children can prepare the soil, then create a small butterfly garden so they can enjoy the butterfly visitors.

Language Activity / Poem

This little caterpillar
nibbles a leaf.

[Wiggle index finger of right hand – the caterpillar.]
*[Hold left hand flat, palm up – the leaf. Crawl the "caterpillar"
over the "leaf."]*

Turns into a chrysalis
all nice and neat.
Inside the chrysalis,
changes occur.

[Wrap the left hand over the right index finger.]

A butterfly grows, and
soon will emerge

*[Make a butterfly with your hands. Hold your hands in front of
you, palms up. Cross your wrists and cross your thumbs. Press the tips of
your thumbs together to create the butterfly head. Your hands are the
butterfly wings. Flap them to make it fly.]*

Crafts and Projects

THUMBPRINT CATERPILLARS

What You Need
- washable ink pads (1 per child)
- thin line markers
- paper

What to Do
Give each child paper and an ink pad. Have the children press one thumb to the ink pad, then to the paper. Make a line of prints for the segments of a caterpillar. Then, the children can add eyes, legs, and antennae.

After doing this activity, you might like to show the children a photo or drawing of a real caterpillar – so you can see where the legs are and how many!

• •

EGG CARTON CATERPILLARS

What You Need
- egg cartons – precut into varying lengths (Also, you might want to use a pencil tip to poke small holes at one end for the pipe cleaner antennae.)
- paints and brushes
- pipe cleaners – pairs, cut into short lengths
- marker or "googly eyes" and glue

What to Do
After covering the table, give each child an egg carton to paint as she/he wishes. When the paint's dry, provide pipe cleaner pieces to add as antennae, as well as some sort of eyes.

When the caterpillars are finished, encourage the children to compare their varying lengths. Which ones are longest? Shortest? Put the caterpillars in size order. How do real caterpillars grow longer? (by eating) Which ones are the youngest? Oldest?

GROWING BUTTERFLIES

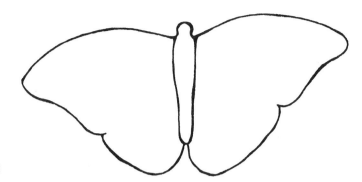

What You Need
- strong paper plates (1 per child)
- glue
- rice
- foam peanuts
- large pasta shells
- paint and brushes
- markers
- small paper butterfly outline (1 per child)

What to Do
Give each child a few grains of rice, a foam peanut, a pasta shell, and a butterfly outline. Explain that these things represent the different stages of a butterfly's metamorphosis (egg, caterpillar, chrysalis, adult). Invite the children to use the paints and markers to color these parts. When dry, ask the children to glue the pieces (in correct order) in a circle on the paper plate.

PRETTY FLYING FLOWERS

What You Need
- large paper butterfly outlines (1 per child) (Body length should be just slightly shorter than the length of the chopstick.)
- several colors of liquid paint – thinned to a fairly watery consistency
- plastic pipettes or straws
- chopsticks (1 per child)
- long, thin paper strips (1/4-inch wide by 6-inches long)
- pencils – 1 per child
- glue

What to Do
First, have the children fold their butterfly papers in half (so they can see how both halves are the same). Then, using the pipettes, instruct them to apply one drop of paint to just ONE side of the butterfly. Repeat with other colors, adding a drop at a time to the SAME side of the butterfly. After several colors have been applied, help the children to fold their butterflies in half again. Open them to reveal the accurate color symmetry.

When the paint is dry, help the children to use the glue to add a chopstick to the center of the butterfly (as a body AND a place to hold the butterfly to make it "flutter in the wind"). Also, they might wrap a long, thin paper strip tightly around a pencil, then let it go to form a curly tongue (proboscis).

TISSUE PAPER BUTTERFLIES

What You Need
- plastic contact paper – precut into large butterfly shapes (top and bottom sheet for each butterfly) – 1 set for each child
- tissue paper – several colors – small bits are fine
- black construction paper – precut into butterfly bodies to be added to the center of each of the butterflies
- hole punch and yarn

What to Do
Provide one piece of precut, butterfly-shaped contact paper for each child. First, give them the black bodies to add to the center. Then have the children press small bits of different colored tissue paper onto the entire surface of the butterfly. When finished, add the top layer of contact paper (sandwich style). Punch a couple of holes in each butterfly, add yarn, and hang them from the ceiling.

Snack

FRUIT SMOOTHIES

What You Need
- blender
- variety of soft fruits – bananas, strawberries, etc.
- apple or other fruit juice
- ice cubes
- optional – yogurt or milk
- cups and straws

What to Do
Mix all the ingredients together in the blender until smooth. Provide cups and straws for the children, so they can pretend to be butterflies sipping sweet flower nectar.

Independent Play Idea
Use masking tape to form large butterfly outlines on a table top. Provide various colors of stickers. Challenge the children to apply the stickers to the wings in "butterfly fashion" (symmetrical – with a yellow sticker, for instance, in the opposite spot on both wings).

Book Ideas

CHILDREN'S FICTION

Caterpillar Caterpillar, by Vivian French, Candlewick Press, 1993 – a multi-level book about the life cycle of a butterfly; includes detailed information about specific kinds of butterflies.

From Caterpillar to Butterfly, by Deborah Heiligman, Scholastic, 1996 – the story of a child's experience with raising a painted lady butterfly in her classroom, nice for three and four-year-olds.

I Wish I Were a Butterfly, by James Howe, Gulliver Books, 1987 – an artistically illustrated tale of a cricket who feels ugly until appreciated by a spider.

A Monarch Butterfly's Life, by John Himmelman, Children's Press, Grolier Publishing, 1999 – based on scientific facts, describes the life cycle of the monarch butterfly.

The Very Hungry Caterpillar, by Eric Carle, Philomel, 1987 – a classic and entertaining story about a caterpillar who eats all the wrong things, good for counting and days of the week skills, too.

CHILDREN'S NONFICTION

The Butterfly, by Sabrina Crewe, Raintree Steck-Vaughn Publishers, 1997 – extraordinary photography, presents lots of butterfly information with easy-to-read text.

Butterflies, by Emily Neye, Scholastic, 2000 – a simple, informative, and visually appealing book that describes butterfly diversity, life cycles, and more.

Butterflies!, by Darlene Freeman, McClanahan Book Company, 1999 – describes butterfly metamorphosis, body parts, and defenses.

Crinkleroot's Guide to Knowing Butterflies, by Jim Arnosky, Simon & Schuster Books, 1996 – a nature guide, introduces readers to various types of butterflies and moths, includes basic anatomy, identification tips, and simple natural history facts.

Monarch Butterfly, by Gail Gibbons, Scholastic, 1999 – a careful description of the monarch butterfly's life cycle and migration.

The Prince of Butterflies, by Bruce Coville, Harcourt Children's Books, 2002 – an extraordinary, imaginative story about a boy who became a monarch butterfly while he was working to save the species from danger.

Waiting for Wings, by Lois Ehlert, Harcourt Children's Books, 2001 – vivid graphics, recounts the life cycle of butterflies with rhyming verse.

Where Did the Butterfly Get Its Name?, by Melvin Berger, Scholastic, 2003 – provides information about the physical characteristics, habitat, behavior, and life cycle of butterflies in a question-and-answer format.

RESOURCE BOOKS FOR ADULTS AND CHILDREN

Hide a Butterfly, by Jean C. Echols, GEMS series, University of California, 1986 – a teacher's guide for preschool to kindergarten, includes directions for assisting children to construct a flower garden and butterflies.

The Kids' Science Book, by Robert Hirschfeld, Williamson Publishing, 1995 – an activity book, includes a great section on butterflies, especially good craft ideas.

Peterson's First Guides: Butterflies and Moths, by Paul Opler, Houghton Mifflin, 1998 – a condensed field guide that contains the most commonly seen species.

Peterson's First Guides: Caterpillars, by Amy Bartlett Wright, Houghton Mifflin, 1998 – a condensed field guide that contains the most commonly found caterpillars.

BUTTERFLIES: FLYING FLOWERS

We've been learning about butterflies – their bodies, life cycles, eating habits, and beauty.

Continue the Learning at Home

High in the mountains of Mexico each winter, millions of monarch butterflies gather in trees. There are so many butterflies, and they're so closely packed, that they make the trunks and branches of the trees look orange and black!

The monarch butterflies rest there until early spring, when they set out for their northern homes once again. An individual monarch butterfly may fly up to 3000 miles on its tiny wings!

Make a Monarch Butterfly Tree

Use the very simple butterfly outline (left) to copy and cut ten or more butterflies. Provide orange and black markers or crayons and ask your child to color the monarch butterflies. Finally, use tape to fasten the butterflies to a nearby tree – and pretend it's winter in Mexico!

Produced and copyrighted by Vermont Institute of Natural Science, 2005.

From Flower to Fruit

Focus: Flowers become fruits through pollination. Many flowers are attractive to insects, birds, and other animals responsible for spreading pollen from blossom to blossom.

Objective: To learn to appreciate the beauty of flowers and discover the connection between flowers and fruit – an important cycle in nature.

Extra Information for Adult Leaders

DIGGING IN...

The **flower** to fruit cycle shows a plant's need to create and fertilize seeds, as well as to ensure that the seeds travel to locations where they can germinate. The structures and colors of flowers and fruits are often a plant's attempt to attract or discourage insects and animals. Inconspicuous flowers are often found on species that do not need to attract animals to ensure successful completion of the cycle. Flowers attracting insects advertise in all colors except red (insects cannot see red), including ultraviolet, and often have markings that lead the insect to the nectar. Those flowers designed to attract birds often use reds, and night-blooming flowers, such as honeysuckle, four-o'clocks, and many species of cacti, have light-colored petals to increase visibility.

The petals of a flower surround the **pistil** (in female flowers), the **stamen** (in male flowers), or both. The stamen consists of an **anther** (the pollen producer) mounted on a **filament**. While some plants self-fertilize, most attempt to increase their chances of genetic diversity and survival through **cross-pollination** (using pollen from one plant to fertilize another plant of the same species). Plants that depend on fertilization by wind, including many grasses and trees, produce pollen in mass quantities. In the case of the birch tree, for example, millions of pollen grains may be released by a single birch catkin (male flower). Wind-pollinated flowers have long filaments to expose their pollen to air currents.

Plants that attract animals for pollination must provide a food reward, and most offer nectar as an alternative to pollen, which, while nutritious, is energetically expensive for the plant to produce. The nectar, pistil, and stamen are placed to maximize the quantity of pollen brushed onto the animal's body. Depending on the pollinator, bright showy petals, perfume, or both may be used to advertise the presence of nectar.

Successful fruit production relies on the transfer of pollen from the anthers or the pollinator to the pistil, which contains the flower's female parts (the **stigma**, **style**, and **ovary**). The stigma, lifted above the ovary by the style, offers a sticky collection platform for pollen. Every plant species has a distinctive signature to its pollen, which may be a particular shape and/or a chemical coating. Only pollen grains that match the species of plant they land on are permitted by the stigma to grow a **pollen tube** down the style to reach the ovary and to release male genetic information into the flower's **ovules**.

If fertilized, the ovules will mature into seeds, and the ovary will become the fruit. Technically, apples, acorns, tomatoes, and maple seeds may all be considered fruits, as they all consist of seeds wrapped to varying degrees in the protection of the plant's ovary. Lightweight seeds are often dispersed by the wind, and some, like maple seeds, are equipped with adaptations to prolong their journey through the air. Plants that encase their seeds in fleshy fruits, such as apples, oranges, or blueberries, must develop adaptations to advertise fruit ripeness to discourage consumption of unripe fruit whose seeds are not mature. Additionally, they must create seeds that pass through an animal's digestive tract unscathed. If seeds survive the rigors of dispersal and land in an appropriate location, they will germinate, flower, and begin the cycle again.

Indoor Activities

THE STORY OF APPLES

Objective:	*To introduce the concept of the flower to fruit cycle.*
Materials:	• children's picture book: *The Apple Pie Tree* by Zoe Hall
Activity:	1. Read the book aloud and discuss it with the children.
	2. Have the children stand up and pretend to be growing apples.
	3. Talk them through the following stages (events):

- tightly closed bud *[arms around body, body tucked near ground]*
- growing stem and opening petals *[stand up, open arms outward]*
- hot sun, cold wind, hard rain *[shake]*
- bee comes to visit *[tickles neck]*
- loses petals *[drop arms to sides]*
- tiny fruit with seeds remains *[fists to chest like seeds]*
- apple grows larger *[elbows out]*
- apple drops to ground, then is covered by winter snow *[fall to ground]*
- in warmth of spring, apple decays and releases seeds *[spread body out]*
- sprout again into little plant *[hands wiggle up above head]*

Talk about the importance of the bee. The bee carries the pollen from one apple blossom to another. This is called "pollination."

FELT FLOWERS

Objective:	*To introduce the parts of a flower by assembling a felt flower as a group.*
Materials:	• felt board
	• felt flower pieces (see page 72 for patterns)
Activity:	1. Tell the children you are going to put together a flower and look at its different parts.
	2. Begin with the flower stems and leaves.
	3. Add the flower bud to one stem and the flower petals to the other.
	4. Finally, place the pistil and stamens within the flower petals.

Talk about how flowers are just one part of a plant. Point out that the blooming flower comes from a bud, like the one you have placed on your plant. Ask the children why they think the flower petals are brightly colored (to attract pollinators). Point out that the seeds are made in the pistil and that pollen is produced in the stamens.

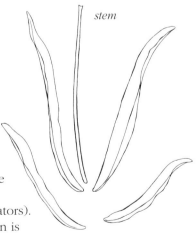

stem

four basil leaves

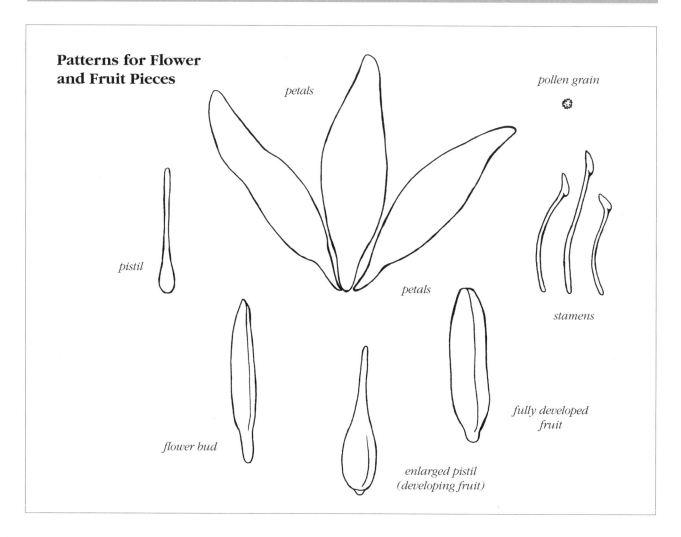

Patterns for Flower and Fruit Pieces

petals

pollen grain

pistil

petals

stamens

flower bud

enlarged pistil (developing fruit)

fully developed fruit

TAKE APART A FLOWER

Objective: *To observe closely the different parts of a flower.*

Materials:
- flowers – 1 per 2 or 3 children (Large petaled flowers, like tulips or lilies, are best.)
- hand lenses
- 1 small sharp knife

Activity:
1. Give each small group a flower to examine. Ask the children to notice the stem, leaves, and flower color.
2. Ask the children to count the petals, then remove them one-by-one. What colors do they see in the petals?
3. Remove the stamens. If they still contain pollen, tap the pollen off.
4. Look closely at the pistil. Then have an adult carefully cut the ovary in half, lengthwise, to look for eggs/seeds in the ovary.

Talk about the flower parts you see. Review the names and functions of the parts with the children (petals, stem, leaves, bud, stamen, pistil). If they're present on your flowers, point out the lines or darker areas on the individual petals – these help to guide the insect pollinators to the center of the flower and the nectar and pollen.

"POLLINATION PALS" PUPPET SHOW

Objective: *To show nature's helpers in the pollination process.*

Materials:
- puppet show script (see the end of unit)
- puppets: red, white and yellow flowers, hummingbird, bee, and bud (see the end of unit)
- puppet stage
- masking tape

Activity:
1. Prepare a puppet stage by taping the flower and bud puppets to the stage.
2. Present the puppet show.
3. Afterwards, show the children the flowers and ask them to recall how each one was pollinated.

Talk about how the flowers need help to spread their pollen around. Mention that in nature flowers reward their helpers with a sweet drink of nectar. The nectar provides energy and nutrients to the pollinator. In exchange, the helpers share pollen with other flowers. Most flowers *need* pollen from *other* flowers in order to develop into fruits. (Some plants produce new flowers from their established **bulbs** or roots.)

FELT FRUITS

Objective: *To help children understand how a flower becomes a fruit.*

Materials:
- felt board or other surface for assembly
- felt flower pieces from "felt flowers" activity on page 72

Activity:
1. Before beginning the activity, assemble the flower on the felt board.
2. With the children, place a pollen grain on the pistil.
3. Tell them, that, as time goes on, the flower will die, but the pistil, which holds the seeds, will grow.
4. Remove the petals, leaving the pistil behind.
5. Add the second pistil to the picture – showing the seeds and fruit growing.
6. Lastly, show the fully developed fruit.

Talk about how, even when a flower's petals fall off and die, part of the flower still continues to grow and that part (the fruit and seeds) will ultimately produce new plants.

POLLEN MATCH

Objective: *To understand that each flower requires a specific type of pollen.*

Materials:
- copies of flower illustrations with shapes in the center (You may want copy these onto colored paper or color these ahead of time.)
- yellow pollen pieces from paper or felt (shaped to match flower center)
- double-sided tape

Activity:
1. Post individual flowers around the room. Put tape on the flowers to allow children to stick pollen shapes to the flowers.
2. Gather the children into a circle and distribute pollen shapes.
3. Tell the children that they are going to pretend to be pollinators traveling from flower to flower. They must move around the room until they find a flower that their pollen shape matches.
4. Allow the children to complete the task, helping them match the shapes to the flowers.

Talk about how, in nature, plants can tell the difference between their pollen and that of another kind of plant. One plant's pollen may have a special shape, like ours did, or it may have a special chemical coating that makes it identifiable to its own kind of flower.

LOOKING INSIDE FRUITS

Objective: *To examine the inside of several fruits.*

Materials:
- several common fruits (apple, orange, peach, etc.)
- knife and cutting board
- photos of the flowers of some of the fruits used, if possible

Activity:
1. Display before the children a variety of familiar fruits. Ask them to predict what they'll find inside all of them (seeds). Also ask the children to recall how the fruit and seeds are formed (from the pollinated flower). Show the flower photos, too.
2. Allowing the children to choose, one by one, cut open and look inside each of the fruits. Any surprises?
3. Count the number of seeds inside each fruit.
4. Which fruit has the smallest seeds? Largest?

Talk about the fact that a fruit is simply a fleshy part of a plant, which surrounds and protects the seeds inside. When animals eat the tasty fruit, they help distribute the seeds to new locations.

FLOWERS AND FRUITS FOR EVERYONE

Objective: *To encourage the children to use their developing understanding of the relationships between flowers and fruits to create their own imaginary flowers and their associated fruits and seeds.*

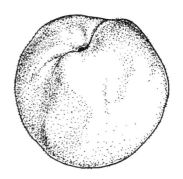

Materials:
- 1 piece of white paper per child
- colored construction paper
- glue or glue sticks
- scissors
- crayons, markers, or paints
- cotton swabs cut in half
- powdered yellow chalk
- variety of seeds

Activity:
1. Prepare the white papers as follows. Turn the paper sideways, then use a ruler and marker to make a line dividing the paper into two equal parts (left and right). Draw a stem in the lower section of one of the halves.
2. Encourage each child to use art materials of her choice to create her own flower on the half of the paper with the stem, and its corresponding fruit on the other.
3. Encourage the children to dip cotton swabs in chalk and attach them to their pictures as stamens.
4. Have the children choose seeds to glue inside their imaginary fruits.

Talk about the many different flower designs made by the children (including colors, shapes, sizes). Ask them about the fruits they created. Do they taste sweet? Juicy? Talk about what the powder on the cotton swab is (pollen) and what the dots in the center of the flower are (eggs). Remind the children that the seeds in their fruits will grow from eggs and the seeds, in turn, will produce new plants – and new flowers, too!

Outdoor Activities

WE'RE GOING ON A FLOWER HUNT

What You Need
- copies of the flower hunt card illustrated on page 77 or one you create yourself

What to Do
Using flower hunt cards to guide children's explorations, take the group outdoors to hunt for various types of flowers. Work in small groups of up to four children, with an adult guiding each group through the card.

Remind the children not to pick any flowers, but rather to observe them where they grow. After all the groups are done, everyone will go on a "guided tour" of all the flowers found.

• •

FLOWER MATCHING

What You Need
- flower matching cards

What to Do
Several days before you want to lead this activity, prepare several flower matching cards for each of the children. Make the flower matching cards by collecting blossoms from nearby common flowers and pressing them between waxed paper and heavy books. After they're pressed, add a stiff paper backing and contact paper to each card. Try to choose a time and location when many flowers are in bloom.

Outside, give each child a flower card and invite him to search for the flower that matches the one on his card. After a child has found that flower (don't pick it, please), he can return to you to get another card.

• •

POLLEN COLLECTORS

What You Need
- cotton swabs
- variety of garden or wild flowers

What to Do
Give each child a cotton swab. Find a variety of wild or garden flowers. If the flower has pollen, collect a bit on the swab and bring it to another flower of the same type. What color does the pollen turn the tip of the swab?

FLOWER HUNT CARD

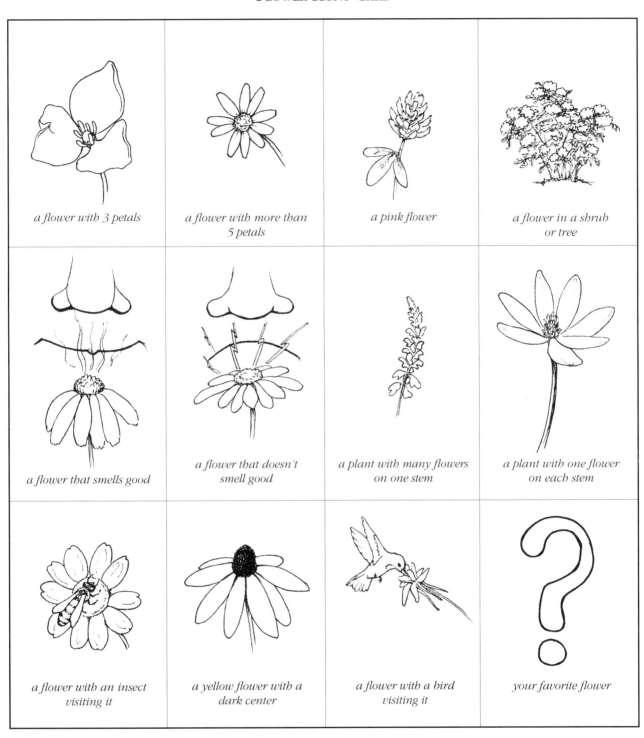

a flower with 3 petals	a flower with more than 5 petals	a pink flower	a flower in a shrub or tree
a flower that smells good	a flower that doesn't smell good	a plant with many flowers on one stem	a plant with one flower on each stem
a flower with an insect visiting it	a yellow flower with a dark center	a flower with a bird visiting it	your favorite flower

Produced and copyrighted by Vermont Institute of Natural Science, 2005.

FRUIT FIND

What to Do

Take a walk in search of fruits (you may wish to scout the route beforehand). Look for bushes with berries on them; nuts or pinecones on the ground; maple seeds high in trees; green apples just starting to grow; and other fruits or nuts.

Depending on the season, you may encounter few fruits and nuts, or many. Talk with the children about why they saw what they did – and what they might expect in the coming months. (In spring, plants are just flowering, so they have not had much time to set fruit. In the autumn, fruits abound. It's harvest time, and the plants have had all summer to develop lots of fruits.)

• •

MOTHER NATURE, MAY I?

What to Do

Here's an outdoor flower counting game. Although it's important to have permission to pick flowers, it's also important to make sure there are plenty of flowers to continue to grow before you pick any. So, while visiting a place where it's okay to pick flowers (permission granted), help the children to determine exactly how many flowers is plenty to pick. A good number is ten; if you can count ten of the same flower from the spot where you're standing, then it's okay to pick one flower. The children might ask, "Mother Nature, may I please pick one flower?"

We Care about . . . Flowers and Fruits

Because young children often learn best by collecting, touching, experiencing, and giving, it is difficult to limit their learning by telling them not to pick flowers. Instead, teach children some basic guidelines about when – and when not – to collect. Public plantings and neighborhood gardens are off limits – they take a lot of work and are for everyone to enjoy! Wild flowers in parks and preserves may also be off-limits. But there are places (along roadsides, in open parks, and perhaps even in the schoolyard) where picking is allowed.

The best rule for the children to remember is to ask first. If the answer is "Yes, you may pick," teach the children to pick flowers only where there are more than one of the same kind of flower. Remind the children to pick only flowers that they'll use in a project (or give away). Also, make sure the children learn how to pick just the flower, not the whole plant.

Language Activity / Rhyme

(To the rhythm of "Patty Cake")

Little seed,	*[pat legs and clap hand]*
Little seed,	*[pat legs and clap hands]*
In the dirt.	*[pat legs and clap hands]*
Grow into a plant and make a bud first.	*[circle head with arms, palms together, to make a bud shape]*
Open	*[pull palms apart and begin to separate arms]*
And	
Flower	*[continue opening arms until arms are open at the shoulders]*
And pollinate with bees	*[buzz like bees]*
The flower turns to fruit for my friends and me!	

[smile and pretend to eat fruit]

Crafts and Projects

PRESSED FLOWER BOOKMARKS

What You Need
- flowers – 1 or 2 per child
- plain white paper
- a big pile of books for pressing
- scissors
- contact paper – cut into 2 x 5 inch strips – 2 per child
- sample 2 x 5 inch paper strips – 1 per child

What to Do

Outdoors, in a suitable place, help the children to collect flowers for pressing. (Small, relatively flat flowers work best.) Help the children to sandwich the flowers between sheets of white paper, to press them for several days under the weight of the books.

Once the flowers are ready, ask the children to use the paper strips to practice arranging the flowers. Then help each child to place the flowers on one contact paper strip, adding the top strip to finish the bookmark.

TORN PAPER FLOWERS

What You Need
- green construction paper
- various colors of tissue paper
- glue

What to Do

Provide the children with green construction paper and various colors of tissue paper, and invite them to create flowers. Use glue to affix the flowers to the paper.

FRUIT PRINTS

What You Need
- variety of fruits – each cut in half
- tempera paint
- brushes
- construction paper

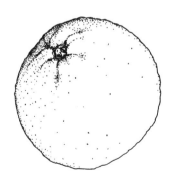

What to Do

Collect a number of fruits and cut each in half. Using tempera paints to coat the flat face, have the children create fruit prints. Afterwards, the children can practice matching the painted prints with the actual fruits.

BOOK OF SEEDS

What You Need
- illustrations: apple, pumpkin, watermelon, orange, and/or nectarine (1 per child)
- seeds (apple, pumpkin, sunflower, orange, and/or nectarine (1 per child)
- paper (2-3 sheets per child)
- strong craft glue
- scissors
- crayons or markers
- stapler

What to Do
To prepare, create a book for each child by folding two or three sheets of paper in half and stapling them on the fold. Give each child a set of fruit illustrations. Encourage the children to color in the fruits and cut them out. Next, help the children glue the appropriate seed inside each fruit. Once the fruit drawings are dry, use a glue stick to attach each fruit to a separate page in the book. With older children, you may want to help them label each fruit.

Independent Play Idea
Provide a variety of seed catalogues, garden magazines, glue, paper, and scissors (optional). Allow children to cut or tear pictures of flowers, fruits, and vegetables from the magazines, so they can create flower and fruit creations of their own.

Snacks

FRUIT FLOWERS

What You Need
- paper plates
- variety of seasonal fruits (grapes, strawberries, apples, melon)
- celery stalks

What to Do
Cut the fruits into thin slices. They will become the center and petals of the flowers. Cut the celery stalks in half lengthwise. Give each child a plate with a celery stalk "stem" on it and a selection of fruit. Encourage the children to make "edible flowers" using their fruit. After appropriate admiration, eat the masterpiece!

NATURE TASTES

What to Do
Serve a variety of fruits and/or flowers – nasturtiums, violets, apples, strawberries, etc.

Book Ideas

CHILDREN'S FICTION

Growing Vegetable Soup, by Lois Ehlert, Harcourt, Brace, Jovanovich, 1987 – a story of plant growth and its connection to food told with minimal text, full of bright collages.

Miss Rumphius, by Barbara Cooney, Puffin Books, 1982 – a lovely book about one woman's life from girlhood to old age and how she scattered flower seeds wherever she went.

The Apple Pie Tree, by Zoe Hall, Blue Sky Press, 1996 – an excellent, simply written description of an apple tree's progress from flower to fruit, includes a nice apple pie recipe, too.

The Rose in My Garden, by Arnold Lobel, Green Willow Books, 1984 – describes a garden with a verse that builds, with wonderful pen and ink drawings.

The Tiny Seed, by Eric Carle, Simon & Schuster, 1987 – brings the reader through the life cycle of a flowering plant, with collage artwork.

CHILDREN'S NONFICTION

Flowers and Friends, by Anita Holmes, Marshall Cavendish, 2000 – discusses flowers and pollinators with simple text and lovely photos.

The Apple and Other Fruits, by Millicent Selsam, William Morrow, 1973 – good for teachers; includes interesting photos and explanations.

The Flower Alphabet Book, by Jerry Pallotta, Charlesbridge Publishing, 1988 – this beautiful alphabet book includes flower folklore.

RESOURCE BOOKS FOR ADULTS AND CHILDREN

Color in Plants and Flowers, by John and Susan Proctor, Everest House, 1978 – gives detailed information for adults about the role of color in plants and includes many big, excellent photos.

Plant, by David Burnie, Alfred A. Knopf, 1989 – with top-notch photos, addresses the simple ("what is a plant?") to the complex ("the story of wheat"), an excellent resource book for easy-to-find facts about plants.

Plants and Plant Life, by Jill Bailey, Grolier Educational, 2001 – includes lots of information for adults and older children with great photos and diagrams, gives a rather one-sided description of genetic engineering.

PUPPET SHOW SCRIPT

"Pollination Pals"

Bud – Ooh! What a pretty color you are!

Red Flower – Why, thank you! When you blossom, I bet you will be a pretty color too!

Bud – I hope I turn out blue. That's my favorite color!

White Flower – *[sigh]* I wish I had a little more color to me!

Yellow Flower – Oh . . . white's not so bad – I think you look quite nice! *[bee buzzes overhead, zeroing in, and finally landing on Yellow flower]*

Bud – *[agitated]* Yellow! Quick! Shake your stem! An awful bug has landed on you!

Yellow – Silly Bud, it's just a bee!

Bud – Shake it off! The bee is going to eat you!

Yellow – *[bee crawls over flower]* No, no . . . . this bee and I are friends. I let her drink a little of my nectar, and she collects my pollen and brings it to other yellow flowers that look just like me! I need her and she needs me! *[bee flies away]*

Bud – But doesn't the bee hurt you!?

Yellow – No. It's perfectly painless . . . but her feet do tickle a bit! *[hummingbird zooms in and out of the picture]*

Red – This one's for me! *[hummingbird hovers at the opening of Red's flower]*

Bud – *[amazed]* Red! That bug's HUGE!

White – That's a *hummingbird,* Bud. A bird. Not a bug. It has come for Red's nectar and is also a pollinator.

Bud – A pollinator!? What's that!?

White – Pollinators move pollen from one plant to another. Since we flowers can't walk – or fly – the animals, and sometimes even the wind, carry the pollen for us!

Bud – Gee . . . pollen sure seems important!

White – It is! Without pollen, the seeds that are inside all of us cannot grow. We all produce seeds so that new flower plants can grow next year. *[hummingbird flies away from Red]*

Red – I am red to attract birds – they LOVE the color red! – and Yellow is the favorite color of many insects.

Bud – White, when will your pollinator come!?

White – Not until the night time. My white petals make it easy for my friends, the moths, to find me in the darkness. My cousins in the rainforest even use bats for pollination!

Bud – Wow! We flowers sure have lots of friends! I can't wait to find out who mine will be!

White – Be patient, Bud. You're a little bud now, but soon you'll open into a big, beautiful, colorful flower. Just wait!

The End

FLOWER PUPPETS

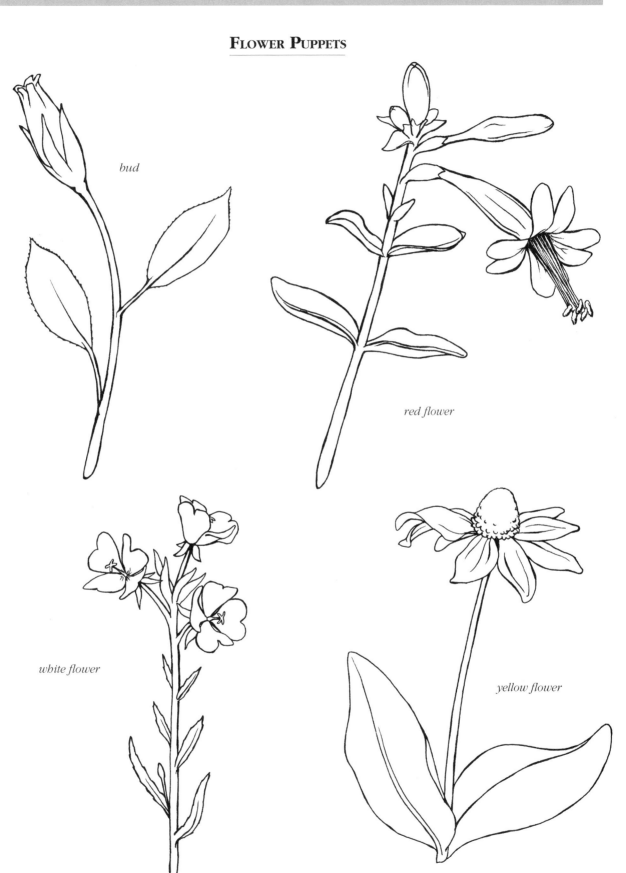

bud

red flower

white flower

yellow flower

HUMMINGBIRD PUPPETS

BUMBLEBEE PUPPET

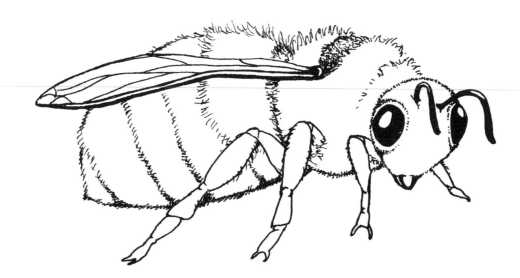

FROM FLOWER TO FRUIT

We've been learning about flowers and how they become fruits. We learned that flowers make seeds when they are pollinated and that the seeds are often stored inside a tasty fruit.

Continue the Learning at Home

Plan an outing to a local garden store. Prepare your child beforehand with a reminder that a store is a walking (not running) place and that the flowers are for looking at, not touching or picking.

Walk among the rows of plants. How many different colors do you see? How many different sizes? Give your nose some exercise. Do any of the flowers have a scent? While you are at the store, don't forget to look at the rows of envelopes full of seeds. How many seeds do you think are in an envelope? Will the seeds grow into flowers or foods (vegetables or fruits)? If possible, your child might handle some of the seeds – especially seed potatoes or corn. (Remember to wash your hands afterward, as some seeds are chemically treated.)

If you can, pick out a small flower or seed packet to bring home. Keep your growing plant in a pot or plant it outdoors. Take care of it together.

More Fun with Flowers and Fruits

As we talked about pollen, we learned that plants use sweet nectar to attract and reward pollinators. You can taste this nectar by nibbling the end of a purple clover flower. The flower we are familiar with is actually a ball of several flowers put together. Gently pull one of these flowers away from the others. It should slip off its base and have a white tip (try again if the tip is green – you may have pulled too hard). Touch the white flower tip to the tip of your tongue. Does it taste sweet? If not, try again, biting gently with your front teeth.

VINS

Produced and copyrighted by Vermont Institute of Natural Science, 2005.

Friends with Frogs and Toads

Focus: Although frogs may vary in appearance and habitat, there are some traits that all frogs share. As amphibians, all frogs depend on water during some part of their lives. The frog life cycle is characterized by obvious changes, as the frog grows from egg to adult.

Objective: Children will discover what makes up the unique body features of frogs. They'll also learn about the frog's life cycle (body and behavior changes).

Extra Information for Adult Leaders

DIGGING IN...

Frogs are some of the most ancient creatures on this earth. Even before dinosaurs, there were frogs. Frogs are **amphibians**, as are salamanders (including newts), toads, and a group of snake-like creatures called caecilians (found in the tropics). The word amphibian means, roughly, "double life" – referring to the fact that virtually all amphibians spend the first part of their life cycle in water, and then most or all of the remainder of their lives on land. Frogs make up the largest amphibian order **(Anura)**, with more than 4,000 **species** found worldwide. In the United States and Canada alone, there are approximately 100 species of frogs.

The frog's life cycle begins with an egg. After hatching, a tiny **tadpole (polliwog)** emerges. The tadpole has a round body, a vertically flattened tail, and **gills** for breathing under water. Many tadpoles are **herbivores** and use tiny scrapers in their mouths to feed on algae and other small plants. Over time, the tadpole grows larger and eventually sprouts hind legs. Later, front legs emerge (lungs develop simultaneously, as the front legs block the gill openings); the eyes bulge and move toward the top of the head; the mouth becomes wide; and the tail is gradually absorbed into the frog's body.

The eyes are two of a frog's most prominent features. Bulging and located high on its head, the frog's eyes permit it to see almost a full circle – very important in evading its many predators. Each eye has a clear inner eyelid that closes up from the bottom and protects the delicate eye as the frog moves through water. Most importantly, the frog's eyes allow it to watch carefully for prey foods (like moving insects). Small insects are the frog's most common meal, although larger frogs will also eat larger creatures, even mice.

The frog's wide mouth is perfect for its life as a **carnivore**. With only two tiny teeth in the roof of its mouth, the fully-grown frog can still grasp slippery animals, as well as its customary insect meals. To assist in swallowing large insects or other prey, the frog's eyes actually sink down into its head, pushing the roof of the mouth down, and moving food to the frog's stomach.

In addition to its well-designed mouth and eyes, frogs possess other **adaptations** for survival. Tiny nostrils, located just above its large mouth, allow the frog to smell. For hearing, frogs have external eardrums, called **tympanum**, located beneath the eyes. Almost all frogs (with the exception of those that use bright colors to advertise that they are poisonous) have **camouflaged** coloration. Almost all frogs have light bellies (to blend with the sky when seen from the below) and darker backs (to blend with the darker colors of ponds, plants, or soils), so they can maintain their camouflage from all angles.

Because of their life cycle, frogs are able to adapt to changing environmental conditions. As young tadpoles, they can exploit the protection and sustenance of the pond environment. Later, as adult frogs, they can take advantage of the shelter provided in more diverse **habitats**. Relatively few North American frogs remain in ponds (water) through their lives. Rather, many hop toward land and forests. In fact, some frogs spend virtually all their time in trees. Tree frogs (like spring peepers and gray tree frogs) have adaptations ideally suited for their arboreal lives, such as suction cup toes and bark-like camouflage.

Small though they may be, frogs are incredibly capable creatures. Thanks to specific adaptations, a changing life cycle and diverse habitat requirements, frogs are truly admirable amphibians.

Indoor Activities

WET AND DRY

Objective: *To imitate the adaptable movements of frogs, from water to land and back again.*

Materials:
- several tubs of water – 1 per 2 or 3 children
- small rubber or plastic frogs (differing colors, sizes and designs) – one per child
- 1 rubber or plastic salamander
- 1 rubber or plastic toad

Activity:
1. Talk with the children about how frogs are amphibians, which means that they spend part of their lives in water and part on land.
2. Have the children move their frogs into the water, then back out again. How would real frogs move in and out of the water? (jumping, using their back legs) How might the frogs breathe in the water? (come to the surface, sometimes floating there) Can frogs see above the water? (yes, using eyes that bulge at top of head) How might the frogs escape from dangerous predators? (jumping and swimming, using their webbed toes and streamlined bodies)
3. While the children have some fun making their frogs go in and out of the water, talk about the times in most frogs' lives when they're in the water (as an egg, tadpole, or mating adult) and when they're on land (as adults).
4. Finally, show the children the salamander and toad, explaining that these animals are amphibians, too. They also spend some of their time in water and some on land.

Talk about the fact that frogs are amphibians, cold-blooded animals that live part of their lives in water and part on land (*amphibios* – double life). They have smooth, moist skin, and long hind legs that make them excellent jumpers and swimmers. Most have some webbing on their hind feet and are found in or near water. As adults, frogs have large mouths. They breathe both through their mouths and through their soft skin (particularly during their winter **dormancy**).

leopard frog

FROGGIE THINGS

Objective: *To notice individual frog characteristics, as well as similarities.*

Materials:
- small rubber or plastic frogs (differing colors, sizes and designs) – 1 per child
- large bull frog illustration

Activity:
1. Pass out the toy frogs, one to each child or pair, and ask the children to sit down.
2. Name a characteristic and ask the children to stand if their frogs show that characteristic. For example, "Everybody with a green frog, stand up" (or hop once). (Notice the many colors of the frogs.)
3. Repeat with other characteristics (four legs, two eyes, big mouth). After each, you might make mention of the results ("I see four people standing. Four people have green frogs. What other color frogs do people have?") For fun, you might throw in a few "no way!" characteristics, like "Everybody with a frog that has two large antlers, stand up."
4. Finally, using the large frog drawing, review the characteristics that all your frogs had in common. Remind the children that these are adult or grown-up frogs; when they're younger, frogs may look very different.

Talk about several characteristics that all adult frogs have in common – smooth (not scaly or furry) skin, four legs, large back legs, two eyes on top of head, ears flat to the head (called tympanum).

SAME OR DIFFERENT FROGS?

Objective: *To notice subtle differences in the appearances of frogs and to match frog sketches.*

Materials:
- illustrations: spring peeper, American toad, leopard frog, green frog, wood frog, and bull frog (2 copies of each)
- index cards

Activity:
1. To prepare, create two sets of frog cards by making two copies of each frog illustration and mounting them onto individual cards.
2. Gather a small number of children (up to 4) into a circle, placing the cards facedown in the center.
3. Help the children to play a "memory" game, with the children taking turns flipping over two cards each in search of a match. Everybody else can ask, "same or different?"

wood frog

4. If the child finds a matched pair of frogs (same), then she takes another turn.

Talk about the ways the frogs look the same and different. Notice details in their appearances, such as feet, markings, and body shape. Be sure to mention that one of the "frogs" in the game is actually a toad. Toads have stubbier bodies and shorter hind legs than frogs. They also have lumpy skin, and some of the lumps, the **paratoid glands** behind the eyes, are poisonous.

JUMPING FROGS AND HOPPING TOADS

Objective: *To compare and contrast the movements of frogs and toads and to imitate their movements while playing a counting game.*

Materials:
- bull frog illustration
- American toad illustration
- blue construction paper puddles – 6 or so

Activity:
1. Look at the two drawings (frog and toad). Ask the children to tell you some ways they're the same, then some ways they're different. Especially, notice the toad's bumpy skin and its relatively short hind legs.
2. In addition to their differences in appearance, the toad and frog move a bit differently. While the frog's extra-long and strong hind legs help it to jump long distances, the toad's shorter legs allow for only short hops. Lead the children in role playing the movements of frogs and toads (large jumps and small hops).
3. Next, play the jumping frogs game. Choose one child to be the leader frog. That child gives the instructions – "Jumping frogs, jump ____ times." The other children must jump the number of times instructed. Repeat with a new child as the frog leader.

4. Finally, play "thirsty toads." Scatter the blue construction paper puddles around the room. Have the children pretend to be toads, hopping about the room. When you say something like, "the toads are thirsty now," the children must hop over to a pond and put their bellies to the paper (to absorb water).

Talk about the bumpy skin of the toad. Because toads often wander far from ponds and other permanent bodies of water, they need to be sure to keep moist. One way they do this is to carry their own water-like liquid inside the bumps on their skin. After even just a small rain, the toads can replenish their water supply by visiting a puddle and absorbing water through the permeable skin on their bellies.

toad

WIDE-MOUTHED FROGS

Objective: *To pretend to be frogs catching foods with sticky tongues.*

Materials:
- singing spring peeper illustration – colored
- masking tape
- yarn – cut into short, 2-inch lengths and tied into tiny bows, if desired

Activity:
1. Look at the spring peeper sketch together. Notice the frog's vocal sac and discuss how it is used.
2. Also look at the relatively large size of the frog's mouth. Challenge the children to open their mouths as big as they can, like "wide-mouthed frogs."
3. Next, discuss how the frog uses its mouth – both for singing and for eating. A sticky tongue springs out from the frog's mouth and grabs flies and other prey. (The tongue is attached to the front of the frog's mouth, rather than the back, like ours is).
4. Give each child a small loop of masking tape to put on his/her fingertip. Practice "springing" the fingers from near the mouth, like frogs sticking out their tongues.
5. Scatter the yarn "flies" (bows) on tables, chairs, etc. Using their fingers as sticky tongues, have the children capture "flies" for their suppers.

Talk about how tiny frogs can make big calls. The frog takes air into its vocal sacs, which inflate. The air is then pushed back and forth from mouth (vocal sacs) to lungs, vibrating the vocal cords and creating noise (the frog's call). Also, the frog's wide mouth serves as an amplifying chamber, directing sound waves great distances. Finally, the frog's big mouth allows it to capture and swallow even relatively large insects.

spring peeper

WINTER SLEEPERS

Objective: *To pretend to be toads getting ready to sleep the winter away.*

Materials:
- brown or black blanket

Activity:
1. Ask the children, "Where do frogs and toads go in the wintertime?" (mostly underground)
2. Tell them that we're going to pretend to be toads, entering our winter burrows, where we'll sleep through the winter.
3. Toads back into their underground forest burrows. So, taking turns holding the corners of the blanket, which represents the forest soil, ask the children to back themselves under the blanket and then pretend to fall asleep there.
4. Optional: Turn this activity into a game. Have one child leave the room for a moment. Four children hold the corners of the blanket. Then choose several "toads" to back themselves under the blanket. Drop the blanket corners carefully now. The child then returns to the room, sizes up the bulges under the blanket, and tries to guess how many toads are hiding there.

green frog

Talk about the slightly different spots where frogs and toads sleep through the winter months. Many frogs dig themselves into the soft mud of stream banks and pond bottoms. Toads hide in forest burrows (perhaps earlier excavated by chipmunks or mice). Tree frogs find winter shelter beneath forest leaves or behind the bark of trees.

FROG EGGS

Objective: *To learn about frog eggs – their appearance and feel.*

Materials:
- several chicken eggs, hard-boiled – 1 per child or pair
- bowl of cooked tapioca or quinoa
- frog eggs illustration (see wood frog sequence cards on page 91)

Activity:
1. Give each child (or pair) a hard-boiled chicken egg. Ask the children what it is, and then have them take it apart. While they are doing this, describe the parts of the egg.
2. Now show the children the picture of the frog eggs. The frog eggs have the same basic parts as the hen's egg.
3. Pass around the bowl of cooked tapioca or quinoa, so the children can touch it to get an idea of what frog eggs feel like.

Talk about the tiny size of frog eggs. The tiny eggs are surrounded by clear, thick jelly shells. The gelatinous envelopes provide support and protection, while also allowing for the exchange of water, **oxygen**, carbon dioxide, and ammonia.
   Frog eggs are usually laid in big masses of hundreds or even thousands of eggs together. Toads lay eggs in long chains. The egg mass is often attached to a stationary stick or plant leaf. Frogs have to lay hundreds of eggs because so many of them are eaten by predators and die due to other environmental factors.

bull frog

GROWING FROGS

Objective:	*To review the life cycle of a frog, from egg to adult.*
Materials:	• wood frog sequence cards
Activity:	1. Using the growth stages sketch, review the stages of a wood frog's life cycle, from egg to adult.
	2. Now give each child a set of frog life sequence cards. Ask the children to put the cards into the proper order, from the egg to the fully grown adult frog.
	3. The children might also add numbers to the cards. And, to practice following directions, you might ask the children to then "color card #1 yellow" and so forth.
	4. Optional – Finish this activity by telling a story about a frog, while asking the children to hold up the appropriate card at the right moment. (For example, "Once upon a time, there was a grown up wood frog. One rainy spring evening, she hopped down to the frog pond. The next week, she laid some eggs near a stick in the pond.")
	Talk about the frog's development, from egg to adult. See the "Digging In" section at the beginning of this unit for in-depth information.

WOOD FROG SEQUENCE CARDS

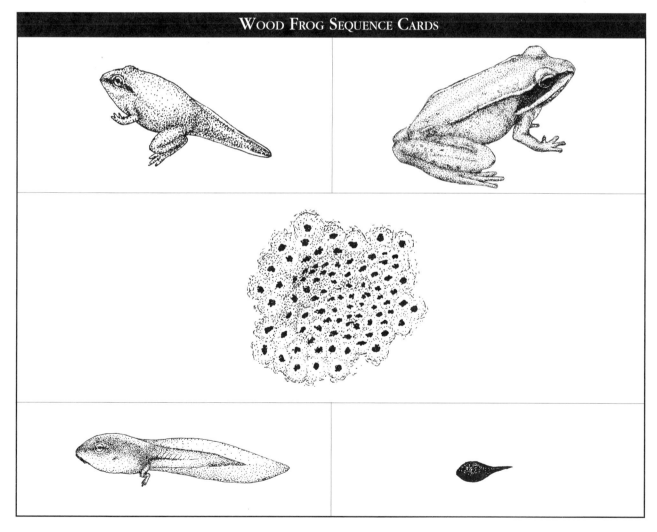

Produced and copyrighted by Vermont Institute of Natural Science, 2005.

FINDING FROG FRIENDS

Objective: *To pretend to be frogs calling to each other.*

Materials:
- copies of frog call cards, 1 per child.

Activity:
1. Children should form a large circle. Give each child a frog call card, making sure there are at least two of each card.
2. All together, review the three calls – "quack," "jug-o-rum," and "peep." Everybody should practice all the calls.
3. Then, individually, whisper each child's call into his ear. (Try to divide the calls equally.)
4. At your signal, the "frogs" sing their calls and hop around until they find their partners who are singing the same song. The children should then crouch down to show they have found their partners.

Talk about how it's almost always the male frogs that are calling. The males make their way to a pond in spring, where they announce their presence and attract females by singing. Several different species of frogs may gather in one pond, but the females will recognize the distinct call of their own potential mates.

FROG CALL CARDS

Jug-o-rum

Quack

Peep

Produced and copyrighted by Vermont Institute of Natural Science, 2005.

Outdoor Activities

SUPER JUMPERS

If a boy were a frog....

What You Need

- small section of rope
- tape measure
- small 1-inch frog toy
- "If a boy were a frog" illustration

What to Do

Using the rope as the starting marker, challenge the children to jump as far as they can in just one jump. Measure their jumps, and perhaps record the measurements in a simple bar graph display.

There's a South American frog that can jump 40 times its own body length. Show the children how far that would mean the one-inch frog could jump. Next, show how far that would mean for one of the children. Can the children match that feat?

Explain that one reason frogs can jump so far is that most have hind legs that are as much as twice the length of their bodies. Show the "If a Boy Were a Frog" illustration to illustrate your point.

• •

HULA HOOP HOPPERS

What You Need

- several variously colored hula hoops (or colored yarn circles.)

What to Do

Arrange a variety of colored hula hoops on the grass, touching each other. Choose one child to be the "frog." The adult provides hopping directions for the frog – "Start in the yellow hoop. Hop inside the blue hoop," and so on. Pick up speed as you go.

• •

GOING ON A FROG HUNT

What You Need

- simple frog catching equipment – like yogurt cups, kitchen strainers, nets if you have them
- large, deep-sided collection basin (If it's too shallow, the frogs will hop right out.)

What to Do

Talk to the children about proper frog catching behavior – be mindful of boundaries, keep your hands wet, be gentle and careful, share your frog catches with others back at the basin. It's always best to hold frogs close to the ground, just in case they slip out of your hands. You might ask the children to imagine how frightening this must be for the frogs!

One idea is to practice frog handling, even before you go to the pond, by using plastic frogs. The children can demonstrate gentle holding and careful release. "Frog squeezers" can be given directions for more considerate handling.

With adult supervision, allow the children to have some fun catching frogs. As they capture them, encourage all the children to look closely at the frogs. Notice their habitat, movement, and appearance. Finally, and most importantly, when you're finished observing them, release the frogs back to where they live and belong.

Language Activity / Song

(To the tune of "I'm a Little Teapot")

I'm a little tadpole, hatched from an egg   *[two hands form egg]*
I've got a tail, and soon I'll grow some legs   *[hand shows tail, then count]*
One, two, three, four   *[place hands and feet on ground]*
Then I'll lose my tail,   *[look for missing tail]*
And a tadpole I won't be   *[shake head no]*
Because I'll be a big frog like my mommy!
RIBBIT!!

Crafts and Projects

FROG MASKS

What You Need

- paper plates – 1 per child – each with a large mouth hole pre-cut
- large yellow paper circle eyes (maybe best to precut) – 2 per child
- green crayons
- glue
- party favor "tongue"
- black marker (to add nostrils)

What to Do

Have the children color the bottom sides of their plates green. Using the glue sticks, add the two eyes (taking care to place them up high on the face). Add nostril markings.

Now give each child a party favor tongue, so they can pretend to be frogs!

• •

FROG EGG PICTURES

What You Need

- several plastic cups – each filled with a mixture of water and tempera paint
- straws
- paper
- protective plastic under the cups
- sponges for clean up

We Care about . . .
Frogs

Because frogs absorb air and other materials through their skin, it's important to protect their well being by always handling them with clean, chemical-free hands. Children's hands should be free of insect repellent, sunscreen, and other lotions before handling frogs.

What to Do

Remind the children that frog eggs look a bit like a mass of bubbles and tell them they are going to make some "frog egg pictures" using bubbles.

The children first use the straws to blow lots of bubbles into the paint liquid – enough to rise up above the top of the cup. Once the bubbles have reached that height, the children can then place their paper against the bubbles. For multiple-color paintings, repeat this process with other paint colors. (If you are working with very young children, the adult should blow the bubbles.)

FROG'S LIFE

What You Need
- white paper
- blue construction paper, cut in half
- green or brown construction paper, cut in half
- seeds or beads
- strips or squares of green tissue paper
- small pieces of yarn knotted or tied into bows
- copies of frog and tadpole illustrations (1 per child)
- other construction paper
- markers or crayons
- glue

Independent Play Idea
Provide a variety of frog toys, plus some play trees, and perhaps a shallow pan of water (as a pond). Let the children play with the frogs.

What to Do
Have the children glue a piece of blue (water) and a piece of green/brown (land) construction paper onto their white paper. Have them glue the tadpole and frog into the appropriate habitat (tadpole – water, frog – land or water). Finally, ask the children to provide food (green tissue paper "algae" for the tadpole and yarn "insects" for the frog) for their tadpole and frog. If desired, glue a clump of seeds or beads to the picture to signify frog eggs.

Snacks

FROGGIE PRETZELS

What You Need
- 1 1/2 cups warm water
- 1 package dry yeast
- 4 cups flour
- 1 teaspoon sugar
- 1 teaspoon salt
- 1 egg, lightly beaten with 1 tablespoon water
- access to an oven

What to Do
Preheat oven to 425 degrees. Dissolve the yeast in the water in a large bowl. Mix the flour, sugar, and salt in a second bowl. With a large spoon, work the flour mixture into the yeast mixture, turning out onto counter when ready. Knead and work into a smooth dough. Add flour if the dough is sticky; water if the dough is dry.

Give each child a piece of dough to shape into an egg, tadpole, frog, or toad. Place onto greased cookie pans. Paint with egg-water mixture. Bake 25 minutes or until golden brown. Makes about 25 pretzels.

FROG EGGS!

What You Need
- tapioca pudding package and required ingredients
- spoons
- bowls

What to Do
Cook according to directions. Serve the tapioca to the children, pretending the pudding is frog eggs!

Book Ideas

CHILDREN'S FICTION

A Wood Frog's Life, by John Himmelman, Children's Press, 1998 – a superbly written and illustrated story of several years in the life of a wood frog.

Frog Girl, by Paul Owen Lewis, Whitecap Books, 1997 – a Native American tale with a message of respect and colorful illustrations.

CHILDREN'S NONFICTION

Frogs and Toads, by Bobbie Kalman and Tammy Everts, Crabtree, 1994 – an appealing overview of frogs and toads.

Frogs, Toads and Turtles, by Diane Burns, NorthWord Press, 1997 – in a child-friendly way, describes the appearance, habitats, and habits of a variety of frogs, toads, and turtles.

The Frog: Natural Acrobat, by Paul Starosta, Charlesbridge, 1996 – contains lots of information about frogs directed toward a young audience.

From Tadpole to Frog, by Wendy Pfeffer, HarperCollins, 1994 – a nice read-aloud book about frog life cycles with drawings.

The World of Frogs, by Jennifer Coldrey, Gareth Stevens Publishing, 1986 – simple clear text and photographs make this a fine introductory book to frogs.

RESOURCE BOOKS FOR ADULTS AND CHILDREN

Reptiles and Amphibians, by Catherine Herbert Howell, National Geographic Society, 1993 – eye-catching photos and illustrations and information appropriate for older children and adults.

Reptiles and Amphibians, by Andres Llamas Ruiz, Sterling, 1995 – beautifully illustrated, minimally worded, clear explanations.

The Complete Frog, by Elizabeth Lacey, Lothrop, Lee, and Shephard, 1986 – suggests where to look for frogs and what you might see when you find them, and even gives a simple key for telling frogs from toads.

The Tadpole, Raintree Publishers, 1986 – detailed photographs and descriptions document the development of a frog, from egg to adult.

FRIENDS WITH FROGS AND TOADS

We've been learning about frogs and toads – their bodies, habitats, and life cycles.

Continue the Learning at Home

Frogs live many places. Although all frogs must begin their lives (as eggs and tadpoles) in water, many frogs leave that watery habitat for drier places (like forests) once they become adults. There's a whole family of frogs, for instance, known as "tree frogs" because that's their preferred habitat.

But no matter where they live, frogs are "colored for success." Some tropical frogs have vivid colors – electric purples and day-glow oranges. These frogs *want* to be seen, perhaps because they have a foul taste to ward off predators. Most frogs, including those species found throughout the United States, use camouflaged coloration. That is, their body colors match their surroundings, so they are not easily seen.

Frog Camouflage!

Make a bunch of copies of the frogs shown below. Have your child help you to color them different colors, from brown, green, and tan to bright red and purple and then cut out the frogs.

Now, outdoors, using tape where needed, hide the frogs for your child to find. Hide the frogs in the grass, on the bark of trees, on rocks, along fences, etc. When you're ready, invite your child to "go on a frog hunt" in your yard. Which color frogs did your child find first? Which were the most difficult to find?

More Fun with Frogs

Play "leap frog" with your child. One person crouches low to the ground (frog fashion). The other then tries to jump over him, like a frog. Then switch places and continue forward.

Produced and copyrighted by Vermont Institute of Natural Science, 2005.

Growing Up a Bird

Focus: Birds change in dramatic ways from eggs to adults, with each stage designed for survival.

Objective: To discover the unique features of birds, as well as their fascinating life cycles.

Extra Information for Adult Leaders

Those fantastic flyers we call birds have some of the most remarkable **adaptations** for survival in the animal world. Animal adaptations are structures or behaviors that help meet the changing demands of the environment. In other words, adaptations are what animals have or do to help them survive. Some birds are designed to fly great distances; others are adapted to hunt from the air, or stay warm in extremely cold weather. The greatest challenge for all birds is to find adequate food year round. Specially designed bodies help them to meet these challenges.

Most birds have extremely sharp vision. Their eyes are large, held by a ring of bone, like a **reptile's**. They also have a special third eyelid that cleans and protects their eyes. Placement of the eyes differs according to feeding habits and the bird's vulnerability as prey. Most birds have eyes on the sides of their heads, affording them the broad peripheral vision needed to help watch for danger. The eyes of birds of prey (like owls, hawks, and eagles), however, are situated more forward on the head, permitting them to clearly focus on possible prey animals.

The bird's body is supported by a bony skeleton. These bones are hard but not like solid rock. In fact, some of a bird's bones are nearly hollow, a way to reduce weight for flight. Bills help to further lighten a bird's skeleton, allowing them to avoid the heavy jaw structures that many animals use to support teeth.

Bird nests come in many shapes and sizes. They can be tiny cups made of lichen and spider silk; long tunnels that run many yards into the ground; or, in the case of eagles, massive piles of branches that weigh more than a car. But all birds aim for the same circular nest design. Cup nesters turn and push; birds such as herons turn and trample. Both techniques create circular nests. There is also great variety in the places birds build their nests. Kestrels have even been known to lay eggs on tall city buildings, where its eggs perch at great risk on gutters and window ledges.

If a bird is unable to meet the challenge of finding an adequate food supply or to stay warm during a cold winter, it will move seasonally to a warmer clime. This seasonal movement is called **migration** and more than one third of all the world's species migrate. Some birds migrate only a few hundred miles, but many fly thousands of miles each year. Among the many mysteries of migration is the question of how birds know when to leave for their winter homes and when to return in the spring. Factors affecting the urge to migrate include day length, barometric pressure (changing weather), and an internal clock.

Birds prepare for migration by accumulating fat to fuel the arduous flight. They may change their diets in the fall, looking for the highest-calorie foods available. Migration poses great risks, and hundreds of millions of migrating birds never reach their destination. Challenges include fog, strong winds, bright night lights (tall, lighted buildings, and towers), coastal development, and deforestation.

Finally, bird song plays an important role in the annual life cycle of many birds as they initiate courtship and define territorial holdings vital to producing and successfully rearing offspring. Considering the small size of birds, the distances that may separate them, and the many obstacles that act as visual barriers, it is no wonder that songs and calls are birds' most effective way to communicate. The daily song cycle varies. Most birds sing early in the morning, triggered by the amount of available light. Songs serve to attract mates and to mark territories, but other messages are communicated, as well: aggression, alarm, distress, and location of food.

With unique and beautiful songs, impressive migrations, cozy and protective nests, and bodies perfectly designed for their survival, birds are truly remarkable creatures. To learn about birds is to appreciate life itself.

Indoor Activities

IT'S A BIRD!

Objective:	*To examine the characteristics of all birds.*
Materials:	• felt board • felt body pieces created using eagle outline
Activity:	1. Using the eagle outline provided, create a set of bird body parts from felt. 2. With the children's suggestions, assemble a model bird, discussing the number and placement of the body parts.

Talk about the features in the diagram; these are all exterior (or outside) features. Inside, all birds breathe air through their lungs (just like us), are warm-blooded (their body keeps its own constantly warm temperature), have a digestive system (including a pebble-filled **gizzard**) to digest their food, and a heart like us. But, unlike us, birds lay eggs.

• •

EXCELLENT EGGS

Objective:	*To examine the great variety in size, shape and color of eggs.*
Materials:	• eggs of several sizes, shapes, and colors – hardboiled for safe handling (chicken, goose or duck eggs can be collected from health food stores or local farmers.) **Note**: Collecting or handling of wild bird eggs is illegal.
Activity:	While illustrating with the eggs, discuss the following:

1. **Egg Shape** – Round eggs usually belong to birds that build cavity nests where the eggs cannot roll out of the nest. Water birds and waders, as well as swifts and peregrine falcons, lay eggs that have a wide end and a narrow end (an exaggeration of the chicken egg shape). When bumped, the egg's shape causes it to roll in a circle rather than a straight line as a round egg would. This is important because these birds usually construct minimal nests or lay their eggs in precarious places. The pointed shape keeps the precious eggs from rolling off a cliff or away from the nest site.
2. **Egg Color** – Eggs may be camouflaged with the nest or ground cover and vary widely in both pattern and color between clutches. For example, an egg may be pale blue to blend in with sunlight dapples.
3. **Egg Size** – The size of the egg reflects the size of the bird, but big eggs don't necessarily take any longer to hatch. Just as a litter of mammals may contain an undersize specimen, so occasionally may a clutch of eggs.

Talk about size and shape of eggs and how they are determined by such factors as the size and natural history of the bird. Generally, hole-nesting birds like owls and woodpeckers tend to lay round, white, glossy eggs. There is no need to conceal the eggs, and they have little chance of rolling out of the nest. Pigeons and ducks lay oval shaped eggs, similar to chicken eggs. These oval eggs fit well in cup-shaped nests and don't roll as readily as round eggs. Small birds, like the seed and insect eaters, lay small eggs. However, many produce large clutches – sometimes over a dozen eggs. Large birds lay far fewer eggs. For birds such as eagles and vultures, one small clutch (usually two eggs) a year is all they produce, with an interval of several days between laying the first and second egg.

EGGS – BIG, LITTLE, AND IN BETWEEN

Objective: *To consider the amazing differences in sizes of bird eggs among diverse species.*

Materials:
- illustrations of birds throughout this unit
- variety of items for size comparison (banana, toilet paper tube, pencil, etc.)
- ruler (optional)
- egg illustrations copied in a variety of sizes, from 1/2 inch to 3 inches

Activity:
1. Demonstrate to the class how eggs can be different sizes by having the children sequence the egg illustrations from biggest to littlest. Look at the real egg measurements noted next to the bird illustration and compare them to other household items. For example, the width of a chicken egg is the same as a banana or toilet paper roll. An emu egg is as tall as a six-inch ruler. (Egg dimensions indicate height from end-to-end.)
2. Compare the size of the egg with the size of the bird laying it. Imagine what size egg a child or a teacher would lay!

Talk about the correlation between the sizes of the birds and their eggs. The largest living bird, the ostrich, lays an egg that is 4,500 times heavier than that of the smallest, a hummingbird. The very tiniest hummingbird egg measures about one-half inch from end to end, while the ostrich can be over six inches long.

ROLLING EGGS

Objective: *To examine the fact that most bird eggs are not round.*

Materials:
- ping pong balls (1 per child)
- plastic eggs (1 per child)
- straws (1 per child)
- clay or craft dough (optional)

hummingbird: 3 inches
hummingbird egg: 1/2 inch

Activity:
1. On their hands and knees and using the straws to either blow or push, have the children move the ping pong balls from one end of the room to the other. Notice that the ball travels in a fairly straight path.
2. Now, do the same with the plastic eggs. Do they roll straight? (Test your eggs beforehand; if they are very light, you may want to weight them with some clay or craft dough.)

Talk about the fact that most bird eggs are not round. Because they are irregular ovals, the eggs usually roll around inside the nest. If the eggs were round, they would more easily fall out of the nest.

WHAT'S INSIDE AN EGG?

Objective: | *To discover what the inside of an egg looks like.*

Materials: |
- 1 raw egg per class
- 1 hard-boiled egg
- paper plate

Activity: |
1. Demonstrate to the class what is inside an egg by breaking it open on the paper plate. Talk about what you observe inside the egg using the diagram as your guide. (**Note:** Do not allow the children to handle raw eggs, which may contain salmonella bacteria.)

   All bird eggs have hard shells that help protect them from the parent's weight as they are incubated. The thickness of the shell varies according to the weight of the parent. All egg shells contain pores through which oxygen, carbon dioxide, and moisture can pass.

   - Beneath the shell are two thin, white membranes (skins) that protect the developing embryo from bacteria or other contaminants that might enter through the shell's pores. The membranes also prevent moisture from evaporating from the egg.

   - The membranes separate to form an air bubble at the blunt end of the egg. This bubble cushions the embryo during development and provides the first air an older chick will breathe before hatching.

   - The **albumen**, or egg white, provides the developing chick its main source of nourishment and water for about the first 2/3 of its growth.

   - The yellow **yolk** feeds the embryo during the last stages of development. Attached to the yolk are two white **chalazae**, twisted strands of protein that suspend the yolk in the center of the egg, preventing it from hitting the sides of the shell.

   - Look carefully, and you might notice a white **germinal spot** on the yolk (about the size of a pinhead). This germ spot, if fertilized, eventually develops into the embryo.

2. Observe most of the same features inside the hard-boiled egg.

Talk about the various parts and purposes of the egg. Whatever their size and shape, all eggs have the same internal structure.

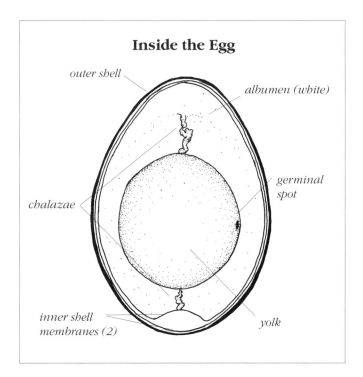

Inside the Egg

outer shell — albumen (white) — germinal spot — chalazae — yolk — inner shell membranes (2)

IMAGINE HATCHING: A GUIDED IMAGERY

Objective: | *To help the children imagine the struggle chicks face before they are free from their protective shell.*

Materials:
- children's jackets or sweaters
- crackers

Activity:
1. To prepare, distribute the crackers around the room.
2. Read the following guided imagery to the children. Have them begin by curling up in a ball on the floor with their sweater or jacket over their bodies.

> Imagine you are a turkey chick getting ready to hatch. Hatching from your egg begins invisibly. You are still completely enclosed in your shell. So, remove your shoes and then tuck your jacket or sweater over and around your body so it is dark and warm inside. Right now you are facing the narrow end of your egg. Your first task is to turn around so that your beak is pointing toward your egg's wide end.
>
> With a sudden movement of your head, peck at your **air sac**. Take a deep breath. This is the first time you are able to breathe air. Once your lungs are working, you can call to your mother from inside your egg. This call alerts your mother that you are ready to enter the world. Peep loudly like a baby bird!
>
> Using your egg tooth (a small bump on your beak) and your powerful neck muscles, you try and break through your strong shell. Make several attempts, stopping for long rests between blows.
>
> Having made an initial break in your shell, you make the crack bigger, extending it sideways. After each peck, stop and turn yourself slightly by pushing with your feet against your jacket (shell). This eventually allows the wide end of the shell (jacket) to be pushed away. Large pieces of shell fall away from the egg as you struggle to finish your labors. Your brothers and sisters may have already hatched.
>
> You finally begin to emerge from your egg. From now on, things happen quickly. You hook your toes over the lip of the shell and then, having gotten a good grip, start to push with your feet and shoulders. With a few heaves, the egg's wide end is lifted away. With your feet clearly visible, you give another push, and the flat end of the egg comes away, sitting like a hat on your head. With a final push, you tumble out of the shell that has protected you during the past three to four weeks of incubation. Fluff your feathers to dry them. They will provide an insulating jacket that will keep you warm. Now the race is on to eat and grow! You leave your nest almost immediately, search for something to eat (look for those crackers), and soon you are able to fly.

3. After reading the imagery, discuss how it would feel to be an **altricial** baby bird (such as a robin, an owl, or a woodpecker), which hatches in a poorly developed state. This little chick is helpless and depends completely on its parents for food. Then talk about a **precocial** bird (such as a pheasant, a chicken, or a duck). This chick is well developed on hatching and can soon fend for itself and even fly.

Talk about how birds grow up. Ground-nesting birds hatch in a well-developed state (have feathers, eyes open, can walk, fend for themselves). However, the newly hatched young of tree- and hole-nesting birds are completely helpless. They have well-developed digestive systems, but everything else about them is unfinished, including their eyes. This does not last for long. Fueled by a staggering supply of food – parents may make up to 1,000 trips between them a day to feed their nestlings – the babies grow at a great rate. The young may increase their weight by ten times in ten days, and their development is so fast that they quickly catch up with birds that hatch with all their feathers.

FEATHERS MAKE BIRDS DIFFERENT!

Objective: | *To explore the special qualities of feathers.*

Materials:
- feathers (craft feathers, game bird feathers, etc.) – 1 for every 1 or 2 children
- feather illustration
- magnifying glasses

Activity:

1. Pass out the feathers and have the children explore their characteristics with their fingers. As the children describe the parts of a feather, show them the feather illustration.

2. Have the children gently pull apart the web of the feather. Use the magnifying glasses to see the tiny **barbules** that project from the **barbs**. Have the children try to zip the feather together by pinching and drawing their fingers along the separated barbs from the shaft to the outer edge. Discuss how birds oil and groom themselves.

3. Challenge the children to blow on their feathers to keep them from touching the ground.

Talk about the unique structure of feathers. They are the one feature that separates birds from all other animals. Like hair, claws, and horns, feathers are made from a protein called **keratin** that gives them their great strength and flexibility.

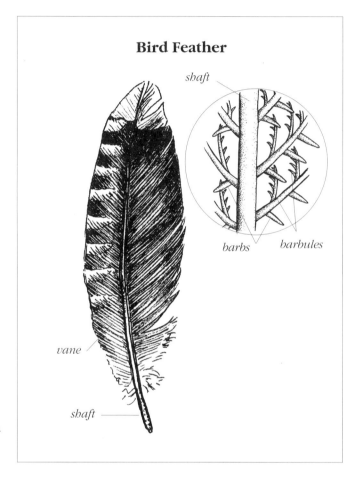

Bird Feather

Feathers start their growth as pulp inside tubes known as feather sheaths. The tip of the feather gradually emerges from the growing sheath, unrolling and splitting apart to form a flat **blade**. Feathers come in four main types: down feathers (soft, finely divided feathers that trap a layer of air to provide insulation), body feathers (streamline a bird's body), tail feathers (for steering, balance, and display), and wing feathers (smooth the flow of air over the bird's wing and shaped to provide power for flight). Although many of them are plain or dull, others are beautifully shaped and colored structures.

Close examination of a feather reveals these parts: the **shaft** (the central hollow tube that gives the feather its rigidity); barbs (the parallel strands that attach on either side of the shaft and create the feather's flat surface. Many of a bird's feathers have barbules, small extensions that fringe the length of each barb. A feather's smooth surface is formed when **barbicels**, tiny hooklets on the end of the barbs, interlock, holding the barbules and barbs together. Some types of feathers, like **down**, do not have barbules or barbicels, which accounts for down's fluffy, rather than smooth, texture.

When birds **preen** they are cleaning and rearranging their feathers, keeping them in good order for flight. Many birds have a gland above the base of their tails that secretes oil. The birds use their beaks to spread the oil on their feathers while preening. Besides being designed for flight, feathers also insulate and waterproof a bird's body and enable it to conceal itself, attract a mate, incubate eggs, and stay balanced on the ground.

THE BEST BEAKS

Objective: *To investigate beak differences by comparing how well different utensils work to obtain different foods.*

Materials:
- utensils and tools, such as slotted spoons, tweezers, straws, nutcrackers, toothpicks, tongs, tea strainer spoon
- foods in various containers, such as rice floating in water, gummy worms in oats, nuts in shells, jelly beans in pudding, grapes floating in water, juice in a bottle, shells in sand, oatmeal on bark

Activity:
1. Set out an assortment of foods in different containers.
2. Give each child a different "beak" (utensil) and ask the children what foods they might eat, given the designs of their "beaks." Have them try to find the foods they can pick up using only their beaks.

Talk about the advantages and disadvantages of specialized beaks. Bird beaks are modified in various ways for obtaining specific types of food. There are wide scoop-like bills that ducks and geese use to dig for submerged plant and animal food. The slender bills of some songbirds are very good at reaching insects in bark crevices, while the broad, short bills of flycatchers scoop insects out of the air during flight. Hummingbird beaks and tongues can suck in nectar and are also used to capture small insects inside flowers. Hawks, eagles, and owls all have sharp, curved beaks that are well adapted to tearing the flesh of their prey. As you talk about beaks, use the "*Small Wonders* at Home" page at the end of this unit for reference.

penguin: 3 feet
penguin egg: 4 inches

goose: 2.5 feet
goose egg: 3 inches

BIRD FEET ARE NEAT

Objective: *To create bird feet, showing the proper number and placement of toes.*

Materials:
- chenille pipe cleaners (2 colors)
- scissors
- sticks

Activity:
1. To prepare, cut two sets of four 5-inch sections of pipe cleaner of the same color for each child.
2. Help the children to twist the sections together to form a four-toed bird foot with two toes forward and two toes back. Twist all four together to form the leg.
3. Now repeat the foot-building to create a foot with three toes forward and one toe back.
4. Finally, have each child twist her bird feet onto a stick. Display.

Talk about how birds use their feet in a variety of different ways: to walk, hop, run, perch, swim, and to catch or grip their food. Most birds have four toes, with the first toe commonly facing backward and the other three forward, which works well for perching. Many other birds, like owls, parrots, and woodpeckers, have two toes forward and two back.

Outdoor Activities

KEEPING AN EYE AND EAR OUT FOR BIRDS

What You Need
- binoculars (either professional or homemade, such as toilet paper tubes taped together)

What to Do

Step outdoors and listen for the songs of birds. Encourage children to focus by cupping their hands behind their ears ("fox ears"). Try imitating some songs. Have children use binoculars to observe what the birds are doing (flying, perching, bathing . . .). Try observing birds at different times of day. Keep a journal to record bird activity. When are they most active? How do they eat? What do they sound like?

BIRDS IN FLIGHT

What You Need
- several colorful scarves or crepe paper streamers – enough for two per child
- tape player and several different tempos of music

What to Do

Tie the corners of colorful scarves or paper streamers to the wrists of the children. Step outside, and ask the children to flap their colorful wings. Pretend to fly around while moving in response to the music. Different kinds of birds fly in different ways – some fast, some slow, some smooth, some jumpy, for example:

hawks – soar, barely flapping their wings
geese – flap slowly, with strength
ducks – flap quickly
woodpeckers – dip up and down as they fly

NEST BUILDING

What You Need
- picture book, *Birds Build Nests* by Yvonne Winer
- craft dough, 1 egg-size ball per child
- scrap material (paper, straw, pipe cleaners, tissue, string, etc.)

What to Do
Read the picture book *Birds Build Nests* aloud to the children. Talk about the different ways nests are built. Outside, hand each child a glob of craft dough. Take a walk and pretend to be a parent bird looking for natural materials to build and line your nests. Have the children construct their nest with found and supplemented scrap material using the dough as a base.

• •

EGG-SPOON RACE

What You Need
- hard-boiled eggs – 1 per pair
- 1 raw egg
- spoons – 1 per child
- 2 ropes or other boundary markers

robin: 10 inches
robin egg: 1 inches

What to Do
Outdoors, run an egg race. Pair up children, give each pair a spoon, and have them stand behind one of the boundary lines. Give one child in each pair a hard-boiled egg to balance on his spoon. That child must walk to the other boundary line and back, transfer the egg to his partner (using hands is fine), who then does the same. See how many times each team can do that. Try running. Finally, after dropping many boiled eggs, ask the children to imagine what might happen to real (unboiled) bird eggs if they were dropped like this. Demonstrate by dropping the raw egg.

chicken: 1.5 feet
chicken egg: 2 inches

We Care about . . .
Birds

If you feed birds or provide water to them, be sure to keep your feeding area clean to prevent the spread of **avian** diseases. According to Cornell University, feeders should be washed in hot, soapy water, then rinsed in a dilute bleach solution (1 part bleach: 9 parts water). Make sure the feeder is dry before you re-hang it. Hummingbird feeders should be cleaned with hot water once a week. If you provide water to the birds, be sure to change the water and to clean the birdbath regularly. Also, periodically rake and remove seed hulls to discourage **rodents** and to prevent birds from eating spoiled foods.

Language Activity / Rhyme

Five little ducks went out one day,
Over the hills and far away,
Mother duck called "quack, quack, quack,"
But only four little ducks came back.
Continue counting down to zero little ducks, then "all the little ducks came back."

Crafts and Projects

BIRDS OF MANY COLORS

What You Need
- food coloring
- squeeze bottles or eye droppers
- coffee filter (1 per child)
- scissors
- simple bird patterns
- paper towels

What to Do

Spend some time watching or looking at pictures
of birds. Help the children appreciate their many colors.
Using scissors and a simple bird pattern, help the children cut simple bird shapes out of coffee filters.
Place the silhouette on top of a folded paper towel, and, using food coloring – one drop at a time – let the
children color their silhouettes.

> **Independent Play Idea**
> Allow the children to build nests
> in various areas of the room by
> providing a selection of plastic eggs
> and "nesting materials." These could
> be any number of things, including
> boxes, small sticks, blankets,
> fabric scraps, paper scraps.

SEQUENCING CARDS

What You Need
- copies of barn swallow sequencing cards (see next page) (1 per child)
- scissors
- coloring materials
- envelopes

What to Do

Give each child a set of the barn swallow sequencing cards. Give them time
to color the set, then help them cut the cards out. Challenge the children to sequence
the cards, to create a story of barn swallows nesting, laying eggs, hatching, and
growing up. Provide each child a labeled envelope to bring their cards home in.

emu: 6 feet
emu egg: 6 inches

SWALLOW SEQUENCE CARDS

Produced and copyrighted by Vermont Institute of Natural Science, 2005.

Snack

EDIBLE BIRD NESTS

What You Need
- 1 package butterscotch chips
- 1 can chow mein noodles
- jelly beans
- sauce pan, large spoon, heat source

What to Do

Melt the butterscotch bits in the pan. Let cool. Add noodles and stir. Give each child a small handful of the mixture and have him shape it into a nest. Add jelly bean bird eggs, and eat!

Book Ideas

CHILDREN'S FICTION

Quiet, by Peter Parnall, Morrow Junior Books, 1989 – simple text and unusual illustrations describe quiet interactions with wildlife.

White Snow, Blue Feather, by Julie Downing, Bradbury Press, 1989 – a very simple story describing the wonders of a winter afternoon.

CHILDREN'S NONFICTION

How Do Birds Find their Way?, by Roma Gans, HarperCollins, 1996 – readers learn about the many ideas scientists have come up with to explain migration's mystery.

Hummingbirds in the Garden, by Roma Gans, Thomas Y. Crowell, 1969 – gives information appropriate for young children about ruby-throated hummingbird.

A Kettle of Hawks and other Wildlife Groups, by Jim Arnosky, Lothrop, Lee & Shepard Books, 1990 – a nice read-aloud book with a poem at the beginning of each section that connects language use with animal behavior.

Loon at Northwood Lake, by Elizabeth Ring, Soundprints, 1997 – describes a pair of of loons raising young.

Outside and Inside Birds, Sandra Markle, Bradbury Press, 1994 – a photographic close-up about the behavior, habits, and characteristics inside and outside birds.

Tiger with Wings: the Great Horned Owl, by Barbara Juster Estensen, Orchard Books, 1991 – a long book full of gorgeous illustrations and natural history of the great horned owl.

RESOURCE BOOKS FOR ADULTS AND CHILDREN

Bird, David Burnie, Alfred Knopf, 1988 – hundreds of photographs present an intimate look at the world of birds in encyclopedic fashion.

Bird Talk, by Roma Gans, Thomas Y. Crowell, 1971 – describes songs and lifestyles of some common songbirds.

Birds and Their Nests, by Gwynne Vevers, McGraw-Hill, 1973 – describes all types of bird nests and who makes them.

Bird World, by Struan Reid, Millbrook Press, 1991 – a catalog of birds based on habitat and geographic location.

GROWING UP A BIRD

We have been learning about birds and their life cycles – from egg to adult.

Continue the Learning at Home

One topic we have explored is how birds use their beaks as specialized tools for finding food. See if you and your child can match the birds below to the foods they eat (answers below). For an added challenge, cut out each picture and glue it to a separate index card. Spread the cards out, face down, and take turns turning two cards over at a time. When you match a bird to its food, keep the pair. If the bird and food do not match, turn the cards back over. Whoever finishes with the most pairs wins!

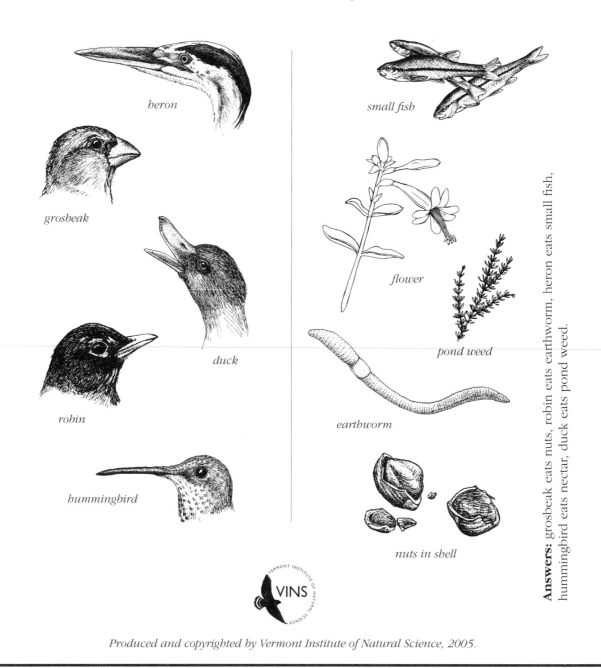

heron

small fish

grosbeak

flower

duck

pond weed

robin

earthworm

hummingbird

nuts in shell

Answers: grosbeak eats nuts, robin eats earthworm, heron eats small fish, hummingbird eats nectar, duck eats pond weed.

Produced and copyrighted by Vermont Institute of Natural Science, 2005.

ANIMAL HOMES

ANIMAL HOMES

A good home is one of the most important things in life. Young children know this, and wild animals do, too. Homes provide far more than simple shelter from the elements. They offer a hiding place from predators; an area to store food; a place to raise babies; and a safe spot to escape from the cold rain, blazing sun, and other weather hazards. Without adequate homes, animals could not survive.

Young children are naturally curious about animal homes. They compare a chipmunk's burrow to their own cozy beds. They imagine what it might be like to live in a home as busy as a beehive. They marvel at the abilities of owls to find and capture food during the dark hours of night, while they sleep peacefully. These comparisons from child to animal are rich with opportunities for empathy, as children imagine lives in the wild different – yet also quite similar to – their own.

Lessons in this theme describe and compare a variety of animals and their homes. From the tiny tunnels a mouse makes through snow to the huge home ranges of a moose, children learn that animals live in a variety of places in a variety of ways.

Bats and Beyond

Focus: Bats are fascinating creatures: unique among mammals in their ability to fly, their method of finding and catching food, and the locations of their homes.

Objective: To become familiar with the bodies and lives of bats and to come to celebrate bats, rather than fear them.

Extra Information for Adult Leaders

With over 1,000 **species** around the world, bats account for nearly one quarter of all **mammal** species. Bats are found on every continent but Antarctica. They eat a variety of foods and come in a variety of sizes. The smallest bat, the Kitti's hog-nosed bat, weighs less than a penny and can fit into a walnut shell. The largest bat, the flying fox of Asia, has a wingspan of six feet and weighs up to 2 pounds. Among all this diversity, there is one thing all bats have in common: they are the only mammals that have developed flight (flying squirrels glide, but they cannot fly).

Bats are categorized into two groups: **megabats** and **microbats**. The megabats are found in tropical regions of Asia, Africa, Australia, and some of the South Pacific island chains. They rely on their large eyes and keen sense of smell to help them find food – primarily fruit, nectar, and pollen – in the dark. One species also uses a primitive form of **echolocation** to navigate. Although, as their name implies, megabats are generally larger than microbats, there is some overlap in size between the two groups.

Microbats are found on every continent except for Antarctica. The microbats are primarily composed of insect eaters, although some species are known to eat fish, rodents, frogs, fruit, nectar, and even mammal blood. Microbats are uniquely adapted to finding their prey using echolocation. They fly with their mouths open, emitting incredibly high-pitched calls that are inaudible to humans. These **ultrasounds** bounce off of objects, and their echoes return to the bat. Microbats use these echoes to help them accurately locate potential meals and to avoid bumping into obstacles as they swoop through the darkness. The unusual spikes, flaps and folds of skin that characterize many microbats' noses are thought to help direct the ultrasounds as they leave the bats'

mouths. Large ears maximize the bats' abilities to hear echoes returning from objects.

All bats need safe, quiet homes where they can rest, groom, and, in the case of bats inhabiting colder regions, **hibernate** (many bats also migrate to avoid cool weather and dwindling food sources). Caves, the undersides of bridges, old mines, and vacant buildings are just a few of the places that bat colonies call home. Individuals can also find a safe spot to sleep under loose tree bark or in tree cavities. During the day, and actually much of the night, bats rest by hanging from their feet, with their heads pointing down. They will upright themselves when they need to defecate. Bats also give birth in an upright position, catching the baby bat in their wings. Then they'll hang upside down again to hold and nurse their babies. Within a month, the baby bats will be able to fly on their own.

Bats contribute to the environment in a variety of ways. Many tropical plants, including banana, papaya, mango, and avocados, rely upon bats for pollination. Bats are also believed to be responsible for scattering up to 95% of the seeds that sprout into new trees in the rainforest. Microbats are considered important factors in pest control. So important, in fact, that some homeowners and farmers build special bat houses to encourage bats to colonize their property. In Canada and the northern United States, the little brown bat consumes up to one-half of its body weight each night.

Bats are an integral part of many environments all over the world. Not only is their lifestyle unique, but they help the environment through seed dispersal, pollination, and insect control. As children and families learn more about bats and experience life as a bat, it is hoped they will welcome them into their world.

DIGGING IN...

Indoor Activities

STELLALUNA

Objective: *To read a story about a bat and a bird, then to compare the two.*

Materials: • *Stellaluna* by Janell Cannon

Activity:
1. Read the *Stellaluna* book aloud to the children, allowing them to make observations and comments along the way.
2. Then take some time to compare birds and bats. How are they alike? How are they different?

Talk about the fact that birds and bats belong to two different animal groups. Birds have feathers and hollow bones. They hatch from eggs. Bats, on the other hand, are mammals. Their bodies are covered with fur. They give birth to live young, and mothers feed milk to their babies (called "pups"), much like human babies. Both birds and bats sometimes migrate south to warmer climates where food is abundant throughout the winter.

little brown bat

WINGED WONDERS

Objective: *To think about some of the animals that fly and the unique wings of each.*

Materials:
• bat illustration
• bird illustration (see "Growing Up a Bird" unit in Growth and Change)
• flying squirrel illustration (see "Chipmunks and Their Cousins" unit in Animal Homes)
• butterfly illustration (see "Butterflies: Flying Flowers" unit in Growth and Change)
• access to chalkboard or large paper for writing
• folding fan (optional)

Activity:
1. Ask the children to list the animals they know that fly. Write the list on a chalkboard or paper.
2. Ask the children, "What is the name of the body part that allows these animals to fly?" (wings)
3. Compare the wing structures of the following flying creatures. Show pictures to illustrate the wing features.
   • **Birds** – Feathers are connected at one end to the skin near the wing bones, so the wing opens and folds closed like a folding fan. Feathers are perfect for flight. They're lightweight (hollow shaft). They can be groomed and then returned to their original shape. The feathers are replaced when they get worn out. An individual bird has thousands of feathers on its body.
   • **Insects** – Wings are flat or nearly so, and they do not bend or flex much. Usually only adult insects have wings. For some insects, wings not only help the insect to fly, but also provide color and produce sounds to attract mates (butterflies, grasshoppers, crickets).

- **Bats** – Wings are made of a very thin skin, stretched over long fingers. A bat's wings are very lightweight (like a bird's) and can fold in next to its body. Bats can tuck and shape their wings, so they can fly very fast – at speeds up to 65 mph!
- **Flying Squirrels** – Don't have wings and don't really fly. Instead, they glide. Instead of wings, flying squirrels have loose skin that they can stretch out between their feet to form a parachute-like tool.

Talk about how birds, bats, and insects have developed different solutions to the same problem – how to fly.

BAT WINGS

Objective: *To look more closely at the bat's wing structure and to recognize its similarity to the human hand.*

Materials:
- bat illustration (enlarged to focus on wing structure)
- black construction paper – 1 sheet per child
- white chalk
- scissors
- measuring device that is approximately 1-inch long, such as a block or a paper clip

Activity:
1. One at a time, ask each child to place his/her hand (with fingers outstretched) on the piece of black paper. Using the chalk, trace the child's hand.
2. Now ask the child to use the chalk and measuring device to extend each fingertip (except the thumb) by several inches. For example, use the chalk to extend the fingertip the length of three blocks.
3. Draw a line across the thumb, then connect the ends of the remaining four lines to draw in the edges of the bat's wing.
4. Have the child use scissors to cut out the bat's wing.

Talk about the fact that a bat's wing is similar to a human hand, with a thin skin membrane stretched between the fingers. This gives a bat excellent flexibility and range of movement in its wings, allowing the bat to easily maneuver in midair (while catching insects) and to fly swiftly. The bat's thumb can move freely, and it is sometimes used like a cotton swab to clean out the bat's ears!

BATS BIG AND SMALL

Objective: *To begin to appreciate the diversity and value of bats.*

Materials:
- bat illustration or bat picture
- a quarter
- bat outline
- 6-foot square of cloth or paper to use to create bat silhouettes
- black paint (optional)
- paint brush (optional)

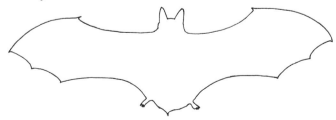

Activity:

1. To prepare, use the bat outline as a guide to create two bat silhouettes, one with a 6-inch wingspan and the other with a 6-foot wingspan (wingtip-to-wingtip). The silhouettes may be made of paper or cloth and can be painted black for effect.

2. Using the bat picture or illustration as inspiration, help the children to notice the various body features of a bat.

3. Ask the children to tell you some things they know about bats. Discuss any questions or misconceptions that might arise. Below are some things you might chat about:
   - Virtually all bats are the most active at night (which is also when most insects are active).
   - Most bats eat insects, sometimes thousands in a single night. Other bats eat ripe fruit, flower nectar, fish, and frogs. Vampire bats bite sleeping cattle and horses with their tiny teeth then lap the blood that oozes out. As a result of their eating habits, bats help to spread seeds, control pesky and dangerous insects, and pollinate crops.
   - Bats do not try to tangle themselves in people's hair. They do, however, grab insects that are attracted to warm bodies like ours, such as mosquitoes. Bats can carry rabies, as can virtually all mammals. Never handle a bat without protection.

3. Show the two cloth or paper bat silhouettes, explaining that one represents the world's smallest bat, while the other represents the world's largest bat.

4. Have the children practice measuring the bats' wingspans – the small one in finger widths and the large one in handspans.

5. Finally, pass around the penny for the children to hold in their hands. That's about as heavy as a small bat.

Talk about the smallest bat. It's called a Kitti's hog-nosed bat. It lives in Thailand and weighs less than .07 ounce. The largest bat is the giant flying fox, which lives in Asia and weighs slightly more than two pounds.

HUNGRY BATS

Objective: *To pretend to be bats searching for foods.*

Materials:
- copies of bat illustrations – 1 per child (cut out in advance) **Note:** You can turn these into puppets with a wide craft stick.
- lots of flowers, real or plastic or paper
- lots of fruits, real or plastic or paper
- lots of insects, plastic or paper

Activity:

1. Place the flowers, fruits, and insects in various places throughout your room.

2. Give each child a bat sketch. Tell them they are going to pretend to be hungry bats searching for food.

3. At your signal, have the children flap their wings and fly about the room, picking up flowers, fruits, or insects to eat.

Talk about how bats often use their wings to capture insects while in flight. They eat their food immediately (rather than storing it for later consumption).

BIG EATER BATS

Objective: *To appreciate how much bats must eat to survive.*

Materials:
- large 50-lb bag of potatoes
- bathroom scale
- several buckets or other sturdy containers
- a photograph of a little brown bat (optional)

Activity:
1. Tell the children that bats eat an enormous quantity of food, considering their small size. Many bats eat as much as half their body weight in food every night.
2. Use the scale to weigh a child. Calculate half the child's body weight.
3. Now have the children use the scale, buckets, and potatoes to measure that amount of food (half the child's body weight).
4. Repeat for other children, as desired.

Talk about how a little brown bat might eat as much as 1,200 insects in a single hour. Just imagine how many mosquitoes we might have if not for bats!

· ·

HOME TO A BAT

Objective: *To learn about the unique places that bats call home.*

Materials:
- picture book showing caves
- illustration of a tree with needles (see "Year of a Tree" unit in Growth and Change)
- illustration of a tree with leaves (see "Year of a Tree" unit)
- picture of a house
- picture of a bridge
- illustration of a bat house

Activity:
1. Ask your students about where they sleep at home – in a bed with a pillow, for example.
2. Show the children a picture of a cave from a book. Ask if they know what they are looking at (a cave). Share with the children that this is one of the places where bats sleep.
3. Show them the tree pictures. Did they know that some kinds of bats can also live in trees? (under the bark, in the branches, or among the leaves and needles)
4. Show them the pictures or sketches of the houses and bridges. Bats use homes that people build for them, too.
5. Finally, show the children the sketch of the bat house. Sometimes people make special houses for bats, just like they might do for birds!

Talk about how bats in North America hang upside down in their homes as they rest. Their bodies have special adaptations that allow them to do this. Some people build bat houses because they really like bats or because they want to attract bats to their communities to eat insects.

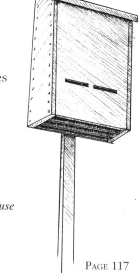

bat house

BEING BATS AT HOME

Objective:	*To imagine what it would be like to live in a cave or under bark.*
Materials:	• 3 or 4 large sheets of cardboard or heavy poster board (brown or black if possible) • glue sticks • a stack of brown construction paper • sheet or parachute • flashlights • scissors (for teacher)
Activity:	1. To prepare, cut the poster board or cardboard into an irregular, shape, like an oversize piece of bark. 2. In small groups have the children tear pieces of construction paper and use glue sticks to glue them to the poster board, to give it a bark-like texture. 3. When the giant "bark" is completed, help the children to lean it against a wall and to take turns fitting themselves under it. 4. Also make a cave using a parachute or sheets and tables. Try to squeeze the whole group into the cave.

Talk about how the children felt in the cave and under the bark. Was it crowded? Talk about how caves are often dark, damp places, and how many times bats hang high above the floor. Talk about how high above the ground the bats are in the trees. Do the children think it would be scary to be so high up? Bats are used to it.

• •

GO BAT, "THIS ISN'T YOUR HOME!"

Objective:	*To imagine being a trapped bat suddenly set free.*
Activity:	1. Ask the children to be bats who are somehow caught indoors. How might they feel? 2. Now, open the windows and doors, so the bats can feel the fresh air. 3. Invite the bats to follow the fresh air and fly outside!

Talk about how this is just what you should do if a bat somehow gets caught inside your house. Close the doors to the rest of your house, open the outside doors and windows, and let the bat find its way out.

We Care about . . .
Bats

Many people try to encourage bats to stay in their yard either because they are interested in bats, or they want bats to eat their insects. Many organizations offer free plans for building bat houses, and there are several companies that make reasonably-priced, bat house kits that you can build with your class. To attract bats, the bat house should be mounted facing the south and 12-to-18 feet above ground.

Outdoor Activities

LISTEN UP, BATS!

What You Need
- cup or bucket of water
- several marbles or stones

What to Do

Explain to the children that bats rely on their hearing to an extraordinary degree. Help the children to cup their hands behind their ears, so they can become better listeners. Ask the children to close their eyes. Then, keeping their eyes closed, they should listen to the adult, who will drop several marbles into the water. How many marbles were dropped?

ECHO BALL

What You Need
- rubber or plastic ball

What to Do

Help the children to sit in a semicircle on the grass, with their legs spread out in V-fashion. They're the "moths." Now choose one child to sit opposite the moths; this child is the "bat." To play, child one (the bat) chooses another child (the moth) to roll the ball toward him, announcing "bat!" as the ball starts rolling. The moth catches the ball, then returns it to the bat, announcing "moth!" as she releases the ball.

BEEP BEEP BAT

What You Need
- blindfolds – 2 or more
- gym-type cones to mark boundary lines (optional)

What to Do

Have the children form two lines about ten feet apart, facing inward. Choose two children to be the bats. The two bats begin at opposite ends of the lines (actually in the space defined by the two lines). Blindfolded, each bat tries to walk to the other end, all the while saying "beep, beep." If one bat bumps into the other, she says "Bat!" If a bat bumps into somebody in the line, the person says "Tree!" Continue until both bats reach the opposite ends. If you like, you can have more than two bats at a time.

Language Activity / Rhyme

1 little bat, all alone,
Tries to remember how to get home.

2 little bats flying high above trees,
Find their lost friend, and then there were three.

3 little bats got stuck in a hat
Chewed a hole out, now how about that!?

4 little bats flew to the moon,
Didn't come back, 'till halfway past noon!

5 little bats, taking a break,
Slept and they slept, until halfway past eight!

6 little bats, feeling grumpy,
Had a flight that was quite bumpy.

7 little bats swinging on a vine
Played outside 'till way past bedtime.

8 little bats, tired as can be
Look for their mommas way up in a tree.

9 little bats, full of bugs
Snuggle up for some bat hugs.

10 little bats, giving a yawn,
Sleep in their cave as the day starts to dawn.

Crafts and Projects

CLOTHESPIN BATS

What You Need
- wooden clothespins (1 per child)
- glue
- copies of the mother and baby bat illustration
  (1 per child)
- black and brown crayons or markers
- scissors

What to Do
Have the children color in the bat illustration. Help them cut it
out, and fold the mother bat's wings around the baby bat. Glue a clothespin
to the back of the bat, with the clip side of the clothespin lined up with the bat's feet.
Now the children can hang their mother bat and her baby upside down in the room.

BAT MOBILES

What You Need
- bat outlines
- crayons
- scissors
- string or yarn
- two thin and straight sticks (about 10 inches long) for each child
- hole punch

What to Do
Prepare the sticks by connecting them X-fashion. Tie a string to the ends of the sticks, as well as one in the center (to hang the mobile). Now have the children color and cut out the bat pictures. Punch a hole in each picture, then use the string to hang them in a mobile.

Snacks

BAT FRUIT

What You Need
- roll of fruit leather (about 1 per child)
- bat-shaped cookie cutter

What to Do
Take a roll of fruit leather and cut out simple bat shapes. Enjoy.

BUG AND FRUIT MIX

What You Need
- gummy insects
- variety of dried fruits (such as apples, apricots, raisins)
- knife or kitchen scissors

What to Do
Cut the larger dried fruits in half or quarters. Mix dried fruits and gummy insects together and serve each child a handful. Remind children that most bats can eat either fruit or insects.

Independent Play Idea

Surrender one section of the room to cave creation. Provide a variety of supplies: blankets, tables for draping, blocks for creating entryways, paper bats, and clothespins for hanging items. Also, allow the children to build houses using the giant bark they created in "Being Bats at Home."

Book Ideas

CHILDREN'S FICTION

A Promise to the Sun, by Tololwa M. Mollel, Little, Brown, 1992 – an African tale about a bat's broken promise to the sun and how this shapes the behavior of all bats to come.

Bat Loves the Night, by Nicola Davies, Candlewick Press, 2001 – a beautifully written and illustrated description of one bat as she wakes, searches and captures food, and returns to her baby.

Stellaluna, by Janell Cannon, Harcourt Brace, 1993 – a sweet story about an orphaned baby bat who tries to blend in with a family of birds – good for introducing the similarities and differences between birds and bats.

CHILDREN'S NONFICTION

Bats, by Gail Gibbons, Scholastic, 1999 – another classic by Gibbons, very informative yet readable for young children, covers bat anatomy, hibernation, foods, value to people, and more.

Bats for Kids, by Kathryn T. Lundberg, NorthWord Press, 1996 – an informative non-fiction book for children about bats.

Outside and Inside Bats, by Sandra Markle, Simon & Schuster, 1997 – a very informative book about bats, including exceptionally fine photographs.

RESOURCE BOOKS FOR ADULTS AND CHILDREN

America's Neighborhood Bats, by Merlin Tuttle, University of Texas Press, 1988 – a great introduction to bats for adults, includes many good photos.

Bats: Explorer Books, by Lisa deMauro, Trumpet Club, 1990 – a good, easy to read resource book for adults and older children.

Zipping, Zapping, Zooming Bats, by Ann Earle, HarperCollins, 1995 – natural history of bats from echolocation to how they manage to hang upside down, nice illustrations.

BATS AND BEYOND

We have been learning about bats: their unique bodies, their different sizes, how and what they eat, and how they move. We have even compared bats to other animals.

Continue the Learning at Home

Take a bat walk! Venture out on a late spring, summer, or autumn afternoon, around dusk, and when there is a full moon. Look for the flitting silhouettes of bats against tree tops, over fields, and over damp areas. Bats are also attracted to the insects that gather near streetlights (or stadium lights at sporting events). Your local nature center may be able to offer advice on where to find local bats and may even offer evening bat walks.

More Fun with Bats

If you don't have any luck finding bats around your home, don't worry, you can still create a "bat night" of your own. Check a bat book out of the library. Pack a flashlight, a blanket, and a snack in your bag (don't forget to put on bug repellent!). Go to the park or your own backyard, spread out your blanket, and read your bat story. Lie on your backs and look at the stars. Take a short walk without your flashlight (how do **you** see in the night?). Enjoy a snack in the dark.

Produced and copyrighted by Vermont Institute of Natural Science, 2005.

Chipmunks and Their Cousins

Focus: Chipmunks and squirrels, while similar in many ways, are distinguished by their physical differences and choice of nesting site. Their behaviors, such as climbing in trees, gathering and storing nuts, and even chasing each other, are easily observed and imitated.

Objective: To learn about some similarities and differences between chipmunks and squirrels: what they look like, the foods they eat, how they move, and more.

Extra Information for Adult Leaders

DIGGING IN...

Several varieties (**species**) of squirrels are found in the continental United States and Canada. Squirrels can often be easily observed in woodlands, backyards, quiet parks, and even busy streets. Depending on the particular setting and food availability, chipmunks, gray squirrels, or red squirrels may be most familiar to children. Although each is distinct in name, size, coloration, and behavior, all three share enough traits that they are considered to be closely related and are grouped by scientists under the heading of squirrels.

Squirrels are all members of the **rodent** mammal family. Rodents are distinguished by their upper and lower **incisors**, paired front teeth that grow throughout the animal's lifetime to combat abrasion from hard foods. Without the continual growth of these important front teeth, a squirrel would soon lose its ability to gnaw on hard foods, like nuts. All the species of squirrels also share a similar footprint: four toes on the front feet, five toes on the back. In general, squirrels can be placed into two groups: **ground squirrels** and **tree squirrels**.

Ground squirrels live in earthen burrows and include groundhogs and eastern chipmunks. Chipmunks, true to their ground squirrel name, spend much of their time in underground burrows that can extend up to three feet deep and up to 25 feet long.

They re-use the same burrow year after year. A typical burrow will have multiple chambers with specific uses, such as food storage or nursery. Every burrow has several exit doors, often hidden under tree roots or fallen material. To add to the **camouflage** of their burrows, chipmunks carry all tunnel diggings away from the excavation site.

Groundhogs, also known as woodchucks, live in similar but larger burrows, venturing above ground only for feeding purposes. Rather than storing food for winter, groundhogs store large amounts of body fat for winter dormancy. A true hibernator, the woodchuck reduces its winter energy demands by greatly slowing its circulation and respiration, and dropping its body temperature to barely above freezing (40 degrees Fahrenheit). Surviving on its stored body fat, the hungry woodchuck emerges in spring – ready to begin the intense feeding cycle one more time.

While groundhogs **hibernate**, chipmunks spend the majority of the winter season in a state of **torpor** or **dormancy** in their burrows. They will sleep from three to seven days at a time, then wake to feed on food stored in their burrows. On warm winter days (often in February in New England), chipmunks will venture outside to forage. In preparation for their winter rest, food is gathered and stored in late summer and autumn, and includes a variety of seeds and nuts.

Tree squirrels focus their lives, including their nests, around trees. This group includes gray squirrels, red squirrels, and southern and northern flying squirrels. Because they are relatively rare and nocturnal in their activities, flying squirrels are not easily observed. Gray squirrels, on the other hand, are frequently and easily seen. Gray squirrels make their homes exclusively in trees, either in holes abandoned by other animals or in twig and leaf nests

chipmunk

constructed high in tree branches. To survive the winter, gray squirrels bury nuts and other food in the ground; each piece is buried separately in a small pit and patted down. The gray squirrel later uses its sense of smell to locate the nuts. Like the chipmunk and red squirrel, a gray squirrel's diet varies from season to season and includes flowers, fruits, nuts, and occasional insects, birds, bird eggs, and plants.

Red squirrels also remain active in winter, tunneling under snow to access **caches** of pine cones and nuts stored under tree roots and in burrows. Unlike gray squirrels, which nest exclusively in trees, red squirrels may create nests in the ground or in trees, often lining their nests with cedar bark. A pile of pine cone **scales**, called a **midden**, is one of the most common signs a red squirrel has been active in an area.

Although their food preferences are similar and their territories overlap, red squirrels, gray squirrels, and chipmunks may not be seen together in all areas. Red squirrels prefer mixed forests, with hardwood and conifer trees offering both nuts and pinecones. Eastern gray squirrels prefer hardwood forests containing oak and hickory trees. (Hickory nuts offer gray squirrels one of their best energy sources) Chipmunks prefer immature forests with plenty of undergrowth for hiding from predators.

Regardless of which type you encounter, squirrels provide an excellent opportunity for up-close observation of the life of a mammal.

Indoor Activities

DO YOU KNOW CHIPMUNKS AND THEIR COUSINS?

Objective: *To become more familiar with the appearances of chipmunks and squirrels.*

Materials:
- chipmunk, gray squirrel, red squirrel, woodchuck, and flying squirrel illustrations – colored by an adult to mimic the real animals
- recording of chipmunk, red squirrel, and gray squirrel sounds (optional)

Activity:
1. How many children have seen a chipmunk before? What does it look like? Show the chipmunk drawing and point out the details – size, shape, color, whiskers, tail, stripes, etc. Does anybody know the sound chipmunks sometimes make? ("chip, chip, chip"). Play a recorded chipmunk call, if available, or, alternately, have the children practice imitating the chipmunk's call.

2. Next, show the drawings of the gray squirrel and red squirrel. How many children have seen these squirrels before? What makes them look different than the chipmunk? Play the recorded sounds the red squirrel and gray squirrel make.

3. Finally, show the photos of the woodchuck and flying squirrel. Explain to the children that all these animals are "cousins" or members of the same squirrel family.

4. Tell the children that they will be focusing on learning about the types of squirrels that are found in your area. (Be sure to adapt this portion to your area).

Talk about where each kind of squirrel spends most of its time – in the trees or on the ground? Red, gray, and flying squirrels are tree squirrels, while chipmunks and woodchucks are ground squirrels. Examine the sketches again and notice the body types/shapes of the tree squirrels versus the ground squirrels.

woodchuck

CHIPMUNK COATS

Objective:	*To study the placement of the chipmunk's stripes, then design a coat to match the pattern.*
Materials:	• brown paper grocery bags – 1 per child – precut as noted below • a few extra bags • precut black and white construction paper strips 1 inch wide by 11 inches long; 4 of each color for each child • glue or glue sticks • chipmunk photo or illustration
Activity:	1. Prepare the grocery bags by cutting up the center of one side, then cutting a head-hole in the bottom of the bag. Cut two armholes. The bag will now look like a vest. Turn the bag inside out if there is writing on it. 2. Provide glue and black and white paper strips for the children. Ask them to study the chipmunk picture(s), then to repeat the correct stripe pattern on the backs of their coats. 3. Have the children tear tails out of the remaining paper bags and glue them to their coats. **Talk about** how the stripes of a chipmunk help to camouflage it from enemies because the animal's shape seems broken into smaller, unrecognizable pieces.

CHIPMUNK CHEEKS

Objective:	*To appreciate the expandability of chipmunk cheeks.*
Materials:	• large edible sunflower seeds (60 per child or pair) • large corn kernels (31 per child or pair) • small bowls to hold the seeds and kernels • clear plastic cups or baggies
Activity:	1. Seat the children in small groups, where they have easy access to the bowls of seeds or kernels. Give each child a clear cup or baggie. 2. Help the children to each count 31 corn kernels into their cups or baggies. 3. Now help them to count 60 sunflower seeds into each cup or baggie. 4. Tell the children that these represent the number of sunflower seeds or large corn kernels a chipmunk can carry in its mouth at one time! 5. Pretend to be chipmunks by filling your cheeks with air and making them as big as you can. Now, like hungry chipmunks, munch the sunflower seeds. **Talk about** how the cheeks of the chipmunk can stretch and expand, so they can carry lots of food in just one trip. Ask the children, "Did you know that a chipmunk's cheek has pouches that extend down the sides of its neck?"

red squirrel

MYSTERY BAGS

Objective:	*To try to guess what's inside a bag, using only the sense of touch.*
Materials:	• several small brown paper or cloth bags • small food item for each bag – pine cone, flower bulb, acorn or other nut, apple, mushroom
Activity:	1. Seat the children in a circle. 2. Without peeking, have each child feel the item inside one bag. Don't say what's inside until the bag has made it all the way around the circle. 3. Can they guess what's inside? Repeat with other food items.

Talk about these items as foods for chipmunks and squirrels. What would a chipmunk have to do to gather each food? (climb a tree, dig underground, etc.) Try pantomiming these actions.

• •

WHO'S GOT THE NUT? GAME

Objective:	*To guess who's got the nut.*
Materials:	• 1 large nut (like a walnut) in its shell
Activity:	1. Seat the children in a circle and have everyone hold their hands behind their backs. 2. Choose one child to stand or sit in the center of the circle ("the guesser"). 3. Now walk slowly around the outside of the circle, pretending to place the nut in every child's hands, but only really doing so in one – "the hider." 4. After you've made it all the way around the circle, then the guesser tries to guess who is holding the nut. Three guesses. 5. Next time, the nut hider gets a chance to be the guesser. Continue until all the children have the chance to hide and guess.

Talk about how chipmunks and squirrels use their mouths, not their paws, to hold nuts. Chipmunks fill their cheeks with nuts, while red and gray squirrels carry them one-by-one in their mouth.

• •

WHERE DID GRAY SQUIRREL HIDE THE NUT!?

Objective:	*To find a hidden nut by shape.*
Materials:	• 6 large green or brown felt squares to symbolize grass or soil • a large nut (like a walnut) in its shell • 2 or 3 other objects with shapes and sizes different than a walnut (fork, square block, piece of play food)
Activity:	1. Gather the children into a circle, with the felt squares in the center. 2. Show the children the nut and other objects. 3. Choose one child to be the squirrel, who then leaves the circle (no peeking!). 4. Distribute the nut and other objects among the children remaining in the circle and have them hide their objects under the felt squares in the center of the circle.

5. Call the squirrel back to the circle. The squirrel's job is to choose which felt square conceals the nut.

6. In addition to looking, the "squirrel child" might be allowed to touch the felt squares. (optional)

Talk about how gray squirrels bury nuts one by one, digging a small hole in the ground, then patting soil on top. Ask the children what sense they used to find the nut (sight, and perhaps touch). Gray squirrels find *their* hidden nuts using the sense of smell.

Outdoor Activities

NUT HUNT

What You Need
- mixed nuts, with shells
- cups (1 per child – labeled)
- nut cracker or hammer

What to Do

Just a little while beforehand, hide lots of mixed, un-shelled nuts outside in a play area. Give each child a cup to represent his "burrow" and have them set their burrow in a special place in the play area, then gather back together as a group. Remind the children of how chipmunks use their cheek pouches to carry nuts and seeds. Tell the children that at the signal, they will pretend to be chipmunks searching for nuts to store in their burrow (cup) for winter. Demonstrate how nuts should be carried back to the borrow two at a time in cheek pouches created by holding one nut next to each cheek. The chipmunks continue to search and carry nuts until they're all found.

Come together and count, sort, observe, and talk about the nuts found. Use a nut cracker or hammer to break open some nuts and taste what's inside.

Variation: Play the game again with the same number of nuts. This time, be gray squirrels carrying just one nut at a time (holding the nut near the mouth). Pretend to bury your nuts one by one at the base of a schoolyard landmark, such as a tree, until all the nuts are collected near the landmark. Which method takes longer – gathering nuts like a chipmunk or like a squirrel?

gray squirrel

CHIPMUNKS BELOW AND ABOVE

What You Need
- 3 or 4 12-foot lengths of rope
- nuts

What to Do
Put one length of rope out straight on the ground. Explain to the children that this rope represents the average length of a chipmunk's underground tunnel or burrow. In a real burrow, there would be lots of separate rooms, called "chambers", off the main burrow. Create a couple of chambers by looping the remaining rope. These chambers are used for storing food, sleeping, raising babies, and bathroom purposes.

Put one of the rope pieces on the ground in a slightly curving line. Tell the children to imagine this rope is a branch, high up in a tree. As chipmunks, the children must walk along the branch without falling off. Place another rope near the first one. Have the children try jumping from the end of one rope to the beginning of another (branch to branch). Place a nut alongside one of the ropes; the children have to lean down and pick up the nut (like picking it off the tree) and then continue walking along the branch.

Finally, use all the ropes to form a tree with many branches (as seen from overhead). Ask the children to imagine they're chipmunks being chased through the branches of the tree by a cat, which can be you or another child. Did the children know that chipmunks and their cousins have light undersides to blend in with the sky when they are climbing?

• •

FOLLOWING MAMA SQUIRREL

What to Do
The adult leader demonstrates up to five different movements, in sequence. You say, "This is movement #1." and so on.

1. sit on the ground cross legged
2. hop on one foot to the tree
3. put your arms around the tree
4. crawl to the slide
5. lie on your back on the grass

The leader demonstrates the movements one by one. Then she asks one child to try to do all the movements in correct order.

For very young children, you might simply play "follow the leader," with the adult (or the leader child) demonstrating where to go and what to do. Ask the children, "Why would it be important for a young squirrel to follow its parent?"

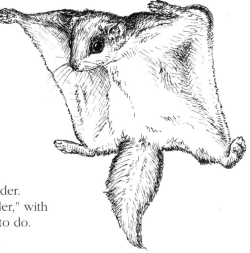

flying squirrel

RED SQUIRREL FEAST

What You Need
- variety of pine cones soaked in water, to soften scales (Pine cones that have not yet fully opened and whose scales are still soft often work best.)

What to Do
Give each child a pine cone. Encourage them to pull off the scales (be prepared for sticky fingers!) and drop them at their feet. Do they see the pile forming at their feet!? Red squirrels eat and store the seeds that are at the base of the pine cone scales and leave the scales behind in piles at their feet. These piles are called middens. Red squirrels often create middens on high places, like stumps or fallen branches – even picnic tables where they have eaten. Seeds and nuts are then stored in caches that are either buried or hidden under fallen branches, trees, or rocks.

• •

SCURRY AND FREEZE

What to Do
Gather your group outside and turn them into chipmunks and squirrels. Tell the children they are to scurry about, pretending to gather and store nuts and nesting material, build burrows, and play with each other. When you shout the name of a potential threat (like hawk, cat, dog, or human) the children must freeze, as a squirrel or chipmunk would, until the danger passes. A call of "safe!" means the children may go about their tasks once more.

We Care about . . .
Chipmunks and Their Cousins

In spite of their reputation as outgoing creatures, squirrels and chipmunks do have boundaries. Often, our curiosity as children and adults cause us to invade these boundaries, causing the animal discomfort and distraction from the task at hand. Preschool is a great age to begin to observe animals from a vantage point that is comfortable for both child and animal.

Gather the children outside during a quiet time in their day, and tell them they are going outside to do some animal watching. To watch animals, however, they must, shhhhhhhh . . . be quiet and creep slowly! Creep outside with the children and gather as a group in a comfortable spot (pillows, carpets, or blankets may help keep the children comfortable and help establish boundaries as well). Lie or sit down and watch the schoolyard. What animal activities do the children see? Encourage the children to quietly point to interesting sights to share them with their classmates. To build patience and observation powers over time, you might repeat this activity twice a week, trying to remain still and quiet just a bit longer each time.

Language Activity / Poem

Using scarves as pretend tails, encourage the children to practice the squirrel tail poem/movement activity below.

Furry little squirrel,
Running along the front porch rail,
You've got a very important body part,
It's there behind you, it's called your TAIL.

Scampering along narrow branches,
You flick it left and right,
Your tail keeps your balance,
You stay safe and upright.

When the drenching rains come down,
Your tail's like an umbrella – pop!,
Held high above your body,
It protects you from the wet rain drops.

Sometimes danger comes nearby,
A fox or dog or child,
Your tail you shake and twitch,
To show you're not surprised.

In summer, the sun can be so blazing hot,
You'd melt without some shade,
But holding your tail up high,
You're cool, you've got it made.

When winter's winds begin to blow,
Bringing cold and snow and hail,
You curl yourself up in a ball,
And feel thankful you've got a TAIL!

Crafts and Projects

CHIPMUNK BEDS

What You Need
- paper bowls (1 per child)
- brown paper lunch bags – used or new (1 per child)
- scissors
- stapler
- tape
- small scraps of brown fabric (burlap or fake fur) or copies of chipmunk illustration (reduced) on page 124 or page 135.
- black permanent markers or crayons
- access to leaves, acorns, or other nuts

What to Do

Beforehand, cut a large (but smaller than the bowl), circular hole in the side of the lunch bags. Give each child a bowl, and have them put it in the paper bag with the opening in the bowl lined up with the hole in the bag. With adult assistance, staple the top of the bag closed. Have each child use the marker to draw lines on the brown fabric (to suggest a chipmunk), or have children color the chipmunk illustration. Now step outside, and have the children search for dry leaves to make a comfy bed for their chipmunk. Add a few acorns or other nuts or seeds, too. Finally, find a nice quiet place for your chipmunk to take its winter rest.

• •

SQUIRREL TAILS

What You Need
- large sheets of sturdy paper (1 per child)
- white, black, and/or brown paint
- paint brushes
- scissors
- hole punch
- marker
- glue
- brown yarn snips (2-inch lengths)
- string (or yarn)

What to Do

Have each child stretch out his arm on the paper. Use a marker to draw a loose outline around the arm. This is now a child-size squirrel tail. Provide paints and brushes for the children to paint their tails. When the tails are dry, have the children make them "furry" by gluing on many snips of the brown yarn. Finally, punch holes and add string to tie the tails around the children's bodies. Go play!

• •

CHIPMUNK POCKETS

What You Need
- chipmunk face illustration – 1 per child
- lunch size paper plates – 1 per child
- plastic baggies – 2 per child
- markers, crayons, or paints
- scissors
- glue
- stapler
- pipe cleaners
- peanuts in shells

What to Do

Provide markers, crayons, or paints for the children to color their chipmunk faces. Using glue, the children can then attach the faces to the paper plates. Staple the pipe cleaners to the faces as whiskers. Finally, staple the baggies to the sides of the faces, like two chipmunk cheeks.

Give the children peanuts to place inside their chipmunk cheek pockets.

Snack

CHIPMUNK MIX

What You Need
- variety of shelled nuts (peanuts, almonds, pecans)
- variety of shelled seeds (pumpkin, sunflower)
- variety of fruits (raisins, dried apples, dried cranberries, dried blueberries)
- gummy insects (optional)
- zip-top bags
- large bowl and spoon for mixing

What to Do
Check to see if any child has a peanut allergy and eliminate the nuts if necessary. Package the different ingredients in bags (at least one bag per child). Hide the bags around the room or outdoors. Gather the children together and tell them they are chipmunks gathering food for the winter. Each child must scurry around the classroom and look for a bag of food for the winter. When the food is found, the children return to the circle and sit down with their bags. When all the food has been found, add the ingredients, one by one, to the bowl. Identify each ingredient as it is added and have the children help with opening the bags and stirring. All (nuts, seeds, and fruits, even insects) are foods that chipmunks might eat. Give the children time to enjoy their treat. Which ingredient is their favorite?

RED SQUIRREL CONES

What You Need
- pretzel rods (1 per child)
- almond slices
- peanut butter or soft cream cheese

What to Do
Smear peanut butter or cream cheese on the outside of the pretzel. Roll in almond slivers. Children can pretend to be red squirrels and pick the almond slivers off of their pretzels – like scales off a pinecone. The only difference is, the whole pinecone is edible!

Independent Play Ideas
1. Provide lots of nuts to hide in a sand box or sand table and/or to weigh with a balance scale.
2. Use large (appliance size) boxes to build a child-size chipmunk burrow with side chambers.

Book Ideas

CHILDREN'S FICTION

Chipmunk at Hollow Tree Lane, by Victoria Sherrow, Scholastic, 1994 – an informative description of a chipmunk family's activities.

Chipmunk Family, by Lois Brunner Bastian, Grolier, 2000 – entertaining and informative.

Chipmunk Song, by Joanne Ryder, Puffin Books, 1987 – an imaginative story about a chipmunk-size child and the seasonal activities of chipmunks.

How Chipmunk Got His Stripes, by Joseph and James Bruchac, Dial Books, 2001 – chipmunk teases bear until he finally takes a swipe at him!

Night Gliders, by Joanne Ryder, Bridgewater Books, 2001 – investigate the world of the flying squirrel through this poetry book.

Stripe: The Story of a Chipmunk, by Robert McClung, William Morrow, 1951 – an accurate story of chipmunks in their natural habitat – very nice even if a bit old.

The Tale of Squirrel Nutkin, by Beatrix Potter, Fredrick Warne, 1976 – classic Beatrix Potter tale of a squirrel who would rather play with owl than gather nuts.

CHILDREN'S NONFICTION

Animals and Their Hiding Places, by Jane R. McCauley, National Geographic Society, 1986 – text and photos describe animals' techniques for camouflage, including chipmunks.

The Raggedy Red Squirrel, by Hope Ryden, Lodestar, 1992 – includes photographs and descriptions of a red squirrel interacting with its environment and raising its babies.

RESOURCE BOOKS FOR ADULTS AND CHILDREN

Nature's Children: Chipmunks, by Merebeth Switzer, Grolier, 1986 – a non-fiction description of the lives of chipmunks.

Rabbits, Squirrels, and Chipmunks, by Mel Boring, Gareth Stevens, 1996 – a very appealing children's field guide to many species of rabbits, squirrels, and chipmunks.

Squirrels: Furry Scurriers, by Rebecca Olien. Capstone, 2002 – includes good descriptions of the characteristics of squirrels, including their behavior and relationships with people.

CHIPMUNKS AND THEIR COUSINS

We have been learning about the similarities and differences between chipmunks and squirrels: what they look like, the foods they eat, how they move, and more.

Continue the Learning at Home

Go for a walk around your neighborhood, local park, or nature center and look for signs that squirrels and chipmunks have been near. How many can you find? Circle the clues you find.

More Fun with Chipmunks

At home, encourage your child to hide five nuts inside the house. About three days later, see if your child can remember where the nuts were hidden.

Gray squirrels bury hundreds of nuts each fall, and they can successfully locate the majority of them over the winter by using their powerful sense of smell.

Life Underground

Focus: Although we focus primarily on life at the earth's surface, there is also much plant and animal activity occurring underground. Some animal species even spend the majority of their lives under the soil.

Objective: To explore what it means to live underground – for both animals and plants.

Extra Information for Adog Leaders

Although we are often unaware of it, a tremendous amount of plant and animal activity occurs hidden from view below the earth's surface. For plants, the soil is the domain of the roots, where most plants absorb water and nutrients. Certain **perennial** plants, such as carrots, beets, and sweet potatoes, have modified roots that are used for food storage and/or propagation. Other plants have evolved modified stems that are used for the same purposes. Perhaps the most familiar of these is the potato, which is classified as a **tuber**, or a modified stem. If you compare a tuber and a root such as carrot or sweet potato, you will notice that the tuber has **nodes**, or eyes, while the root does not. Nodes, or joints, are the points on a stem at which a leaf or bud typically emerges (or falls off). They may appear bud-like (as in potato eyes), as scars, or as rings.

Bulbs and **corms** strongly resemble each other. Crocus and gladiolus reproduce and/or store food in corms, which are modified stems. Bulbs are modified stem and leaf layers. Some examples of plants that have bulbs are onions, hyacinths, tulips, and lilies. Lastly, a **rhizome** is a horizontally growing stem that usually grows underground, though rhizomes may also be found above ground. New growth occurs at the joints on the rhizome. Trillium and crabgrass both propagate with rhizomes.

DIGGING IN...

Interestingly, one of the favorite underground foods of many children, the peanut, does not fall into any of the above categories. Rather, the peanut is a seed. After the peanut flower has been fertilized above ground, its stem grows down into the ground, where the **ovary** finishes its development into the peanut in the soil.

Many animals spend part or all of their lives underground, depending on the soil and the layers below it for food and/or shelter. Among the temporary burrowers are **hibernators** and those who create dens to raise young. Woodchucks dig burrows underground for their winter hibernation, and many turtles and frogs burrow into the mud in pond bottoms, taking advantage of shelter below the **frost line** – the point below which the ground no longer freezes.

Other animals seek the safety of a den when raising their young. Female red foxes give birth to and raise their young underground. Although they can dig their own dens, red foxes prefer to use those created by other animals. Like many other animals who create homes underground, red foxes often line their homes with soft material to create a warm, comfortable sleeping area. Once the pups are grown, the den will be abandoned.

Many insects also spend part of their life cycle underground. Notable among these are the cicadas, that spend the **nymph** stage of their life cycle in the soil, feeding on the plant fluids in roots. Some species spend just a few years underground, while others may spend as many as 20 years below the surface. Cicada burrows may be observed as round holes at the base of trees in the summer. Because cicadas tunnel through the dirt in such a way that they do not leave a pile of dirt behind (like an ant mound) cicada holes are even with the ground.

shrew

grub

Finally, there are animals that are adapted to spend their entire lives underground, leaving only for short periods of time, if at all. Moles, earthworms, and shrews find food and shelter, even air and water, underground. Shrews eat a variety of underground foods, including **grubs**, worms, and occasionally other small **rodents**. Moles primarily eat earthworms, and earthworms, in turn, eat decaying plant matter in the soil.

Creatures that live underground have evolved **adaptations** for this life. One of the most common features is a powerful digging tool. Moles have front legs that grow outward from their shoulders, well adapted for a digging motion that resembles the breast stroke, but not well-adapted for life above ground. Cicadas also have forelimbs that are modified for digging. Necessary too, is the ability to rely on senses other than sight. Moles are quite famous for their tiny eyes and weak eyesight. They more than make up for it with their sensitive noses, which can smell the trails of earthworms in the soil. Shrews use stiff hairs around their mouths to detect prey.

Beneath our feet is a flurry of growth, death, decay, and reproduction. Although some of the activity occurs too slowly for us to notice, or on such a small scale that it cannot be noticed without the aid of a microscope, the activity is occurring, and it stretches the imagination to think about what it would be like to live and grow underground.

Indoor Activities

FOODS FROM UNDERGROUND

Objective:	*To examine some foods that grow underground.*
Materials:	• a variety of underground foods – potatoes, yams, carrots (with leaves), beets, peanuts, onions, etc. • cutting board and knife • paint brush (optional)
Activity:	1. Display the underground foods for the children to see, smell, and touch. 2. Ask children which foods they've tasted. Which ones do they like to eat? How do their parents prepare these foods for eating? 3 Use the knife and board to cut open the foods, so you can look inside. Ask the children to predict the interior color of each vegetable. 4. Which of these foods grow underground? (all) Show the children the carrot and describe the plant parts. Introduce the term "root." 5. Use beet juice to paint a design or shape on the back of each child's hand. *(Do not paint on the children's faces as beet juice can be difficult to remove.)*

Talk about the appearance of each food. Any surprises? Notice the tough outer skin. A root is the underground portion of a plant. Its function is to drink up water and nutrients from the soil and to anchor the plant in the ground.

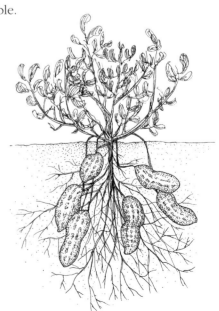

SOIL SOUP

Objective: *To appreciate the many plants, animals, and other natural materials that contribute to soil.*

Materials:
- soup pot and large spoon
- baggies containing various soil components – dried leaves, moss, gummy worms, pebbles, plastic insects, seeds, etc.
- water ready to pour
- bag of soil

Activity:
1 Tell the children they are cooks who are going to help you create a batch of "soil soup."
2. Give each child a baggie (as described above).
3. One at a time, invite the children to add their ingredients to the soup pot, while you stir. Add water last.
4. Compare the bag of soil to the "soil soup" the children created. Does the "soil soup" look like soil? Why not?

Talk about how all the items in the "soil soup" combine and break down into soil, given lots of time and water.

BIG AND LITTLE

Objective: *To judge size by touch alone.*

Materials:
- several underground foods (potatoes, carrots, etc.) – one large and one small of each type
- blindfold
- brown paper bag to hold root foods (so no one can see them)

Activity:
1. Seat the children in a circle.
2. Choose one child to be blindfolded. After the blindfold is on, hand her two samples of the same root food (for example, carrots). Which one is big? Hold it up. Which one is little? Hold it up.
3. Choose another child and repeat the activity.

Talk about the fact that plants and plant parts (like roots) grow at different rates – some get big fast, others grow more slowly (like children). Ask the children, "What might help a plant to grow quickly and get big?" (plenty of water, sunlight, and good soil) "Other than size, are there other things you feel that might help you to tell one root sample from another?" (texture, shape)

LOOK AT THOSE ROOTS GO!

Objective: *To examine roots as they grow.*

Materials:
- clear glass or plastic aquarium
- carrot seeds
- potting soil, mixed with a bit of sand
- paper and tape to cover the outside of the aquarium

Activity:
1. Help the children to fill the aquarium about 2/3 full of soil. Then scatter the carrot seeds at the surface, taking care to especially reach the edges. Cover with a very thin layer of soil. Dampen soil.
2. Wrap the outside of the aquarium with an easy-to-remove paper sleeve.
3. Place the container in a nice, sunny spot. Keep the soil damp, and watch for the seeds to sprout.
4. Continue to care for the carrots. Notice changes. Once the roots are established, remove the paper sleeve every now and then, so you can examine the roots as they grow.
5. Finally, of course, eat the carrots when they're fully grown!

Talk about the growth and changes you see. Remember that the carrot is a root, so one of its jobs is to gather water and nutrients from the soil for the plant.

• •

WHAT'S IT LIKE TO LIVE UNDERGROUND?

star nose mole

Objective: *To imagine what it might be like to live underground and to recognize some animals who do.*

Materials:
- tables
- blankets
- white yarn
- newspaper
- masking tape
- scissors
- mole illustration
- magazine or calendar pictures of animals that live underground (optional)

Activity:
1. To prepare, cut the yarn into a variety of lengths, none longer than the distance from the table to the floor. These will become plant "roots." Also, tear off a large number of pieces of masking tape and attach them to the edge of the table.
2. Ask the children to imagine what it might be like to live underground (darkness, temperature, moisture, tunnels, foods, etc.) Consider the mole – how does it deal with these challenges? What other animals can they think of that live underground? (The book *Deep Down Underground* by Olivier Dunrea is a good introduction to underground creatures. It's listed in "Book Ideas" at the end of the unit.)
3. Have the children help you attach the yarn "roots" to the underside of the tables with masking tape.
4. Larger roots can be made by wrapping newspaper around table legs or attaching strips of newspaper to the underside of the tables.

5. When finished, cover the tables with blankets to create a dark environment. As an optional addition, attach pictures of underground animals to the blanket and roots.

6. Allow the children to explore their underground tunnel.

Talk about what it feels like to explore the underground tunnel. What might it be like to be an animal living under the ground.

CREATING DENS

Objective: *To create a den and reflect on the experience.*

Materials:
- large blankets or sheets
- tables and chairs
- smaller blankets, pillows, and other soft materials (such as jackets and sweaters)

Activity:
1. To prepare, drape sheets and blankets over tables and large chairs to create "underground" dens.

2. Encourage the children to work in small groups to use the smaller, soft materials to create a comfortable place to curl up and pretend to sleep.

3. As a group, tour the different dens. How did the children make their dens soft and comfortable? Ask the children how they feel in their dens. Do they feel safe? Do they feel warm? Do they feel hidden? You may even suggest they take a real nap, or you could read a story to the children while they are in their dens.

Talk about how some animals construct underground dens to stay safe, stay warm, or hide their young. Many animals that create homes underground line them with soft materials, such as dried grasses, to create a comfortable sleeping area.

Outdoor Activities

ROOTING AROUND

What You Need
- a shovel
- a white sheet or piece of cloth

What to Do
Take the children outside to search for different kinds of plants (wild and garden varieties). If you are in an area where you can dig, use a large shovel to carefully dig up the entire plant, taking care to keep the roots intact. Display the plant on a white sheet for the children to examine.

We Care about ... Life Underground

Many animals make their homes underground, and it is not overly difficult to find the entrances to their burrows. These homes often take a lot of work to construct. The children can show their respect for this work by observing with their eyes, rather than with their hands and feet. Encourage the children to look for burrows, to observe their entrances, and to think about the animals that created the structure. Remind them to be careful not to step on the entrance or otherwise fill it in. It is always a good idea to avoid sticking fingers or other objects into the burrows as well.

SEEKING CREATURES

What You Need
- magnifying glasses
- collecting containers of various sizes
- shovel or trowel (optional)
- insect guide (optional)

What to Do
Send the children on a supervised hunt for underground creatures and signs of underground life. Signs of underground life may include holes such as burrows and ant hills. Underground creatures may be accessed at the surface by carefully overturning rocks, sticks, logs, pieces of bark in a garden, or, if possible, digging with a shovel or trowel. Results may be best if the soil is dug while moist; it will be softer to dig and more likely to contain activity. Share your finds with each other.

It will be important, during the activity, to remind the children to replace the stones, sticks, and bark as they move them. Also, remind the children to be gentle with their finds. Release everything near the site of capture when you are finished with it.

Language Activity / Song

(To be sung to "She'll Be Coming around the Mountain")

I wish I was a <u>mole</u> underground
Yes, I wish I was a <u>mole</u> underground
If I was a <u>mole</u> underground, I'd <u>root that mountain down</u>
Yes, I wish I was a <u>mole</u> underground.

Continue on, replacing the underlined words with other underground animals and their actions. For example, "worm – nibble all around," "snake – slither underground."

Crafts and Projects

UNDERGROUND VEGETABLE PRINTS

What You Need
- variety of underground vegetables (such as potatoes, carrots, and radishes)
- tempera paints
- plates
- paper
- knife

What to Do
To prepare, cut the root vegetables in half horizontally and/or lengthwise. For slippery vegetables, you may wish to cut notches on top to create a gripping surface. Spread some tempera paint on a plate, and use the vegetables to make "vegetable prints" of varying sizes and shapes. Afterwards, ask the children to match each print with the correct vegetable.

SPROUT A POTATO

What You Need
- potatoes (number depends on size)
- large plastic cups (1 per child, plus spares)
- damp potting soil
- water source
- permanent marker
- knife (for teacher)
- cutting surface

What to Do

To prepare, cut the potato into chunks, making sure each piece has an eye. Make sure you have one chunk per student. Label the cups with the children's names. Plant a spare, just in case.

Have the children help you fill the cups about 3/4 full of soil. Place the potato chunk in the center of the cup, with the eye facing up. Cover the eye with two to three inches of soil and give it some water.

To care for your potatoes, keep the soil damp. Enjoy the plants when they sprout. You may also want to dig up the spare sprout to show the children what is happening below the surface. To prolong their lives, transplant the sprouts outdoors. If you are lucky, they will flower.

• •

CARROT TOP

What You Need
- carrots with the leaves attached
- lids or plant saucers
- knife (for an adult to use)
- cutting surface
- water source

What to Do

With the children, cut off the top inch or two of the carrot, leaving the leaves attached. Fill the lid or saucer with water and stand the carrot top, leaves up, in the water. Make sure the carrot top has water at all times. Watch what happens.

Independent Play Idea

Provide multiple samples of several different root vegetables. Encourage the children to sort them by size, shape, texture, color, and weight.

Snacks

BEET OR SWEET POTATO CHIPS

What You Need
- beets and/or sweet potatoes
- vegetable oil
- salt
- baking sheet
- bowl
- access to an oven
- sharp knife (for an adult)
- cutting surface

What to Do
Slice the beets and/or potatoes thinly. Toss in a bowl with a couple of tablespoons of vegetable oil and a little salt. Bake about 20 minutes in a 400 degree oven. Allow to cool and enjoy.

ANTS ON A LOG

What You Need
- celery sticks
- peanut butter and/or cream cheese
- raisins
- table knife

What to Do
Have the children help you spread celery stick "logs" with cream cheese or peanut butter. Add raisin "ants" to the top and enjoy a crunchy snack.

Book Ideas

CHILDREN'S FICTION

Bear Underground, Betty Boegehold, Doubleday, 1980 – an adventure of a small teddy bear inside an ant colony.

Deep Down Underground, by Olivier Dunrea, Macmillan, 1989 – an amusing counting description of animals underground.

Eany, Meeny, Miney Mole, by Jane Yolen, Harcourt Brace Jovanovich, 1992 – a charming story of a mole curious to see above ground.

Mole's Hill: a Woodland Tale, by Lois Ehlert, Harcourt Brace, 1994 – a story of how a mole keeps her underground home.

CHILDREN'S NONFICTION

Tops & Bottoms, by Janet Stevens, Harcourt Brace, 1995 – a bright and bold book about the parts of plants above and below ground.

Under the Ground, by Gallimard Jeunesse, Scholastic, 1999 – describes the underground environment and some of its inhabitants.

Walkabout under the Ground, by Henry Pluckrose, Grolier, 1994 – a very nice book that encompasses a view of life and human activities underground.

RESOURCE BOOKS FOR ADULTS AND CHILDREN

Discovering Shrews, Moles, and Voles, by Jill Bailey, The Bookwright Press, 1989 – in-depth information appropriate for children, including photos and diagrams.

Mammals, by Carson Creagh, Time Life Books, 1996 – a general mammal reference book with a section on "burrowers."

Nature's Children: Woodchucks, by Laima Dingwall, Grolier, 1986 – gives facts on many aspects of woodchuck's lives.

LIFE UNDERGROUND

We have been learning about plants and animals that live underground and have been imagining how it might be to live there ourselves.

Continue the Learning at Home

Ants have fascinating underground colonies and, because their homes are easily located, make great creatures to observe. Find an anthill near your home and conduct this simple observation/experiment. Search your kitchen for four different small food items, such as salt, sugar, bread crumbs, or raisin bits. Find an active ant hill and create a small pile of each food item, each at a different location, about six inches from the hill. Get down on your hands and knees and observe the ant hill's activity for a moment. If the ants do not quickly find your food, leave the hill and return in about half an hour. What are the ants doing? Which is their favorite food? How do the ants carry food back to the nest?

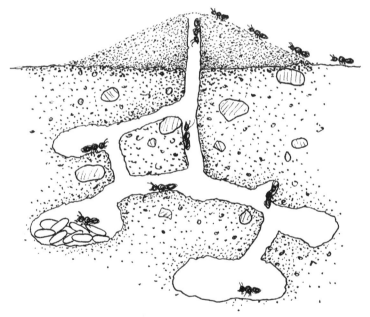

Did You Know . . .

Many species of ants use scents, or pheromones, to mark a trail along the ground to follow back to the nest. More than one ant can follow this pheromone trail, and ants often travel one behind another to a fruitful food source. If you wash away part of the trail, the ants will mill about in confusion until the trail has been re-established.

Produced and copyrighted by Vermont Institute of Natural Science, 2005.

The Snow's My Home

Focus: Snow and its properties are fascinating on their own, but snow is also interesting to investigate in the animal context. Some animals have adapted their behavior to turn a challenge into a unique advantage.

Objective: To investigate the qualities of snow and to discover some of the reasons why snow is helpful to many animals.

Extra Information for Adult Leaders

Snow can be so beautiful as it drifts from the sky, especially if it is falling on a moonlit night. To animals that remain active through winter snows, however, it can be a challenge or a distinct survival advantage, depending on the animal.

Snow crystals develop when moisture condenses and freezes on tiny particles of dust floating in the atmosphere. When the crystal is heavy enough, it floats to the ground. As snow falls throughout the season, it accumulates and changes composition. Cold, dry air or wind and additional accumulation cause snow crystals to fragment and pack into a tightly interlocked lattice. A layer of space between the **snowpack** and the frozen ground develops throughout the winter. This space, the **subnivean layer**, provides small mammals and even birds protection from cold weather and predators. The snow provides excellent insulation. Although it is not uncommon for the temperature in northern climates to dip well below zero, a good snowpack will allow the subnivean layer to remain at a constant temperature just at, or a fraction of a degree below, zero. In addition, the subnivean layer provides the added benefit of being a shelter from the wind.

Mice, voles, and shrews take advantage of this sheltered space beneath the snow. Here, they are more likely to avoid predation, though a fox or coyote with a good nose won't be deterred by snow. The mostly **insectivorous** shrews are one of the most common, but rarely seen, mammals. Related to moles, shrews live primarily in tunnels underground. In the winter, they tunnel under the snow, rarely coming onto the surface. They start mating in January, and nests may be found underground or in protected spots under logs or in woodpiles.

Mice, in contrast, frequently travel above ground and on the snow's surface. In the winter, deer mice and white-footed mice feed on stored **caches** of nuts (oak, hickory, beech, and walnuts), pine seeds, wildflower seeds, and the dormant winter shoots of herbaceous plants. They frequently have caches of up to eight quarts of seeds in log piles, knotholes, and underground holes! They also rely heavily upon insects in the winter, including beetles, flies, and moths in adult and larval stages.

For some mammals who spend their lives primarily underground, such as the short-tailed shrew and the star-nosed mole, the onset of snow doesn't change their habitat choices at all. The subterranean insectivores benefit from snow cover only in the sense that it raises the **frost line**, enabling them to tunnel closer to the earth's surface than they could without snow cover.

Snowshoe hares are uniquely adapted to living with snow. Reduced daylight triggers their brown summer coat to shed and be replaced by a coat that is pure white so that they will be **camouflaged** and more difficult for an owl, fox, or coyote to distinguish against a snowy white background. Large, wide feet give the snowshoe hare its name and enable it to stay above the snow, where it can reach buds and twigs to feed on and quickly hop away into dense spruce-fir underbrush when a predator is nearby.

Even some birds have adapted to snowfalls. Ruffed grouse and ptarmigans, frequently dive below the snow's surface to wait out a storm or stay warm for the night. Owls, crows, finches, and kinglets will bathe in the snow. Great horned and snowy owls have excellent vision and hearing and have little problem locating a mouse or snowshoe hare, plunging fiercely into the snow and grabbing their prey with vice-like talons. Next time you are out and about in the snow, keep an eye out for signs of animal activity in the wintry world.

DIGGING IN...

Indoor Activities

"SNOW'S MY HOME" PUPPET SHOW

Objective: *To learn how snow can help small animals stay warm, find food, and avoid predators.*

Materials:
- mouse and hare puppets (see end of the unit)
- evergreen branch
- tape
- script (see end of unit)
- white cardboard or foam board stage cut with a slanting tunnel

Activity:
1. To prepare, fold the cardboard and cut a tunnel as indicated in the illustration below. The mouse puppet should fit into the tunnel. Color the bottom of the tunnel brown and add some weed seeds with glue. Also, tape a small evergreen branch to the stage so it stands above the top.
2. Perform the puppet show for the children.

Talk about the benefits of snow for the mouse and hare. How do the snow and the hare's fur work together to protect the animal? (camouflage)

MOVE THE MICE

Objective: *To practice moving pretend mice through their tunnels under the snow.*

Materials:
- white bed sheet
- several cardboard wrapping paper tubes, cut in half lengthwise, and taped securely to the floor in a star-like arrangement (cut side up)
- ping pong balls

Activity:
1. Make sure the wrapping paper tube tunnels are arranged so their ends are close together (with the other ends pointing outward), and their cut sides are up.
2. Put all the ping pong balls in the center of the tunnels.
3. Carefully cover the balls and tubes with the white bed sheet.
4. Now challenge the children to get down on their hands and knees, each finding one ping pong ball "mouse" to gently guide down one of the tunnels toward the edge of the sheet. The mice should eventually "pop" out the side.

Talk about how mice, voles, and shrews use tunnels to travel under the snow. Subnivean is a special word scientists use to describe life under the snow.

FINDING FOOD

Objective:	*To pretend to be mice searching for food under the snow.*
Materials:	• white bed sheet • several small plastic containers with lids • pretzels or other edible treat
Activity:	1. Place a pretzel in one of the containers. 2. Then mix up the containers, scatter them within a small area on the floor, and cover them with the white bed sheet. 3. Invite one child to pretend to be a mouse searching under the snow for food. On hands and knees, the child crawls under the sheet. One by one, he opens the plastic containers until he discovers the one with the food inside. 4. Refill and replace the containers and invite a new "mouse" to give it a try.

Talk about techniques mice might use to find food, like seeds, under the snow. It can be very dark under the snow, so the mice have to use their sense of smell to find their food.

HOPPING HARES

Objective:	*To have fun and practice coordination and color recognition skills.*
Materials:	• white bed sheet • old white socks, balled, and each marked with a different color circle • add ears and whiskers to make the socks look more like hares (optional)
Activity:	1. Have each child grab a corner or edge of the sheet, stretching it flat between them. 2. Place the sock "hares" into the center of the sheet, designating a certain color hare for each child. 3. Now have the children stretch and snap the sheet (snow), so the socks (hares) hop about. 4. The children try to hop the hares off the snow until only one hare remains (the winner).

Talk about how the hare's extra furry feet help it to stay on top of the snow. Foxes' feet sink into the deep snow, but hares' feet stay on top. Why is that?

summer snowshoe hare

MELTING SNOW

Objective: *To discover what happens to snow indoors and to illustrate that much of snow is air.*

Materials:
- three identical bowls, measuring cups or jars marked with numbers
- snow
- ice cubes
- paper and pen
- white coffee filters

Activity:

1. With the children, fill cup #1 to the top with soft snow.

2. Fill cup #2 to the top with tightly packed snow.

3. Fill cup #3 to the top with ice cubes.

4. Bring the cups inside. Ask the children what they think will happen to the snow and ice? Write down their responses.

5. As the cups of snow and ice begin to melt, ask the children about what's happening and why. Ask the children for other observations. Can you guess which cup will become all water first? Record the guesses.

6. Now ask the children to predict what the water level will be when the snow and ice are all melted. Mark their predictions with masking tape pieces.

7. Wait until all the cups' contents have completely melted. Why are there different levels of water? (The snow has lots of air in it.) Illustrate this concept by showing the children another container filled with small crumpled pieces of paper. Remove the papers, flatten them out, and put them back into the container. See how much less space they fill now? That's because the papers used to have lots of air between them – just like snowflakes – and now they don't. The packed snow and the ice cubes didn't have quite as much air between them so water levels should be higher.

8. Ask the children if they think the water in the cups is clean. Pour the water from each cup through the coffee filter and examine the residue from each.

9. Finally, ask the children what they think will happen when the water is put back outside. Do it and watch what happens.

Talk about the fact that in a typical snowstorm, there is only about one inch of water for every ten inches of snow. You might compare and chart snow falls and melts in your classroom. After a while, the kids may recognize that a wet snow will result in more water. Record the temperature, too, so the children can notice that the driest snows occur when it's really cold, while the wetter ones are close to freezing temperatures.

summer weasel

MELTING ICE: IT TAKES TIME

Objective: *To compare the melting rates of ice placed in different spots indoors.*

Materials:
- several identical cups of ice (not cubes)
- pie plates or other dishes to hold the ice as it melts to water

Activity:
1. Prepare several cups of ice beforehand. Empty these cups onto the plates.
2. Have the children place the ice blocks in various locations indoors – some warmer, some cooler (for example, on the windowsill, under the table, near the heater, in the freezer).
3. Help the children to compare the different melting rates.

Talk about why some of the ice melted faster. Discuss temperature and its effect on ice.

MELTING ICE: JUST ADD WATER

Objective: *To compare the ice melting power of cold, warm, and salt water.*

Materials:
- plastic bowls or containers, filled with colored water and frozen (1 per child or pair)
- eye droppers
- sources of cold, warm and salt water
- trays or pans to place the ice bowls in

Activity:
1. Remove the bowls, and give each child (or group) a block of colored ice. Also give each child an eyedropper.
2. One at a time, provide access to the three forms of water, allowing the children to compare the melting power of each.

Talk about the melting effects of each. Discuss the fact that salt lowers the melting temperature of ice (that is, it melts at a colder temperature).

winter weasel

MELT IT QUICK!

Objective: *To use your body to melt a baggie filled with snow.*

Materials:
- small zip-top bags, filled half-way with snow (1 per child)

Activity:
1. Give the children snow baggies, with the instructions that they should use their bodies to melt the snow to water as quickly as possible. (You may want to set some guidelines, like no putting it in mouths or down pants.)

Talk about how the children were able to melt their snow. Which parts of their bodies were warmest? Whose snow melted the fastest? Where did he or she put it? How long would it take the snow to melt if we didn't touch it?

Outdoor Activities

WOLF AND MOOSE TAG

What to Do

In snow, have half the children pretend to be moose (with long legs) walking through the snow. (Walk normally.) The other children pretend to be wolves (with shorter legs) trying to run after the moose. ("Walk" on hands and knees.) Notice how difficult it is for the wolves to run through the deep snow, while the moose have little trouble.

- -

MEASURING WINTER SNOWS

What You Need
- several large clear soda bottles with the tops cut off
- permanent magic marker
- yardstick
- poster board and markers or colored paper

What to Do

First prepare the snow gauges. Mark the sides of the plastic bottles in half-inch increments. Place the snow gauges outside in various locations – in the open, under a pine tree, near a building, etc. Keep them there. At the end of each snowfall, check the snow gauges to see how much snow fell in each location. Record your findings on an indoor graph. Also use the yardstick to measure and compare snow depth in a variety of areas around your building (next to building, on the lee side, in a snowdrift).

- -

ARE YOU HUNGRY, LITTLE MOUSE?

What You Need
- sunflower seeds

What to Do

Outdoors, in mostly undisturbed snow, search for long squiggly lines that indicate mouse or vole tunnels. (A vole is a small, mouse-like rodent with just a short tail.) When you find a tunnel, follow its course. If the snow's deep enough, you might also find a number of holes leading to the surface. These "escape holes" allow the mouse to come up and get fresh air every now and then. Carefully scrape away the top of the tunnel at one point, so you can look inside. Drop in a few sunflower seeds for the mouse to eat later. Come back later to see if they've been eaten. Also, leave some sunflower seeds just outside the tunnel entrance, on top of the snow. Watch for visitors.

HIDDEN SNOW CREATURES

What You Need

- construction paper – cut several mouse shapes from each color (including white)
- illustrations of a weasel and a snowshoe hare in summer and winter
- poster board and markers or colored paper for graph
- mammal field guide, for reference (optional)

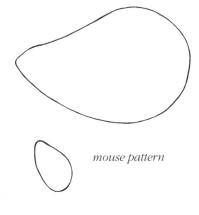

mouse pattern

What to Do

To prepare, color the summer snowshoe hare brown and the back of the summer weasel brown. (You may want to look at a mammal field guide for reference.) Also prepare the mouse shapes and place them outside, scattered around the yard. Show the children the pictures of the hare and weasel in summer and winter. What happens to their fur in winter? Why would this be helpful to these animals? Explain that now we're going to go outside, in the snow, to play a game that will show us how helpful it is to blend in with the snow. Outside, have the children search for colored mice for a specified amount of time. Indoors, count how many mice of each color were collected. Graph the results. Discuss which colors were easiest to find. Why weren't many white mice discovered?

Also note that camouflage is helpful to both the hunter (weasel) and the hunted (hare).

Language Activity / Guided Imagery

Snowflake Journey

Gather the children in a standing circle (make sure they have room to move). Lead the group in the movements described as you read the imagery below.

You are a tiny speck of dust, sitting on top of a dried weed in the middle of a big field. Feel yourself move as the wind blows the weed you're on. [sway back and forth]

The wind blows colder and harder now. The strong wind blows you sideways [shuffle your feet and move sideways]. *The wind is carrying you closer and closer to the wall of a big barn nearby. Then, suddenly, the wind lifts you up, up, up* [jump three times].

Now you're high up in the sky, above the field, the barn, the trees below [look down]. *The wind carries you up higher and higher, up into the center of a big dark cloud* [cover your eyes with your hands]. *Here, inside the cloud, there are millions, even billions of other dust particles like you – all knocking and bumping into each other* [hold your elbows with your hands and pretend to bump into other dust pieces]. *It's crowded inside this cloud!*

It's also very wet and cold inside this cloud [shiver]. *Soon some water vapor – teeny, tiny little drops of water – begins to freeze on you, and you begin to form little feathery arms of ice* [put your arms out from your sides now].

Soon you have six beautiful arms growing longer and wider, so big that you become too heavy to stay up in the cloud, and you begin to float down toward the ground [pretend to float gently down now]. *Look around you – you can see hundreds, even thousands of other snowflakes almost like you. They all have six sides or arms, but each one is special – just like you!*

Crafts and Projects

SNOWY SCENES

What You Need
- dark construction paper
- white paint
- white glue
- glitter
- cotton balls
- white paper

What to Do
Have the children make their own snowy scene pictures using the white materials on a dark background.

• •

GLITTER SNOWFLAKES

What You Need
- dark construction paper
- chalk
- glue
- glitter

What to Do
Using the dark paper and chalk, have the children sketch different kinds of snowflakes. An adult might do this part for younger children. Apply glue to the lines drawn, then sprinkle with glitter.

• •

BEADED SNOWFLAKES

What You Need
- pipe cleaners (3 per child)
- white or clear plastic beads (lots of them!)
- white thread and scissors

What to Do
Help the children twist the three pipe cleaners together in the middle, and then spread out the pipe cleaners to form the six arms of a snowflake. Thread several beads onto each arm of the snowflake, leaving a half-inch or so to fold back over the last bead. Add a length of thread to each flake and hang them from the ceiling.

Snack

SNOWMEN

What You Need
- cottage cheese
- apple slices
- raisins
- chow mein noodles
- spoons (1 per child)
- plates (1 per child)

What to Do
Line up three small, round circles of cottage cheese on each plate. Provide apple slices (hats), raisins (eyes, nose, mouth), and chow mein noodles (arms). Have the children create and eat their snowmen.

Independent Play Ideas

1. Fill the sand table with snow. Watch and touch it as it melts. Add toys and other props for sleds, people, vehicles, etc.

2. Freeze water in large (lasagna-type) pans or similar plastic containers. Provide miniature cars, people (skaters), and other toys for pretend play.

Book Ideas

CHILDREN'S FICTION

Ben's Snow Song, by Hazel Hutchins, Annick Press, 1987 – a tale of a winter family picnic.

First Snow, by Emily Arnold McCully, Harper & Row, 1985 – the adventures of the mouse family during the first big snow of the year (no words).

The First Snowfall, by Anne and Harlow Rockwell, Scholastic, 1987 – a little girl tells the story of the year's first snowfall, from the time she observes the first snowflakes fall.

Oh!, by Kevin Henkes, Greenwillow Books, 1992 – a rhyming story describes children and animals playing in the snow.

Snowballs, by Lois Ehlert, Scholastic, 1995 – simple and pleasant.

Stopping by the Woods on a Snowy Evening, by Robert Frost, Penguin Putnam, 2001 – a lovely reprint of the famous poem with exceptional illustrations by Susan Jeffers.

The Snowman, by Raymond Briggs, Random House, 1978 – a lovely, magical and wordless story about a snowman's arrival, departure, and adventures in between.

The Snowy Day, by Ezra Jack Keats, Viking Press, 1962 – a nice and simple story about a young boy's fun in the snow.

White Snow, Blue Feather, by Julie Downing, Bradbury Press, 1989 – a nice book for younger children, points out the many colors of winter.

CHILDREN'S NONFICTION

In the Snow: Who's Been Here?, by Lindsay Barrett George, Greenwillow Books, 1995 – a very nice read aloud book about finding animal signs in winter.

Summer Coat, Winter Coat: The Story of a Snowshoe Hare, by Doe Boyle, Soundprints, 1995 – describes the foods, habits, and life of a snowshoe hare.

Who Lives in the Snow, by Jennifer Berry Jones, The Court Wayne Press, 2001 – explores the world of mites, spiders, shrews, voles, chipmunks, foxes, and other animals that live in the snow in winter, describing their homes, habitats, and survival techniques.

RESOURCE BOOKS FOR ADULTS AND CHILDREN

Discover Nature in Winter, by Elizabeth Lawlor, Stackpole Books, 1998 – a good reference book for teachers, lots of activities and information about snow, stars, plants, and animals in winter.

Exploring Nature in Winter, by Alan Cvancara, Walker & Co., 1992 – a good reference book for teachers, describes how plants and animals adapt to the challenges of winter, and excellent instructions for winter shelter building.

Snow Watch, by Cheryl Archer, Kids Can Press, 1994 – an excellent, easy-to-use source for fun snow related activities, mostly appropriate or adaptable for young children.

Whose Tracks Are These? by James Nail Roberts, Rinehart, 1996 – a clue book of familiar forest animals, good introduction to tracks.

PUPPET SHOW SCRIPT

"Snow's My Home"

Hare – *[On top of the snow, near the tunnel entrance]* Hey, Mouse. It's me, Hare. You in there, Mouse? Can you come out to play?

Mouse – *[At the bottom of the tunnel]* Oh, hi, Hare. No, I don't want to come outside today. It's too cold.

Hare – Aw, come on, Mouse, it's not that cold. Sure, the wind's blowing a bit . . . And the sun's not warming things up much today . . . But . . . we can run and jump and move around lots – then we'll get warmer. See, like this. *[hare hops and jumps]*

Mouse – No, I don't feel like running around today, Hare. I'm cozy down here. I don't want to come out.

Hare – But it's great out here, Mouse. We'll have fun.

Mouse – I don't think so, Hare. Whenever I go up out of my tunnel in cold weather like this, my feet get cold and my tail, too. Don't your feet and tail get cold in weather like this?

Hare – No. Why, my tail's just a little fluff of fur. It's always warm.

Mouse – Not my tail. My tail hasn't got much hair on it at all. It's long, nearly bare, and it drags through the snow and gets cold.

Hare – Well, I can't understand why your feet would get cold. My feet – well, they grow extra hairs in the fall, so they stay warm in the winter. And those hairs also help me to stay on top of the snow, so I can run away from foxes and other animals who like to chase me. Don't your feet grow extra fur, too?

Mouse – No, as a matter of fact, my feet don't grow extra fur for winter. They get cold! So, no, Hare, I don't want to come outside today. It's too cold.

Hare – But, Mouse, you must be hungry. If you come up here, we can walk on top of the snow and reach high. Why, we can reach branches that we'd never be able to reach in the summertime. *[reaches up to nibble some evergreen twigs]* Don't you want to eat some tasty twigs with me?

Mouse – No, Hare, not today. Besides, I've got plenty of food down here under the snow. There are leaves and seeds from last summer's flowers. I never go hungry down here.

Hare – Oh, Mouse. I give up! You just won't come up, will you?

Mouse – Nope.

Hare – Alright, then I'm coming down. Here I come! *[struggles to squeeze into the tunnel]* Ah, shucks, Mouse, I can't fit. I'm too big to climb into your tunnel.

Mouse – *[Giggling]* Hey, that's exactly what Fox said yesterday. He smelled me from above the snow, but he couldn't squeeze into my tunnel to get me. Ha! And when he tried to dig me out, I just scurried away down one of my many long tunnels.

Hare – Gee, Mouse, it sounds like living under the snow is perfect for you. And living on top of the snow is perfect for me. So . . . I guess we'll have to wait until spring to play together again. See you then! I've got to hop now. Bye, Mouse.

Mouse – Bye, Hare. See you when the snow melts!

The End

MOUSE PUPPETS

SNOWSHOE HARE PUPPETS

winter snowshoe hare (white)

summer snowshoe hare (brown)

THE SNOW'S MY HOME

We've been learning about snow and the different strategies animals use to survive in it.

Continue the Learning at Home

Gather together a couple of pom-poms or scraps of felt, or perhaps a small plastic animal toy. On a snowy day, go outside with your child and work together to construct a "home" for your creature out of the snow. Does your home have a place to sleep? Does it have pathways? Has your creature stored food in its home?

If you do not get frequent snow in your area, use pretend snow made out of some cotton batting, cotton roll dressing, and cotton balls to create a snowy scene indoors.

More Fun with Snow

Learn more about animals in the snow by checking a book out of your local library. Two suggestions are: *In the Snow: Who's Been Here?*, by Lindsay Barrett George or *Who Lives in the Snow*, by Jennifer Berry Jones. Both books talk about animals and snow.

Produced and copyrighted by Vermont Institute of Natural Science, 2005.

Owls: Nighttime Hunters

Focus: Owls have many adaptations that help them hunt at night and hide by day.

Objective: To investigate many of the adaptations that help owls make a home out of darkness.

Extra Information for Adult Leaders

Owls are uniquely adapted to their role of **nocturnal** hunters. Their eyes are huge, to maximize low light levels, and they have distinct **facial disks** that help concentrate sound. Some owls, like the great horned owl, have tufts of feathers on top of their heads called **ear tufts**. Although these feathers have "ear" in their name, they are not the owl's true ears. Owls do not have external ear parts like we do. Rather, they have ear openings in their skull that are covered by the feathers on the owl's head, making the owl's ear openings indistinguishable from the rest of its head.

Not only do they have superior night vision and hearing, owls also have feathers that are adapted for nearly silent flight. The surfaces of their feathers are fuzzy, or velvety (unlike the surfaces of most feathers, which are smooth). This velvet surface helps dampen the sound of feathers rubbing together. The forward edges of the owl's largest flight feathers are fringed, reducing air turbulence and sound. All combine to help an owl fly so silently that you may not realize it is near until it swoops by your ear.

Some people believe that owls fly silently to surprise their prey, but it is more likely that silent flight helps owls continue to hear their prey as they fly toward it. This is especially important for owls hunting in northern regions during the winter months. These owls often must hunt their prey under the snow, depending solely on their hearing to locate their prey. A silent flight might mean the difference between accurately locating a winter meal and missing the target.

Owls live in a wide variety of environments throughout North America. The smallest owl, the elf owl (5 1/2 inches tall) lives in desert lowlands and canyons and makes its home in woodpecker holes in cacti and trees. The elf owl primarily eats insects,

DIGGING IN...

although it will also eat mice and lizards.

Another owl that can be found in desert areas, as well as other open environments such as prairies and grasslands, is the burrowing owl. This owl nests in burrows, either digging its own or using those prairie dogs and pocket gophers have abandoned. The snowy owl, common primarily in far northern latitudes (although they can be driven south when their food source, mostly rodents, becomes scarce), lays eggs right on the ground, often with very little lining in the nest.

Barn owls also prefer open areas but not those as cold as the snowy owls. They nest in tree cavities and buildings, and also do not line their nests. The eastern screech owl, found in open woodland, **deciduous** forests, and other areas with moderate tree or scrub cover, has an interesting twist on the **cavity nest**. Screech owls are known to blind snakes and bring them live to the nest, where the snake feeds on debris from the chicks and larvae. The snakes apparently do not harm the chicks and help keep parasites down in the nest. Finally, well known to many is the great-horned owl, which lives in wooded habitats where it nests in trees and hunts mammals from perches (they have also been known to eat birds, fish, and **amphibians**).

During the day, when owls are not in their nest, their **cryptic coloration** helps them blend in with their environment. In addition, owls will squint their eyes to cover the **iris** and stand tall, holding their feathers close to their bodies, making them extremely difficult to discover. Often you will hear owl calls or find **owl pellets** before actually seeing the bird. Perhaps the challenge of spotting an owl makes it that much more of a thrill to discover they are active in a neighborhood.

Indoor Activities

NO HIDING FROM THESE EYES!

Objective: *To compare our eyes to owl eyes.*

Materials:
- owl glasses – old sunglasses with the halves of 4 inch foam balls glued to each lens hole, then colored like eyes
- index card with a large star on one side and a circle on the other

Activity:

1. Ask the children, "When do owls come out?" (night because they are nocturnal) "Do you think owls can see in the dark night?" (yes, because their eyes are specially adapted for nighttime sight)

2. Compare our eyes to an owl's eyes. An owl's eyes are very large in proportion to its head size. Put on the owl glasses, and explain, "If an owl was as big as I am, and its head was as big as mine, then the owl's eyes would be this big!" Why do owls need to have such big eyes?" (so the eyes can gather as much light as possible, even on a cloudy, moonless night)

3. Ask the children to reach up and hold their chins still – no moving their heads. Now, keeping the head still, look at the ceiling, the floor, the door, etc. People can do this because our eyes have muscles attached to them so they can move. But inside an owl's head so much space is taken up by the really big eyes that there's no room for muscles, so an owl's eyes can't move. Instead, the owl has to move its head every time it wants to look in a new direction. (Try that.)

4. Have the children stand or sit in a line, all facing the same way. Move behind them and ask them to look at the card you're holding ***without moving their shoulders***. What shape do they see? If they were an owl, they could turn their heads to look over their back with no problem. They could even keep going to look over their other shoulder! (That's 270 degrees, or 3/4 of the way around.)

Talk about why excellent eyesight is so important to an owl. (hunts in the dark, needs to see little mice and other animals) Also, owls can move their heads so far around because they have about twice as many bones (vertebrae) in their necks as people do.

burrowing owl

OWL EARS

Objective: *To practice locating sounds as a hunting owl would.*

Materials:
- blindfolds (1 per child)

Activity:
1. Have children sit down and then put on their blindfolds. Instruct the children NOT to move their heads, to hold them still while listening.
2. Move to a new spot in the room and make a soft sound (like snapping fingers).
3. While holding their heads still, ask the children to point towards the sound they hear.
4. Try again, but this time encourage the children to cup their hands behind their ears ("owl ears") and to turn their heads toward the sound.

Talk about how owls have facial disks, circles of fine feathers around their faces, which help to funnel sounds into their ear openings (behind the eyes, in similar position to human ears). The feathers in the facial disk can by adjusted to help the owl focus sound. Also, although owl's ears do not have external skin (like ours), they are very big. If an owl's head was as big as ours, we could put our entire fist into the ear opening.

USING YOUR EARS TO FIND FOOD

Objective: *To learn what it might be like to be an owl searching for food above the snow.*

Materials:
- ball with bells inside (available at pet stores, or create your own by cutting out a section of a Wiffle ball, adding two jingle bells, and taping over the section that was removed).
- white bed sheet

Activity:
1. Gather the children in a sitting circle. Tell them they are going to pretend to be a coyote or fox searching for rodents under the snow.
2. Choose one child to be the predator and have that child stand up, just outside the circle.
3. Have the rest of the group stretch the sheet out, holding it slightly above the floor.
4. Quiet the group, then *gently* roll the ball under the sheet. When the ball stops rolling, ask the predator where they think the "mouse" stopped moving. Allow them to point to where they think the ball is, then retrieve it. Continue with a new predator. (The teacher should probably retain control of the ball.)

Talk about how the children, like owls, used their ears to locate the "mouse."

barn owl

SILENT FLYERS

Objective: *To discover how an owl flies so silently and why that's important.*

Materials:
- owl feather illustration
- feather illustration (see "Growing Up a Bird" unit in Growth and Change)
- comb
- hand lens
- a length of light gauge wire, about 20 inches long
- 2 pipe cleaners, twisted together at ends, to form a length about 20 inches long
- owl feather (optional) (See "We Care about" section.)

Activity:
1. Tell the children that owls fly almost silently. Why would that be important to an owl? (Both so their prey doesn't hear the owl coming and run away; and also so the owl can still hear where the prey is even while it's flying.)

2. Compare the illustration of an owl feather with the other bird feather illustration. What differences do the children notice between the two? The surface of the owl feather appears fuzzy, and the edge is like a comb. This uneven edge is what allows the air to go over the feather/wing without making a sound.

3. Demonstrate this concept by swinging the wire in a circle first (makes a slight whistling sound), and then the pipe cleaners (silent). Ask the children to raise their hands if they hear a noise. Note the fluffy edge of the pipe cleaner strand.

4. If available, show the owl feather to each child, and ask her to look at the edge of the feather using the hand lens.

Talk about why silent flight is especially important to owls. They hunt at night, when it's quiet because they can't depend on their eyes as much as daytime birds can. They must fly silently to allow their ears to hear.

CALLING ALL OWLS!

Objective: *To recognize the calls of several common owls and to use these calls in identifying the birds.*

Materials:
- a recording of owl calls (CD or tape)
- a player
- owl pictures and illustrations

Activity:
1. Show the owl pictures to the children. Talk about the differences you observe in each owl's appearance.

2. Play the recording of owl calls, showing the picture of each owl as its call is played. Stop the tape/CD after each call and have the children try to imitate the owl's sound.

Talk about some of the reasons why an owl calls. One reason is to defend its territory ("I'm here, you go away"), but more important is to attract a mate, to communicate with young ("I'm coming with food now"), or to announce its presence ("I'm here").

OWL PELLET INVESTIGATION

Objective: *To discover what and how owls eat and examine the contents of owl pellets.*

Materials:
- owl pellets – one pellet per 2-3 children is ideal (These can be ordered through science supply companies. See Appendix A.)
- black construction paper – 2 pieces per pellet group
- glue and Q-tips
- toothpicks or tweezers (for children who might be shy of touching the pellets at first)
- pencils
- several copies of the "Owl Pellet Bone Identification"

Activity:

1. As a group, create a list of foods that owls eat (mice, voles, squirrels, rats, skunks, crickets and other insects, snakes, frogs, rabbits). Explain that owls usually swallow the smaller prey animals whole, coughing up a pellet of indigestible fur and bones a few hours later.

2. Show a sample owl pellet. What do the children expect to find inside the pellet? Why are some bigger than others? (depends on the size of the owl) Why are some dark and some light? (depends on the color of the mouse or other prey animal eaten)

3. Have the children pair up and give each pair two pieces of cardboard – one to separate the owl pellet on, the other to glue pieces on.

4. Then give each pair an owl pellet. Encourage them to work together to gently break apart the pellet, to use their toothpicks to pick away the fur and to discover what's inside (bones, teeth, seeds, hair, pebbles, etc.) Use the bones chart to identify specific bones, if you like.

5. After ten or more minutes of study, hand out the glue and Q-tips, so the children can glue pieces onto the other cardboard.

Talk about how owls swallow their food whole and regurgitate what they cannot digest in the form of an owl pellet. Mention the advantage of being able to cough up pellets – the owl doesn't have to carry the extra weight for the long time it would take before those pieces would be fully digested.

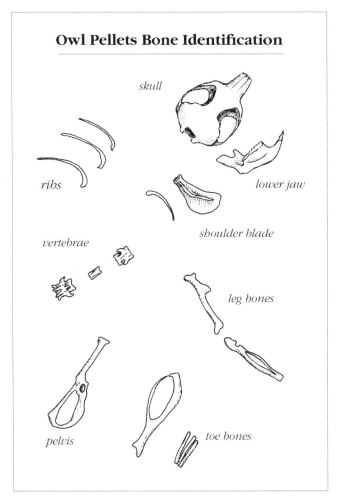

Owl Pellets Bone Identification

skull

ribs

lower jaw

shoulder blade

vertebrae

leg bones

pelvis

toe bones

OWLS LIVE IN MANY PLACES

Objective: *To learn about some of the places that owls call home in North America.*

Materials:
- owls at home illustration (located at end of unit) – 1 copy per child
- pencils or markers
- writing surfaces (optional)

Activity:
1. Hand out the owls at home illustration and encourage the children to find and circle all the owls in their homes.
2. Once everyone has finished, ask the children about what they found in their pictures. Make sure the children understand that the illustration represents many different environments, and therefore many of the owls pictured do not overlap in territory: cacti don't grow with trees!

Talk about how some owls live in trees, others live in cavities, and still others nest on or in the ground (see the "Digging In" section for background). If the children were owls, where would they like to live?

Outdoor Activities

snowy owl

OWL AND MOUSE GAME

What You Need
- blindfold
- squeak toy (preferably a mouse)

What to Do
Form a circle, sitting on the ground. The children in the circle are the mice. Choose one child to be the owl. That person should wear a blindfold and sit in the center of the circle. After the owl is blindfolded, hand a squeaky toy to one child. At your signal, that mouse-child squeezes the squeaky toy, and the owl-child points to the place she hears the sound. The owl (child) gets three tries to point to the right person. Then the mouse becomes the owl, and the game begins again.

SEARCH FOR AN OWL TREE

What to Do
Take a walk in a nearby forest (if you have one) and search for an owl tree. Owls make their nests in other large birds' old nests or inside hollow trees. They also use the branches of other trees to rest during the day. You can usually find an owl resting in a tree if you discover a pile of pellets underneath.

THE OWLS ARE HIDING

What You Need
- owl illustrations in this unit, colored (or owl pictures from a magazine or bird guide)

eastern screech owl

What to Do
Place the color pictures of the owls outside, taping the pictures against the trunks of trees. Invite the children to search for the "hiding owls." Do they blend in with the trees?

We Care about . . .
Owls

Although it is a magical thing to hold and examine an owl feather, it is also illegal to possess owl feathers, or indeed, many other feathers, nests, and bird parts without a permit. Designed to end the commercial trade in bird feathers and bird parts that had resulted in the serious decline in many bird species at the beginning of the twentieth century, the Migratory Bird Treaty Act (MBTA) protects migratory birds and their parts (including eggs and nests) and makes it illegal for anyone to possess migratory bird parts, without a valid permit issued in accordance with federal regulations. Under this Act, all but a few bird species (some game birds, rock dove/pigeon, European house sparrow, and European starling) in the United States are fully protected.

This being said, you may be able to borrow a feather from a nature center or museum, or have a museum educator visit your classroom. Also, depending on your local conservation office, it may only take a reasonable amount of paperwork to obtain a permit to possess feathers for educational purposes. Local nature centers, museums, and wildlife offices can often provide you with more information and contacts regarding feathers in the classroom.

Language Activity / Poem

High up in a gnarled tree,
a gray owl looks at me.

Even so high,
I can feel his eyes

Peering, Glaring, Staring
   and
his ears are listening . . .

For the hustle,
and bustle,
of mice below
the cold, cold snow.

The owl leans,
and then glides
from his perch

silently

until..
feathered toes punch
the snow.

A midnight lunch
of mouse is found.

Independent Play Idea

Leave a tape or CD player and owl call tape/CD out for children to listen to and imitate.

Craft and Project

OWL PUPPETS

What You Need
- brown paper sandwich bags
- circles the size of quarters cut from yellow or brown paper (2 per child)
- scissors
- small triangles cut from yellow paper (1 per child)
- glue
- crayons/markers
- scrap paper
- large circle-shaped patterns

What to Do
Give each child an unopened bag and have them lay the bag down on the table with the opening at the bottom and the bottom flap facing up at the top. Help the children use the large circle patterns to trace and cut out a circle for the owl's head. Have the children glue their circles onto the bottom flap of the bag. The circle represents the facial disc. Allow the children to add two small circles to the head for eyes and a triangle beak. To finish the puppet, encourage the children to cut out and glue (or draw) feathers, wings, and feet for their bird. Have the children practice flying and perching their birds. Let the owls speak.

Snacks

OWL PELLET COOKIES

What You Need
- white flour
- chopped pecans
- 2 sticks of butter
- sugar
- vanilla
- water
- mixing bowl
- large spoon
- measuring cups and spoons
- cookie sheet
- access to an oven
- confectioner's sugar (optional)

What to Do
Mix together 2 cups white flour and 2 cups chopped pecans. Set aside. Cream 1 cup butter. Add 1/2 cup sugar. Mix in 1 teaspoon vanilla and 1 tablespoon water. Gradually add flour/nut mixture to batter. With lightly floured hands, shape dough into small "owl pellet" shapes.

Bake at 325 degrees for 25-30 minutes. If you like, while still warm, roll cookies in sugar (white or confectioners). Enjoy these delicious "owl pellet cookies"!

• •

ANOTHER WAY TO MAKE OWL PELLETS

What You Need
- cotton candy (many grocery and candy shops now carry this in bags or tubs)
- thin pretzels sticks

What to Do
Wrap a small number of pretzel stick "bones" in cotton candy "fur." Shape the package to look like a big owl pellet. When you serve the "pellets" to the children, be sure to tell them to pull the "fur" apart and look for "bones" before eating the whole thing. Be prepared for a sticky, but fun, snack!

Book Ideas

CHILDREN'S FICTION

Owl at Night, by Ann Whitford Paul, G.P. Putnam's Sons, 1985 – a gentle, sleepytime book that contrasts the nighttime activities of owls with the daytime business of people and other animals.

Owl Babies, by Martin Waddell, Candlewick Press, 1992 – a sweet tale of three baby owls, frightened when their mother leaves them alone.

Owl Lake, by Tejima, Philomel Books, 1982 – a strikingly illustrated story of a father owl hunting for food to feed his young family.

Owl Moon, by Jane Yolen, Philomel Books, 1987 – a little girl and her father go owling on a bright winter night.

Screech Owl at Midnight Hollow, by Drew Lamm, Smithsonian, 2001 – relates the daily activities of one of our most common owls.

The Barn Owls, by Tony Johnston, Talewings Press, 2000 – a look at the lives and habits of barn owls, and their long history of residence in a farm barn.

CHILDREN'S NONFICTION

The Moon of the Owls, by Jean Craighead George, HarperCollins, 1993 – a spellbinding journey through the natural world as seen by an owl in the middle of winter.

All about Owls, by Jim Arnosky, Scholastic, 1995 – a visually appealing, yet chock-full-of-information book.

RESOURCE BOOKS FOR ADULTS AND CHILDREN

Barn Owls, by Wolfgang Epple, Carolrhoda Books, 1992 – an entire book dedicated to the natural history of barn owls, specifically one family living in a barn in Europe; factual explanations and many photographs.

Birds of Prey, by Kate Petty, Glaucester Press, 1987 – includes general information about birds of prey and ideas of how to study birds with children.

Tiger with Wings – The Great Horned Owl, by Barbara Juster Esbensen, Orchard Books, 1991 – a nonfiction book about one of the largest and most dramatic owls in New England. Rich with information, it could easily be read in short sections, with the children concentrating on one owl adaptation at a time.

Owls at Home Sheet

OWLS: NIGHTTIME HUNTERS

We have been learning about owl's homes and how they've adapted to living in the darkness.

Continue the Learning at Home

Choose an outdoor site that would be easy to visit in the dark. Take a walk there in the daytime. Look for colors – how many can you find? Listen to the sounds you hear – how many different noises are there in the daytime? Check the site for safety. You will visit it again in the dark. If you like, you can set up a string in the daylight that you can hold onto in the dark. Tie it around trees or other objects along the route you want to take at night. This will guide you when you cannot see.

Prepare for your night hike. It's often cooler at night, so dress in extra layers. Bring a flashlight but save it for emergencies – do not use it for your walk, as it will prevent you from experiencing the dark. Retrace your daytime steps or follow your string. Look for the same colors you found in the daytime. Listen for sounds.

Revisit your site in the daytime again. Do you see it with new eyes now?

Did You Know . . .

Our eyes do not see color well at night?
Unless you are active when there is a bright moon or close to bright lights, you should see colors as shades of gray. The receptors in your eyes that interpret color cannot function without more light than is available at nighttime.

great horned owl

Turtles at Home

Focus: Turtles are reptiles with shells. Their diversity of habitats and remarkable life habits have ensured their survival for thousands of years.

Objective: To understand the importance of the turtle's shell, as well as where and how turtles live.

Extra Information for Adult Leaders

Most people think of turtles as slow-moving animals that carry their homes on their backs. Although the turtle's shell sets it apart from all other **reptiles**, the turtle is much more than merely its shell.

There are more than 250 species of turtles living on every continent except Antarctica and in every ocean except the Arctic. Turtles can be found in lakes, oceans, rivers, ponds, forests, jungles, deserts, and even underground. They range in size from small to tremendous. The eastern bog turtle measures only three or four inches across, while the largest turtles include the Galapagos tortoise (over 500 pounds) and the leatherback sea turtle (over 2,000 pounds).

Turtle, tortoise, terrapin – how do you tell one from the other? Those species that live on land are traditionally called **tortoises**. Those living in water are known as turtles. And any species used for food are called **terrapins**. But as far as biologists are concerned, they are all turtles and fall into these three groups: freshwater turtles, saltwater turtles, and land-dwelling turtles.

Turtles are reptiles. Other reptiles include snakes, lizards, crocodiles, and alligators. Reptiles share several important characteristics. First, virtually all reptiles lay eggs (usually with leathery shells) and have scaly skin. All reptiles use lungs to breathe. Unlike mammals or birds, reptiles are **cold-blooded**, meaning they depend on their environment for heat.

Turtles have been around since the time of the first dinosaurs and have survived primarily because of their shells. Unlike other animals with shells (such as the armadillo), a turtle's shell is fused bone. A turtle's rib cage and spinal cord are actually part of its shell. (The backbone and ribs are easily seen in the inside of the empty turtle shell.) A turtle can never leave its shell, any more than a person could leave his skin. The outside of the shell is covered by a layer of

DIGGING IN...

keratin, the same material as fingernails. It gives the shell its color. The keratin is divided into sections, called **scutes**. As the turtle grows, its scutes also grow (often in growth rings, similar to the growth rings of a tree). In fact, some **herpetologists** (scientists who study reptiles and amphibians) use these growth rings to estimate a turtle's age.

Of course, the most important function of a turtle's shell is to protect its soft body from harm. Some turtles, like the eastern box turtle, can close their shells very tightly to remain safe. Other species of turtles are unable to hide completely in their shells, so they must protect themselves from enemies in different ways. The musk turtle gives off a rank odor, often enough to drive away potential predators. The common snapping turtle defends itself with strong jaws and sharp claws. The spiny soft-shelled turtle buries itself in soft mud or sand, thereby **camouflaging** its body.

While turtles breathe air, using lungs as people do, aquatic (water) turtles do not need as much oxygen as we do. They can stay under water for hours by absorbing oxygen directly from the water.

Instead of teeth, turtles have hard, beak-like jaws that tear at their food. Land-dwelling turtles are mostly **herbivores**, eating plants. Freshwater and saltwater turtles may be either **omnivores** who eat fruit, vegetables, worms, and insects, or **carnivores**,

stink pot turtle

who eat mostly meat or fish. Many species of turtles will even eat carrion (dead animals).

All turtles reproduce in the same way. Some time after mating with a male, the female turtle digs a nest hole into which she deposits her eggs. After laying her eggs, the turtle tamps down the nest hole with soil and abandons it. The sun-warmed earth (not the turtle mother) incubates the turtle eggs. And with most turtles, the prevailing temperature during incubation determines whether the little one will become a boy or girl! Low temperatures (below 70 degrees) produce males; and higher temps (above 85 degrees) produce females. In between those temperatures, both boys and girls are produced.

With only their shells to protect them, baby turtles have been making their way on the earth since the time of the dinosaurs. Turtles live long lives – some species live to be more than one hundred years old! But even a day-old turtle knows its way in the world.

Today many turtles are in danger of extinction due to habitat destruction; hunting for meat, oil, eggs, and shells; predation of turtle eggs and hatchlings; air and water pollution; and diseases from pet turtles being released into the wild. Fortunately, the United States has established federal and state laws protecting turtles and their habitats.

Indoor Activities

DO YOU KNOW TURTLES?

Objective: *To introduce turtles to the children and to allow them to share some of the details they already know about these creatures.*

Materials:
- painted turtle illustration
- the story of the tortoise and the hare (You can get this story from your local library or tell it in your own words.)

Activity:
1. While showing the children the turtle picture, ask them what they know about these amazing creatures. Specifically, ask: How do you know this animal is a turtle? Where do turtles live? What do turtles eat? What else is special about turtles?

2. Ask the children if they have ever heard the story of the tortoise and the hare? Review the story together, or read it aloud if it's new to the children. Talk about the moral of the story – "slow and steady wins the race."

3. If you like, you might encourage the children to act out the story of the tortoise and the hare. Some of the children (the hares) could run fast but need to take breaks to catch their breath; while other children (the tortoises) could move more slowly but without need for rests.

Talk about how turtles move – very slowly! Because of their slow pace, turtles cannot avoid – or run from – certain dangers, like animals who want to eat them. Fortunately, though, turtles have built-in armor to protect themselves against foxes, raccoons, otters, and other predators. At the first hint of danger, many turtles can pull their head, tail, and legs inside their shell. Their shells are bony and hard, and the shell is the turtle's main means of protection. This survival strategy works so well, it has allowed turtles to thrive on earth for a very long time – since before the dinosaurs!

painted turtle

WE ARE TURTLES

Objective: *To pretend to be turtles.*

Materials:
- large brown paper bags (1 for each child)
- markers or crayons
- scissors (for teacher)

Activity:
1. To prepare, cut one big hole in the bottom of each bag (for the child's head) and two on the sides (for the arms).
2. Provide markers or crayons so the children can decorate the top part of their "shells" (one side of the bag).
3. Have everybody carefully climb into their turtle shells, then pretend to
   - crawl slowly
   - tuck in your arms and head when danger approaches
   - sleep inside your shell
   - reach up to tall plants for food
   - dig in the dirt for worms
   - swim

Talk about the reliable protection that turtle shells provide. Other animals have shells, too. Can the children name some? (snails, crabs, clams, beetles, etc.) Remind the children that turtle shells grow with the animals. Turtles do not change or remove their shells. This is unlike hermit crabs and some other creatures, who find new shell homes when they outgrow the ones they are inhabiting.

• •

A TURTLE IS MORE THAN ITS SHELL

Objective: *To look closely at a turtle's body.*

Materials:
- a real turtle shell, if available; or a painted turtle illustration on page 172

Activity:
1. Look closely at the turtle shell (illustration). Notice and name the parts of the shell and body:
   - Top (**carapace**) covers the back of the turtle. The turtle's spine and ribs are attached to this protective upper shell. The carapace may be flat, domed, bumpy, or pointy.
   - Bottom (**plastron**) covers the belly. Some turtles, like the box turtles, have a hinged plastron that enables them to close up very tightly so that no soft body part shows. Snapping turtles have very small plastrons and cannot pull their head and legs inside.
   - Mid/connector section (**bridge**) joins the carapace and plastron.
   - Front and back openings allow the turtle's head, tail, and chunky legs to stick out.
   - Broad, thin covering of scales on shell (scutes) provide color pattern and help camouflage the turtle in its surroundings. Scutes are made of the same material as our fingernails.
   - Sharp beak is used for eating or defense. The beak is similar to that of a bird of prey. Has jagged edges pointing backward to help food go down the throat or to tear it into smaller pieces.
2. Also notice the feet, claws, head, eyes, mouth, and tail of the turtle.
3. Ask the children to reach around to their backs and feel their backbones. If you can, look at the spine of the turtle, which is fused to the inside of the shell.

Talk about the special purpose of each body part: shell – protection; feet – walking; claws – digging for worms or creating a nest; eyes – looking for danger or food; nose – breathing; mouth – beak-like for tearing food (no teeth); tail – balance.

TYPES OF TURTLES

Objective: *To distinguish between the three different types of turtles.*

Activity:
1. Discuss the differences between turtle types.
   - ***Sea Turtles*** are found in oceans and spend almost all their time in water. They only come ashore to lay their eggs. Most sea turtles are very large and can grow to be several hundred pounds. Legs are flattened and have paddle-like flippers.
   - ***Tortoises*** live only on land, usually near deserts and grasslands. They are poor swimmers. These turtles have stump-like legs and high, rounded shells.
   - ***Terrapins*** or freshwater turtles spend part of their time in the water of lakes, ponds, and streams, and part on land. They have many different styles of shells. Their feet are usually suited for both walking and swimming (most have claws and are webbed).
2. Ask the children to crawl around the room very slowly like tortoises. Increase the speed until they are moving as fast as freshwater turtles. Speed up again until they are swimming as fast as sea turtles.

soft shell turtle

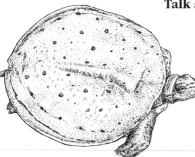

Talk about the fact that land turtles move slowly. In a one-mile race with a turtle, it would take the land turtle five hours to run the course, while a child could do it in ten to fifteen minutes. (This would be the same as a child running 100 inches per second while a turtle can only run three inches per second.) Yet sea turtles can propel themselves through the water at speeds of nearly 20 miles an hour! Their broad flippers make them go fast – the same way we can speed through the water with a set of flippers on our feet.

TURTLE FOODS

Objective: *To discover how and what turtles eat in the wild.*

Materials:
- variety of foods (blueberries, raspberries, gummy worms, broccoli, lettuce, banana chunks, candied fish, chocolate eggs, etc.)
- paper plates – 1 per child

Activity:
1. Discuss with the children the foods different kinds of turtles might eat in the wild. How do they find and capture their food? What tools or body parts do they use to get their meals to their mouths?
2. Distribute the variety of foods onto each child's plate. Have the children pretend to eat like turtles. Have them put their mouths right next to their foods and use their entire hand to push food into their mouths. Use only their lips to crush and chew the foods.

Talk about the variety of foods that turtles may eat. Depending on the type of turtle and the kind of food available in its habitat, turtles may eat only plants, other animals, or a little of both. Just like people, turtles have favorite foods; therefore, it is believed they have a keen sense of taste. Also, turtles can hear quite well. Unlike many animals, turtles can see colors and seem to be particularly sensitive to red.

Different kinds of turtles have different food preferences. Bog turtles like to eat insect larvae and snails; while terrapins prefer shellfish. Snapping turtles consume fish, frogs, insects, crabs, toads, snakes, bird eggs, and small mammals. Tortoises, in their dry land habitats, eat plants; while sea turtles devour jellyfish, eel grass, and fish.

DANCING FOR WORMS

Objective: | *To imitate the unique strategy some turtles use to find their food.*

Activity: | 1. Discuss how wood turtles (found in northeastern North America) have an especially interesting way of finding their favorite food – worms. The wood turtle locates a worm hole, then stands and stomps its front feet in a very regular pattern (two stomps right, two stomps left...). The worms feel the vibrations under the ground and come to the surface to investigate. You can guess what happens next!

2. Have the children pretend to be wood turtles "dancing" to find worms.

Talk about how the chosen foods for different turtles depend largely on where they live – their **habitats**. Most turtles can go for days or even weeks without eating. But when food is plentiful, turtles will eat all they can and may become quite fat. If a wood turtle comes upon a number of worms that have been driven out of their holes by rain, it will bite the head off each squirming worm. Later, the turtle will come back to eat them, one by one.

COLD-BLOODED CREATURES

Objective: | *To understand that the body temperature of cold-blooded animals (like turtles) changes with their surroundings.*

Activity: | 1. Discuss the fact that turtles are members of a group of animals (along with snakes, lizards, crocodiles, and alligators) called reptiles. All reptiles have backbones and scaly skin, bear their young on land, and are cold-blooded. What sets a turtle apart from all other reptiles is its shell.

2. Remind the children that a reptile's body temperature changes with its environment – it is cold-blooded. To speed up the warming process, turtles often bask in the sun. As it warms up, the turtle starts moving in search of food, or to find a friend. If the sun becomes too hot, the turtle retreats into the shade of a tree, under a rock or into a river to cool down.

3. Outside, have the children pretend to be turtles keeping cool (by hiding in the shade) and warming up (moving into the full sun).

Talk about how turtles in northern areas **hibernate** through the winter. As fall approaches and the weather cools, these turtles start to put on extra fat by eating as much as they can. This fat will supply what energy the turtles need through the winter. When the temperature drops still more, the turtles gradually become less and less active. Finally, they burrow deep into the mud at the bottom of ponds or into the loose soil of the forest floor and settle in to sleep the winter away.

Scientists have found that the blood of turtles actually changes and works like the antifreeze we put into our cars in the winter. As a result, the turtle's body temperature can drop to only a few degrees above freezing without harming the turtle's body. In the spring, as the soil and water begin to warm, the turtle's body gradually warms up, too.

EGGS: SAME AND DIFFERENT

Objective: *To distinguish reptile and amphibian eggs.*

Materials:
- grapes or ping pong balls
- sand
- bowls
- cooked tapioca in water
- Extension: trowels, toy turtle, plastic Easter eggs, tiny toy turtles (to fit inside plastic eggs)

Activity:
1. Set up two stations. The first station should have grapes (or ping pong balls) buried in sand (reptile eggs). The second should have cooked tapioca floating in water (**amphibian** eggs).
2. Invite the children to observe, touch, and comment on the two stations. Remind them what an amphibian is (frog, toad, or salamander which spends part or all of its life in the water). Most reptiles, including turtles, lay their eggs on dry land.
3. Extension: Outside, help the children to use trowels and/or a plastic turtle to dramatize the egg laying process. First, dig a hole. Drop several plastic eggs (with tiny turtles inside) into the hole. Cover the eggs with soil. Wait a few minutes, then "help the eggs to hatch" by digging them up, cracking open the eggs, and watching the baby turtles come crawling out!

Talk about how reptiles lay eggs. In the case of turtles, the female digs a nest in the soil or sand with her hind legs and lays her eggs in the nest. She covers her eggs and departs. In a few months, the eggs hatch by themselves, and the turtles (small though they may be) set forth on their voyage to their future homes. A hatchling turtle's life is full of danger. A young turtle could be a meal for a skunk, large bird, or raccoon. Some scientists believe that only one in 100 hatchling turtles live to become an adult.

spotted turtle

Outdoor Activities

VISIT TO A POND

What to Do

Take the children to a pond on a warm, sunny day. Watch for turtles sunning themselves on logs and rocks. Use binoculars to have the children observe the colors and sizes of the turtles. How close to the turtles can you get before they slip into the water?

Note: Wild turtles carry few diseases, but farmed turtles can frequently carry salmonella bacteria, which can cause serious intestinal infections in humans. To avoid salmonellosis, diligently wash hands after contact with turtles or infected water.

• •

TURTLE TERRITORY HUNT

What You Need
- books illustrating woodland, field, river, and pond habitats (optional)

What to Do

Reptiles found in rivers and ponds differ from those found in fields and forests. Go on a hunt around your school or backyard property looking for different kinds of habitats that may support a turtle or two. What kinds of plants and animals do you find living in the water and along the banks? What about at the woodland's edge? What kind of food may be available in the summer for reptiles to dine on? Are there any pet predators nearby? Backyard habitats can be full of surprises, not to mention a few cold-blooded neighbors, too. (If you cannot observe habitats, find books to make observations.)

We Care about . . . Turtles

Because almost half of all turtle species are in trouble today worldwide, it is essential that turtles are left in their natural habitats and not taken from the wild as pets. If too many young turtles are removed from the wild, there won't be enough turtles to replace the older ones, and the turtle population will suffer. So, enjoy observing turtles in the wild but remember to leave them where they live.

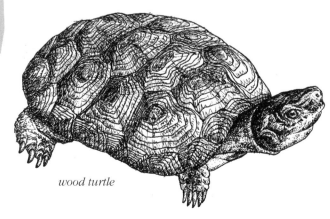

wood turtle

Language Activity

American Sign Language

The Sign for Turtle

1. Make a vertical fist with your right hand, with the thumb on top.
2. Cover the right fist with your left hand – your left thumb should point to your chest. This is the turtle shell.
3. Wiggle your right thumb. This is the turtle head.

The Sign for Egg

1. Make the sign for "h" with both left and right hands (index and middle finger held straight out, touching each other; ring finger, pinky, and thumb curled to palm).
2. Cross your left and right "h" in front of your chest, with the left on the bottom.
3. Make a swift downward motion with your hands separating them until your fingertips point to the floor (the motion is like an upside-down V). This is the egg breaking.

Crafts and Projects

SCALY CREATURES

What You Need
- sunflower seeds
- tempera paints
- paint brushes
- modeling clay or salt dough

What to Do

Help the children mold the clay or salt dough into turtle shapes. Add seeds to the "shells" to make scaly plastrons. If using salt dough, once the dough is dry (overnight), paint the turtles to blend in with their environment.

• •

PAPER PLATE TURTLES

What You Need
- sturdy white paper plates – 2 per child
- cardboard egg cartons – precut the bottom 1/2 inch from each egg cup – 6 or 8 cups per child
- green or brown paper – precut into turtle heads, legs and tails
- glue and paint brushes
- newspaper or plastic tarp

What to Do

After setting up the newspaper or tarp, show the children how to glue their egg carton pieces to the bottom side of one of the paper plates, bumpy side up. (These are the scutes of the shell.) When they're dry, the children should paint the shells as they like.

When dry, the children can add legs, tails, and heads to the inside (top side) of the plates they've prepared. Then glue a second plate to the first, as a bottom shell.

STAINED GLASS TURTLES

What You Need
- precut black or brown large turtle, with holes cut out of shell section (poster board works well; use an Exacto knife to cut holes)
- colored tissue paper (several colors)
- glue and paint brushes

What to Do
Have the children apply glue around each of the precut holes in the shell. They can then tear tissue paper to cover all of the holes. When dry, the turtles can be hung in a window like stained glass ornaments.

Independent Play Idea
Fill your sand table with sand or other loose material. Provide plastic turtles and/or eggs for the children to practice "laying" in the sand. If you don't have a sand table, use a plastic basin of sand.

Snacks

PRETZEL DOUGH TURTLES

What You Need
- pretzel dough – enough for one ball for each child
- 2 eggs

What to Do
While reviewing the anatomy of turtles have children tear off pieces of dough to shape into their own turtle. Put turtle creations on a lightly oiled cookie sheet. Let the dough rise for 30 minutes in a warm place. Preheat the oven to 450 degrees. Then, beat the eggs and brush the glaze over the turtle pretzels. Bake the turtles for 15 minutes, or until they are golden brown. Let cool down and eat them up!

TURTLE EGGS

What You Need
- grapes

What to Do
Tell the children they are predators looking for turtle eggs to eat. Encourage them to pretend the grapes are turtle eggs (with leathery shells). They might even try to suck or eat out the inside of the grapes, leaving behind only the skin (shell).

Book Ideas

CHILDREN'S FICTION

Box Turtle at Long Pond, by William T. George, Greenwillow Books, 1989 – a nicely illustrated book that tells about the events of one day in a turtle's life.

Chickens Aren't the Only Ones, by Ruth Heller, Grosset & Dunlap, 1981 – a brightly colored book describes some of the many egg-laying animals, as well as the diversity of egg sizes and shapes.

Turtle Spring, by Deborah Turney Zagwijn, Tricycle Press, 1998 – a gorgeous book telling the warm-hearted story of a girl who gets a new brother and a surprising pet turtle.

Turtle Tale, by Frank Asch, Dial Press, 1978 – with striking pictures and quick wit, the ups and downs of becoming a wise turtle.

What Newt Could Do for Turtle, by Jonathan London, Candlewick Press, 1996 – a funny story about the friendship of these two animals; not scientifically focused, but not inaccurate.

CHILDREN'S NONFICTION

All about Turtles, by Jim Arnosky, Scholastic, 2000 – a very informative book, beautiful and accurate and answers many questions about turtles.

Look Out for Turtles, by Melvin Berger, HarperCollins, 1992 – a colorful story revealing many turtle facts and encouraging turtle protection everywhere.

My Little Book of Painted Turtles, by Hope Irvin Marston, North Word Press, 1996 – a year in the life of a family of painted turtles – including feeding, hatching, eggs, and over wintering

Nature's Children: Turtles, by Merebeth Switzer, Grolier, 1986 – a fine resource book for children about the lives of turtles, full of photographs.

RESOURCE BOOKS FOR ADULTS AND CHILDREN

Turtles, by Anita Baskin-Salzberg and Allen Salzberg, Grolier, 1996 – an excellent reference book, filled with thorough yet concise biological information, as well as great photographs.

Turtles, Toads and Frogs, by George Fichter, Golden Book, 1993 – a good nonfiction resource book about reptiles and amphibians.

What's the Difference? Reptiles, by Stephen Savage, Steck-Vaughn Library, 2000 – pictures, facts, and information about reptiles.

TURTLES AT HOME

We have been learning about turtles and how they live.

Continue the Learning at Home

Some turtles have some very tricky ways of finding their food. Some even set traps! The common snapping turtle uses a worm-like attachment at the back of its throat to lure unsuspecting fish near its mouth. The snapper's dark color and rock-like carapace helps it camouflage into the backwater of a pond or stream. While remaining still, the turtle opens its mouth and wiggles the worm decoy at passing victims. Eventually, a small fish or frog may become curious enough to venture inside. Like all turtles, the snapping turtle doesn't have teeth, but its strong jaws can easily devour small fish and frogs.

Team up with your child to draw or make the snapping turtle's habitat with several little fish and frogs, as well as the blue water of the pond.

snapping turtle

Produced and copyrighted by Vermont Institute of Natural Science, 2005.

Bees in Their Hives

Focus: Studying bees offers an excellent opportunity to learn about animals that cooperate to live together as a group.

Objective: To discover some of the many fascinating aspects of the lives of honeybees and how their activities and products help people.

Extra Information for Adult Leaders

The honeybee life cycle is a fascinating story of order, efficiency, and social structure. It's mind-bending to think that a small jar of honey is the result of these tiny creatures collecting pollen and nectar from nearly 3 million clover flowers. Bees are common visitors to a flower patch or home orchard and, because they are not aggressive to the casual visitor, they are perfect insects to observe to learn a bit about wildlife behavior.

Three types of bees – the queen, female workers, and male drones – live in a **hive,** each with specific job functions. All bees start their lives as eggs in hexagonal **cells** in a comb. The vast majority of bees in a hive, however, are worker bees. Female **worker bee** larvae hatch from fertilized eggs that are fed **royal jelly** (a glandular secretion produced by worker bees) and **bee bread** (pollen and nectar) by adult worker bees for three days, and honey for two additional days. Larva then spin a cocoon and **pupate**, emerging 12 days later as a sterile worker bee, ready to do the majority of the work in the hive. The **queen bee** is a special female that dominates the hive's social structure. She starts her life as a larva in the comb and like all other larvae is fed royal jelly. Unlike the worker bees, who feed on royal jelly for only a few days, the queen receives royal jelly throughout the 16 days it takes to develop into a mature adult. Due to her special diet, she emerges much larger and stronger than the workers, and longer and slimmer than the **drone** bees. Once the queen emerges, she aggressively asserts her position. She tears open unhatched queen eggs and larvae and attacks other new queens before beginning her primary task – mating and laying up to 3,000 eggs per day. She completely depends upon female workers to feed her throughout this period. Egg laying consumes a tremendous amount of energy, and the queen must be fed every time she lays 20 or so eggs.

Queen bees lay both fertilized eggs that develop into female workers and unfertilized eggs that develop into male drone bees. Drones lack specialized body parts and are unable to even feed themselves, instead relying on workers to provide them pollen. Their only purpose is to mature and fertilize the female queen bee. A typical hive of 10,000 bees will have at most 20 drones at one time.

Worker bees are responsible for nearly all other tasks in the hive. During the first three weeks of their lives they function as **house bees**, cleaning old cells for reuse, producing royal jelly, feeding larvae, secreting wax to build and repair the hive, packing pollen and honey in cells, and guarding the entrance of the hive. The worker is also responsible for feeding drones, and ultimately starving drones that need to die off in the hive before winter. The worker bees build the combs using wax that they produce from abdominal **wax glands**. Their middle legs have hooks on them that are used to pick up the wax and move it to the mouth, where the wax is softened by chewing. Bees are meticulous about cleaning their hives, and a bee hive can be reused year after year.

After working in the hive for three weeks, the house bees venture into the fields to collect pollen for feeding larval bees; at this point they become field workers or **field bees.** The worker bee's legs have special adaptations for pollen collection. The bee's front legs have combs for removing pollen and other materials from the bee's **antennae**. The back legs have **pollen baskets** that are used for carrying pollen back to the hive (look for yellow balls of pollen on the bee's back legs next time you observe one at a flower). All six of the bee's legs have **pollen brushes** that are used to transfer pollen from the worker's body to the pollen baskets.

The field bee locates sources of pollen, such as flowering plants and fruit trees, finding those with strong scents particularly attractive. She sips nectar with her **proboscis,** gathers pollen with her legs, and takes note of where the flower is in relation to the hive. Once back at the hive, the worker lets the other field workers know where the pollen source is, and they take off in search of the pollen. If the bee dances in a circle, called the "Round Dance," she is telling the others that the pollen is close by. If she dances in the shape of a figure eight and is pointing towards the sun when at the middle of the eight, the pollen source is towards the sun. If she does the figure eight and is facing away from the sun when at the middle of the eight, the pollen source is away from the sun.

The nectar that field bees gather is stored in a sac called the **honey stomach**. When a worker returns from the fields, she gives the nectar to the house bees, who spread it throughout the honeycombs. Enzymes absorbed while the nectar was in the bees' bodies break the nectar down into simple sugars. The bees fan their wings to move air through the hive to evaporate the water from the nectar droplets. Finished cells of honey are capped with fresh wax.

Activity in the hive slows down in wintertime, as the bees cluster together to conserve warmth and their movements are slowed by the cold temperatures. Honey sustains them throughout the cold months, then the whole process of egg laying, rigorous hive maintenance, and food production begins again.

Indoor Activities

THE TINY BEE

Objective:	*To pretend to be tiny and big, and to consider what might happen if a honeybee was very large.*
Materials:	• bee illustration
Activity:	1. Talk with the children about what it would be like to be very, very small. Let them pretend to be very little.
	2. Then ask the children what it would be like to be very, very big. Let them parade around as giants.
	3. Show them the bee illustration. Talk together about how bees climb on flowers to gather pollen and nectar. What would happen to the flower if bees were as big as a child? (The bee would crush the flower.)
	Talk about the reasons why bees must be small – to fly, visit flowers for nectar and pollen, hide from hungry birds and other animals, etc. You might ask the children to show you with their fingers the size of a bee.

BEE BODIES

Objective: *To learn about the bodies of honeybees.*

Materials:
- honeybee illustrations, preferably copied onto cardstock paper (1 per child)
- crayons

Activity:
1. Encourage the children to color and observe their honeybee illustrations.
2. Afterward, talk about the parts of the bee.

   - **Three main body parts:** the head, **thorax**, **abdomen**. (All adult insects have the same three body parts.)
   - **Legs:** six legs, like all insects.
   - **Antennae:** feelers; can smell, touch, and taste all at the same time.
   - **Eyes:** compound eyes, which means they see lots of different views at the same time. (Tell the children to try closing their eyes, then opening them very quickly, then move their heads just slightly and repeat. Insects see all those views at the same time with their compound eyes.)
   - **Wings:** allow tiny bees to get around, find food, and escape predators.
   - **Stinger:** used to protect bee or hive from danger, in queen also used to lay eggs.

Talk about the various body parts and their functions.

• •

CLOSE YOUR PROBOSCIS WHILE YOU CHEW!

Objective: *To practice drinking nectar like a bee.*

Materials:
- cups of juice – 1 per child
- straws – 1 per child
- colored construction paper cut into flower petal shapes
- scissors (for adult use)
- tape

Activity:
1. To prepare, attach different colored construction paper petals to each juice cup.
2. Ask the children if they know what bees eat. (They drink nectar from flowers.) In order to reach into the center of the flower, where the nectar is, a bee must have a very special, long, straw-like mouth – called a proboscis. (Practice saying that fun sounding word.)
3. Place a small cup of juice (nectar) for each child on a table. (Each cup can have different colored petals, so each child has his own flower.)
4. Give each child a straw.
5. Explain to the children that because bees only get a tiny drop of nectar from each flower, they must visit lots of flowers every day.
6. Now each child should take just a tiny sip of juice from the cup, then fly around the room for a bit before returning to the juice cup for more nectar.
7. If you like, as the children visit their flowers, stick little loops of masking tape to their legs to represent the pollen collected.
8. Continue until all the nectar juice is gone.

Talk about how bees collect pollen on their legs when they visit flowers for nectar. (Although you can't see them with the naked eye, honeybees have a bunch of hairs on their legs that form pollen baskets to effectively collect pollen from flowers.) Then, when the bee visits a new flower, some of the pollen rubs off onto the new flower – and pollination occurs.

FANTASTIC FEELERS

Objective: | *To discover how a honeybee uses its antennae (feelers).*

Materials:
- film canisters – 1 per child
- cotton balls
- liquid scents like vanilla, lemon, peppermint, etc.

Activity:
1. To prepare, create scent canisters by soaking the cotton balls in the scents before placing them in the film canisters. (Be sure to create at least two canisters of each scent.)
2. Tell the children that a honeybee uses its antennae not only to feel (especially useful in the center of a dark hive), but also to smell and even taste particular flowers (red clover, for instance). Even individual hives have their own unique odors.
3. During this activity, we'll pretend to be bees trying to find the other bees in our hive – using our sense of smell.
4. Give each child a canister (with top removed). Ask the children to sniff the scent, then to visit with all the other honeybees until they find their hive friends who have the same scent.
5. Ask the children to extend their index fingers from the sides of their heads (like antennae) and to smell (touch) the other bees (children) in their hive (group).

Talk about how honeybees use their antennae and sense of smell to find flowers, to know if a bee coming to the hive really belongs there, and to communicate with each other. What body part did the children use to smell the scents in the canisters? (nose) What part would a bee use? (antennae) When beekeepers want to somehow change a hive (add new bees, for instance), they have to smoke the hive not only to calm them but also to mask the original scent of the bees.

• •

HONEY FOR YOU AND ME, BEE

Objective: | *To examine some bee products, as well as a real honeycomb.*

Materials:
- honeycomb piece
- candle
- lipstick
- honey
- floor polish
- orange
- jar of honey with wax included or wax/honey sticks (available at health food stores)

Activity:
1. Display all the objects except the honeycomb for the children to see and touch. Describe any things the children might not be familiar with. Ask the children what all these items have in common? (Bees help produce all of them.)
2. Now show the honeycomb to the children. Let them touch and smell it, as well as look at it very carefully.
3. Finally, give each child a bit of the honey-drenched wax (or wax/honey sticks) to chew. Ask the children to describe the flavor and texture.

Talk about what the honeycomb is made of (wax) and what it contains (honey). Bees have special wax glands where they produce wax to construct cells to house the eggs and larvae, as well as to store the honey they feed to other bees in the hive and save for winter food. When people raise bees for honey, they harvest some of the honey the bees have made during the spring and summer. But careful beekeepers always take care to be sure the bees have enough honey to feed their hive during the winter months.

HONEYCOMBS ARE HOMES, TOO

Objective: *To notice the shapes a beehive contains and to appreciate why the design of beehive cells is so efficient in terms of space.*

Materials:
- 8 to 12 shapes cut from colored construction paper – circle, triangle, square, star, oval, rectangle, hexagon; cut several of each shape (at least four circles and hexagons)
- long sections of rope or masking tape

Activity:
1. Seat the children in a circle. Put all the shapes into the center.
2. Ask the children to sort the papers by shape. (For very young children, you might make each shape a different color.) How many of each shape are there?
3. If possible, have the children help you use the rope or tape to create a large version of each shape on the floor.
4. Ask the children to walk along each shape and to say the name of that shape. (Save the hexagon until last.)
5. Count the six sides of the hexagon with the children. This is the shape bees use to build the cells in their hives.
6. Place the hexagons on the floor or table, putting adjacent sides right next to each other. Do the same with the circles.
7. Show the children how much more efficiently the hexagons fill the available space. That's why bees build hexagonal shaped cells in the hives.

Talk about the advantages of the hexagon. More hexagons can fit into a small space than circles. Plus the hexagons don't leave much space between the cells. That space would have to be built from wax and wouldn't be useful to the honeybees in any way.

• •

"HONEYBEES IN THEIR HIVE" PUPPET SHOW

Objective: *To learn about the different jobs that need to be done in a honeybee hive.*

Materials:
- emerging bee, house bee, queen bee, field bee, fanning bee, and drone bee puppets at the end of the unit
- puppet show script at the end of the unit
- puppet stage

Activity: Present the puppet show to the children.

Talk about the many different types of bees and the many different roles of bees in a beehive.

HIVE ROLE PLAY

Objective: *To appreciate the many jobs of honeybees during their short lives.*

Materials:
- brooms and dusters (for cleaning hive)
- paper fans (for cooling the queen and drying off the nectar)
- bowls and large wooden spoons (for mixing honey)
- small spoons (for feeding young bees and queen)
- cape and/or crown (for queen bee)
- cardboard shields (for guarding the hive entrance)
- puppets from "Honeybees in Their Hives" puppet show

Activity:

1. Explain to the children that there are three different types of honeybees in every hive. As you describe the types of bees, use the puppets from the puppet show to illustrate different features of each type of bee.

2. First, there's the queen – just one queen. Her sole job is to mate (once) and lay eggs throughout her life (up to 3,000 eggs per day, possible for maybe three to five years). She's cared for at all times – fed, kept cool or warm, etc.

3. Then there are the male bees or drones – just a few per hive. Their only function is to fertilize the queen (often from another hive). In autumn, the drones are forced out of the hive by the worker bees to face certain death. More male drones will be produced in the spring.

4. Finally, there are the worker bees – hundreds of them in each hive. The life of the worker bee changes with age. She is involved in hive duties for the first three weeks of her life, producing royal jelly (to feed the larva) and then wax, packing pollen in cells, cleaning house, helping with repairs, tending to the queen's comfort, and guarding the entrance of the hive. Then she starts taking some scouting trips out of the hive and spends her final weeks as a field bee.

5. Now let's play "hive pretend." First choose a queen and give her a cape and comfy place to sit. Then pass out the other tools and assign worker bee jobs – fanning the queen, feeding the young bees, cleaning the hive, guarding the entrance, etc. Take turns being the queen, if you like.

6. Finally, ask the children which kind of bee they'd like to be – a queen or a worker? Why?

Talk about how people, too, have jobs – in the classroom, at home, as adults. Just like in the bee hive, when everyone works together, they can accomplish great things.

Outdoor Activities

WATCHING BEES AND OTHER INSECTS

What to Do

Take the children outside for a walk. Sit quietly near blooming flowers to watch as bees and other insects (and maybe hummingbirds) come to collect the nectar from the flowers. Notice any lines on the flower leading toward the center – these are called "bee lines" and help to guide bees to the nectar.

• •

COLLECTING POLLEN

What You Need
- cotton swabs

What to Do

Visit some blooming flowers. Look carefully for pollen (looks like fine yellow dust). If possible, use cotton swabs to collect a bit of pollen from one flower, and then share it with another of the same kind.

• •

BEE DANCES

What to Do

Explain that bees communicate the whereabouts of nectar and pollen by "dancing." A circle dance means the source is close; a figure eight dance means it's far away. Have the children perform both dances by following the leader.

Because the middle of the figure eight points to the nectar source (flowers), you might hide a honey treat behind a tree or rock and encourage the bees (children) to fly in that direction.

Language Activity / Song

(To the tune of "Hi, Ho, the Derry O")

A bee is on my (knee),
A bee is on my (knee),
Hi, ho, the hive-o,
A bee is on my (knee)

Independent Play Idea

Prepare some simple bee bodies by coloring black and yellow stripes on toilet paper rolls. Use a utility knife to cut two slits in the back of each bee. Use cardstock to cut wings. On half the wings, write a number. On the other wings, draw a corresponding number of dots. Invite the children to practice matching the numbers to the correct dots on the wings. The wings can be slipped into the slits on the back of each bee.

Crafts and Projects

FUZZY BEES

What You Need
- tongue depressor (1 per child)
- small black pom-poms (1 per child)
- medium-sized black pom-poms (1 per child)
- large yellow pom-poms (1 per child)
- black permanent marker
- google eyes
- black pipe cleaners
- wax paper
- scissors (for teacher use)
- strong craft glue

What to Do

1. To prepare, use the permanent marker to draw stripes on the yellow pom-pom. Cut wax paper into a figure eight shape (to form a pair of wings). Make two pairs of wings per child.
2. Give each child a tongue depressor.
3. Have them glue a small black pom-pom, medium black pom-pom, and yellow pom-pom in a row starting at the tip of the stick.
4. Add eyes and pipe-cleaner antennae to the small pom-pom and two pairs of wings to the medium-sized pom-pom.
5. When dry, draw three pairs of legs from the middle pom-pom, wrapping around the bottom of the tongue depressor. (The fuzzy bees created here are fun to use in the Language Activity in this unit.)

• •

BEESWAX CANDLES

What You Need
- sheets of beeswax (these can be found at a craft store)
- candle wick (also found at craft stores)

What to Do

Help the children to create their own beeswax candles by rolling the beeswax around a candle wick.

• •

BEESWAX SCULPTURES

What You Need
- beeswax modeling clay

What to Do

Encourage the children to use beeswax clay to sculpt tiny animals, trees, flowers, and any other things they think of!

Snacks

TOAST OR CRACKERS WITH HONEY

What You Need
- toast or crackers
- honey

What to Do
Enjoy a snack of toast or crackers with honey.

• •

EDIBLE BEES

What You Need
- peanut butter
- powdered milk
- honey
- melted chocolate
- almond slivers
- mixing bowl
- spoon

What to Do
Mix equal parts peanut butter, powdered milk, and honey. Use this mixture to shape into a bee body. Place melted chocolate inside a plastic sandwich bag. Cut a tiny hole in a corner and squeeze out the chocolate to apply dark stripes on the bee's abdomen. Add chocolate chips for eyes and sliced almonds for wings.

Book Ideas

CHILDREN'S FICTION

Cloud Eyes, by Kathryn Lasky, Harcourt Brace, 1994 – the story of a Native American dreamer who found a way to balance his people's need and a bear's need for honey, appropriate for older children, pencil drawings.

The Apple Pie Tree, by Zoe Hall, Blue Sky Press, 1996 – a nicely illustrated story of two sisters and a year in the life of their apple tree, including bees pollinating the flowers.

The Bee Tree, by Patricia Polacco, Philomel Books, 1993 – a girl and her grandfather lead a growing bee chase through their community in order to find the hive, gorgeous illustrations.

Fiona's Bee, by Beverly Keller, Dell, 1991 – designed as a reader for elementary school students including an audio tape; a bit long but a nice story of a girl coming in close contact with a bee.

Honeybee, by Barrie Watts, Silver Burdett Press, 1989 – an easy reader, with beautiful color photographs.

Honeybee and the Robber, by Eric Carle, Penguin Putnam, 2001 – an interactive book that showcases a honeybee's day, which includes an attack on the hive by a hungry bear.

Joyful Noise: Poems for Two Voices, by Paul Fleischman, Harper Trophy, 1988 – a very clever book of poems to be read simultaneously by two adults, has a great bee poem.

CHILDREN'S NONFICTION

I Can Read about: Bees and Wasps, by David Cutts, Troll Communications, 1998 – a rich introduction to bees and wasps, with lots of illustrations.

The Magic School Bus: Inside a Beehive, by Joanne Cole, Scholastic, 1996 – follow the school bus on a fact-filled journey through a beehive, fun and informative.

RESOURCE BOOKS FOR ADULTS AND CHILDREN

A Beekeeper's Year, by Sylvia Johnson, Little, Brown, 1994 – follows a beekeeper through his jobs helping the bees make honey, includes many photos and even recipes!

Hooray for Beekeeping, by Bobbie Kalman, Crabtree, 1998 – a nonfiction introduction to bees and beekeeping, including photos of beekeeping equipment.

The Life and Times of the Honeybee, by Charles Micucci, Ticknor & Fields, 1995 – text geared for teachers (to share highlights with children), provides great photos of a bee's life, inside and out of the hive.

PUPPET SHOW SCRIPT

"Honeybees in Their Hive"

Emerging Bee – Hmmmmm ... I wonder what I'll be doing now that I'm grown up. Perhaps I'm the queen!

House Bee – Open up for some honey! You're almost a full-grown bee!

Emerging Bee – A queen bee, I hope!

House Bee – Ohhhhhh ... I don't think so. There's only ONE queen bee in this hive! You're going to be a worker!

Emerging Bee – What does a worker do!?

House Bee – Well, first you'll stay inside the hive, helping out.

Emerging Bee – How?

Fanning Bee – *[Fanning Bee appears.]* Well, you might fan your wings to move air around the hive. *[Fanning Bee exits.]*

House Bee – Or you could feed the queen or feed the young. Speaking of the queen. ... *[The queen bee wanders by and exits.]*

Emerging Bee – Wow! She's huge!

House Bee – House bees also make wax, clean the hive, and help make and store honey, as well as collect pollen.

Emerging Bee – *[as a drone wanders by]* Who's that bee, with the great, big eyes!?

House Bee – That's a Drone. Drones are male bees. *[the drone exits, and a field bee enters, the House Bee greets the Field Bee.]* Hi, there! How's it going out there!

Field Bee – BUSY! We've found a great patch of flowers. Lots of nectar. Lots of pollen.

House Bee – *[to emerging bee]* When you and I are older, we'll both be field bees. See the yellow pollen on her back legs. We'll take that and store it in the hive. I bet she's got a load of nectar too!

Emerging Bee – Wow! Sounds like I've got a lot of work coming my way! I better see about getting busy!

House Bee – And I'd better check on the other young!

The End

HONEY BEE PUPPETS

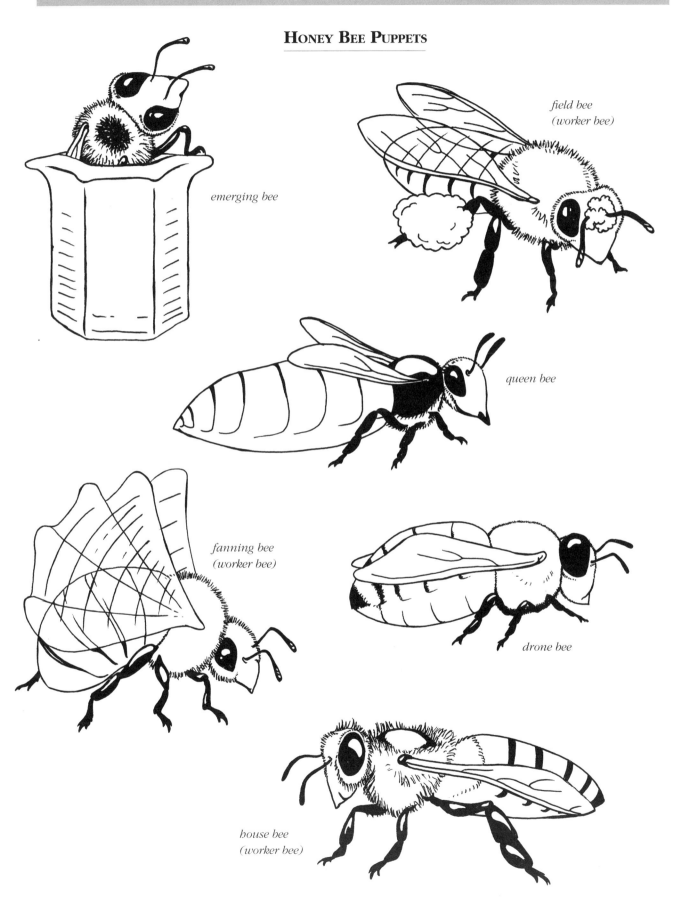

emerging bee

field bee
(worker bee)

queen bee

fanning bee
(worker bee)

drone bee

house bee
(worker bee)

Bees in Their Hives

We have been learning about bees and how they live together in their hives. We have investigated the shapes and structures of hives, as well as the specialized bodies of bees, and the different roles bees play in the hive.

Continue the Learning at Home

We have been learning about the different parts of a bee's body. Bees (and all insects) have six legs and three body parts (head, thorax, and abdomen). Bees, like other flying insects, also have wings. Review the body parts of a bee together by coloring the picture according to the code below:

- color **W** blue (wings)
- color **H** and **T** brown (head and thorax)
- color **B** black (abdomen)
- color **Y** yellow (abdomen)
- color **R** red (eyes)
- color **G** green (legs)
- color **P** purple (antennae)

Produced and copyrighted by Vermont Institute of Natural Science, 2005.

Wiggly Worms

Focus: Earthworms are familiar creatures that deserve a closer look. They have many features and behaviors that help them survive in their underground world.

Objective: To investigate the anatomy and behaviors of earthworms, and conduct simple earthworm experiments.

Extra Information for Adult Leaders

Earthworms – fascinating to some, hated by others – are a common feature in just about any landscape. In fact, one acre of soil can contain more than a million worms. Worms come in many different shapes and sizes – even colors (varying between shades of white, red, pink, brown – even purple). Some of the world's largest earthworms have been known to grow as long as 8 feet!

Worms are **invertebrates**: animals without backbones (insects, spiders, and crabs are other examples of invertebrates). Earthworms are classified as segmented worms because their bodies are divided into many separate sections. Most segments have bristle-like hairs called **setae** that can be moved to help the worm crawl through the soil. The sections toward the head of the worm (the head may be identified by its closeness to the **clitellum**, a swollen band closer to the head than the tail) contain the worm's hearts, of which there are five pairs. Worms do not have lungs, rather, they absorb oxygen through their skin, which must stay moist to facilitate gas exchange. When it rains heavily, earthworms must take refuge above the soil, as water does not contain enough oxygen to keep an earthworm alive. To help preserve moisture in dry conditions, worms are covered in a layer of mucus, which gives them that slimy feeling so many dislike.

The clitellum is used during reproduction. Worms are **hermaphrodites,** but they must still mate to reproduce. When mating, two worms will line up with their heads in opposite directions, and exchange sperm packets (produced in the first twelve segments). The clitellum forms a band of mucus and, as the worm backs out of the band, it slips forward, picking up eggs from the ovaries (located near the clitellum) and the sperm packet. Once free from the worm, the sheath closes around the egg and sperm

to form a cocoon that protects and nourishes the earthworms in their initial stages of development. If conditions are not right for hatching, the cocoon will lie dormant until conditions improve.

The remainder of the worm behind the clitellum is devoted to its digestive tract. Worms do not have teeth, rather, they grind their food in a **gizzard**. Worms play an important role in the environment as **decomposers,** helping speed the process of decay by consuming and digesting decaying plant matter that they find in the soil or below its surface. The plant parts that the worm cannot use are eliminated as **castings**. The castings are mineral-rich and help fertilize the soil as well as nourish centipedes and other soil inhabitants who eat them. Without decomposers like earthworms, dead material would simply accumulate in layers on the forest floor.

In addition to releasing nutrients from decaying plant material, worms also help move air and water into the soil through the tunnels they create. The process of tunneling also mixes the soil. Different worms live in different zones of the soil: some at the surface, others deep below. Night crawlers, for example, live up to six feet below the soil surface and return to the surface each night to drag leaves and other plant items into their burrows to eat.

Earthworms have their predators: along with the birds, several mammals prey on worms as well. Shrews eat worms, and moles can eat three times their weight in worms per day. To avoid being pulled from the ground by an animal seeking a meal, worms use their setae to hold onto soil. Worms do not hear with ears, but rather feel the vibrations of raindrops or predators with their bodies. If a large animal passes by, the vibrations will sometimes send a worm retreating to its burrow. Burrows are also used as retreats during cold weather, when earthworms must burrow below the frost line to survive freezing temperatures.

Indoor Activities

OBSERVING LIVE WORMS

Objective: *To introduce the children to worms.*

Materials:
- live worms (1 per child or pair of children)
- paper plates (1 per child or pair)
- paper towels
- water spritzer bottle
- magnifying lenses (1 per child or pair)

Activity:

1. Give each child (or pair of children) a paper plate with a paper towel on it. As you spray each towel with a bit of water to dampen, explain to the children that you are doing this because too much dryness can hurt a worm's skin. Children should try to keep their fingers damp as they handle the worms, too. Provide magnifying lenses.

2. Put a worm on each plate.

3. Ask the children to observe the worm with their eyes only for one minute. What do they notice?

4. Now the children may carefully touch their worms. Demonstrate proper touching technique.

5. Ask the children to look for the following features or behaviors:

   - **Color** – What color is the worm? Why?
   - **Body** – Can you count the rings or segments around the worm's body? Do they go all around the body?
   - **Underside of the body** – Try stroking the worm's "tummy" from back to front. Can you feel the bristles or what is called "setae"? (There are four pairs of bristles on the lower half of each worm segment. These bristles help to anchor the worm as it moves. They also help the worm to hold itself in a hole if a bird or other predator tries to pull it up.)
   - **The middle of the body** – This thick band or saddle around the worm's middle is called the "clitellum." After two worms mate, a collar-like ring forms here, which is slipped off the worm's head, then its ends join to form an egg sac.
   - **Movement** – Without legs, how does the worm move?
   - **Top and bottom to the body** – How can you find out if there is a top and bottom to the worm's body?
   - **Head and tail end** – How can you tell which is the head and which is the tail? (Watch the direction the worm travels. Also, the clitellum is usually a bit closer to the head end.)
   - **Eyes and ears** – Does the worm have eyes or ears? (no)
   - **Mouth** – Does the worm have a mouth? (yes)

   Talk about other things the children notice about their worms.

Worm Diagram

setae

segment

clitellum

mouth

"HOW LONG IS YOUR WORM?" CHART

Objective: *To measure several worms and make a chart comparing their lengths.*

Materials:
- live worms, as in previous activity
- plastic or wooden ruler for each child
- colored construction paper strips – different color for each child – each 1-2 inches wide and 10 inches long
- poster board or large paper for chart
- pencils
- scissors
- glue

Activity:
1. Using the rulers, ask the children to measure the length of their worms (to the closest inch) and record that number.
2. Then using the construction paper, pencils, and scissors, help the children cut a strip the length of their worm measurement. If they like, the children can give their worms names, which can be printed on the paper strips, too.
3. Glue the paper strips onto a "How Long Is Your Worm?" chart to compare lengths.

Talk about whose worm is the longest and whose is the shortest. Also mention the longest worm in the world – a species found in South Africa, which can be 22 feet long! (You might even make or have ready a paper strip that length!)

MEASURING WITH WORMS

Objective: *To use a "worm" to practice measuring classroom objects.*

Materials:
- worm ruler illustration (1 per child)
- crayons or markers
- scissors

Activity:
1. Give each child a copy of the worm ruler illustration.
2. Have them color the segments different colors, then cut the worm out. For younger children, you may wish to cut the worm out in advance.
3. Encourage the children to use their worm to measure different objects in the room. You can do this in many ways. You can talk about objects that are longer, shorter, or the same length as a worm. You can use the worm's segments to measure blocks or other items. You can line worms up end-to-end to measure a very large object, such as the height of a child or the length of a table. The possibilities are as endless as the children's ideas.

Talk about how you have measured with the worms, and compared the length of objects to the length of the worms. If desired, show the children a ruler or tape measure and demonstrate how people use these tools to measure – after all, not everybody has a worm handy for measuring!

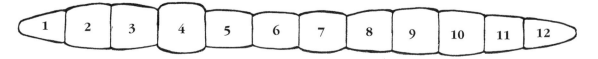

WIGGLE WORMS

Objective: | *To pretend to be worms, wiggling along.*

Activity:

1. Outside or in, invite the children to practice moving like worms. Get down on the ground, with both your knees and your elbows touching the ground. (Your knees and elbows are like the stiff setae which give the worms traction as they move.)
2. Now try wiggling forward, always keeping your knees and elbows touching the ground. First the front stretches out, then the back squeezes in.
3. As leader, you might chant "stretch and squeeze, stretch and squeeze."
4. Hold a worm race, moving from one side of the yard or room to the other.
5. Now try forming a "group worm." Everyone should stand front-to-back, holding the waist of the person in front.
6. When the adult leader says "STRETCH," the children should take tiny baby steps forward – still holding on to each other's waists – until their arms are fully extended. Then the adult leader says "SQUEEZE," and everyone again takes tiny baby steps forward until their arms are pulled in close, bent again.

Talk about how the worm's bristles help it not only to move without slipping, but also allow it to "hold back" when a bird or other predator tries to pull it from its hole in the soil. Worm predators include birds, foxes, turtles, shrews, moles, skunks, and raccoons.

WORM RACE

Objective: | *To watch the movements of worms.*

Materials:
- a large (3-foot-square) piece of paper or cloth, dampened – marked with a small (6 inch) center circle and another circle at the outside perimeter
- water spritzer(s)
- worms, 1 per child or pair

Activity:

1. Tell the children that you're going to hold a worm race. (Again, the children can name their worms if they like.)
2. With great fanfare, begin the worm race by placing all the worms inside the center circle. The first worm to reach the outside circle wins. Encourage the children to cheer for their worms!
3. Keep the contestant worms comfortable by dampening them with a spritz of water should they get too dry.

Talk about the worms' movements. Were the biggest ones the fastest? Did the worms seem to know where they were going?

DESIGN YOUR OWN WORM EXPERIMENTS

Objective: *To design and observe various experiments intended to find answers to children's questions about worms.*

Materials: The following materials are variable, depending on children's questions:
- box that can be divided into 2 halves, bright light and lots of leaves (to create light and dark areas)
- lettuce leaves, carrot peels, apple peels, and other vegetable foods for testing food preferences (You might leave a sample at the top of a worm jar and see if it's taken down below by the worms.)
- spray water bottle

Activity:
1. Ask the children what they'd like to know about worms. Record their questions. Then work together to design and run several experiments to help them answer their questions.
2. Possible questions might be
   - Do worms prefer dark or light areas?
   - Do worms prefer dry or damp areas?
   - Do worms prefer cold or warm areas?
   - Do worms notice color?
   - What foods do worms like best?

Talk about the worms' preferences. How does their natural habitat provide for them? Also discuss the concept of experimentation. You decide what it is you want to find out; you carefully design an experiment to test for that behavior; you observe and record your findings; then you either answer the question OR design another more accurate experiment.

Outdoor Activities

WORM SEARCH

What You Need
- a bucket of damp, loose soil (to put your worms in once they're found)
- small hand trowels for digging (1 per child, if available)
- at least 1 large shovel.

What to Do
Take the children outside to search for worms. Gardens, compost piles, under leaf litter, and other relatively damp dark places are good spots to search. If the ground is especially dry, you can prepare for your search by watering the soil the day before and leaving a board or plastic sheet on top.

Once you've arrived at your worm search area, explain the plan to the children. They will be searching for worms. If they find a worm, they should carefully dig it out of the soil (taking care not to cut the worm with their trowel), then carry it in their hands (or trowel) to the group collection bucket.

After you've collected enough worms for later observations, talk with the children about things they noticed about the worms and where they were found.

WORMS AND SOIL

What to Do

Gather the children together in a tight group. Now choose one person to be the worm. Starting from a point away from the group and with her hands held palms together, the worm slowly winds her way through the group, opening up spaces as she goes. (As the worm passes through, the children move slightly to make room for the worm.) Repeat with a new worm.

DIGGING A WORM TUNNEL

What You Need

- 20 small paper or plastic cups
- 4 buckets or large bowls (two filled with loose soil)

What to Do

Divide the children into two teams for a relay race and have each team form a line. At the front of each line, place one bucket of soil and ten cups. At your signal, the first person in each line fills one cup with soil and passes it to the person behind her. The children in line continue passing the cup until it reaches the last person, who then empties the cup into the bucket behind her and shouts "the dirt's in the bucket!" Then the first person fills another cup and the process repeats. Continue until all cups are filled and passed to the back of the line.

THE ROBIN AND THE MISSING WORM GAME

What You Need

- large blanket or sheet

What to Do

Gather the children around the edge of the blanket. Choose one person to be the "robin." The robin leaves the room or goes to a corner and covers her eyes. While the robin's gone, the adult points to one child to be "the missing worm." That child crawls under the blanket. Then the adult calls the robin to come back. The robin has to look around at the children and try to guess the name of the "missing worm."

We Care about . . .
Worms

As good as they are for the soil, and as efficient as they are as decomposers, there are some areas in North America where certain types of worms are not welcome because they are not native species. When observing worms and creating worm jars, try to use worms that you dig from where you live, rather than purchase, to help ensure that you are not helping to spread worms that do not belong in your environment.

Language Activity / Song

(To the tune of "There Was an Old Lady Who Swallowed a Fly")

There was an old lady who swallowed a worm.
My, oh my, did that little worm squirm!

There was an old lady who swallowed a mole.
She gulped and she gulped and she swallowed it whole.
She swallowed the mole to catch the worm,
My, oh my, did that little worm squirm!

There was an old lady who swallowed a fox.
It pounced and it pounced and it knocked her off her socks!
She swallowed the fox to catch the mole,
She swallowed the mole to catch the worm,
My, oh my, did that little worm squirm!

There was an old lady who swallowed a flea.
But it crawled up her nose and it caused her to sneeze.
She swallowed the flea to bite the fox,
She swallowed the fox to catch the mole
She swallowed the mole to catch the worm,
My, oh my, did that little worm squirm!

There was an old lady who decided to squirm.
She squirmed and she squirmed 'till she shook out that worm.
She shook out the fox and she shook out the flea
She shook and she shook and she shook them all free.
[spoken] AND she never ate another worm!

Crafts and Projects

WORM JARS

What You Need
- large plastic or glass jar or container for each child – half gallon size is great (1 per child)
- rubber bands for jars
- old window screen or lace (precut into squares to cover the tops of the jars)
- bucket of sand
- bucket of purchased potting soil
- cornmeal
- bucket of soil from garden or field
- black paper
- tape
- 2 water spritzers
- lettuce leaves
- worms (at least 1 per child)

continued on next page

What to Do

Set up the materials outside, in assembly line fashion: jar, cornmeal, garden soil, sand, potting soil, water spritzer, cornmeal, garden soil, sand, potting soil, water spritzer. Be careful if you are using glass jars!

Send children through the assembly line, each taking just a handful or two of each material and adding it, in layers, to the worm jar. (The layers will allow you to see how the worms mix soil layers.) When the layers are complete, give each child at least one worm and a leaf of lettuce to add to the top of his worm jar.

Add the screen cap and form the black paper into a sleeve to fit around the worm jar so that light gets in only from the top. Make sure the worm jars are placed in a cool, shaded place. Check them every day. Notice the worms' movements; the way they stir up the soil; the tunnels they create; the foods they prefer; etc. Always remember to put the black cover back on the jar when you're done observing. And, please, when you're finished watching your worms, put them back where they came from.

DOUGH WORMS

What You Need
- homemade craft dough
- paint
- paintbrushes

What to Do

Practice rolling worms with craft dough. Once the children get the hang of it, have them roll a few, then let them dry. The next day, paint the worms bright colors and bring home.

WORM PUPPETS

What You Need
- old socks or tights (cut to the length of a child's lower arm)
- craft glue
- small circles of felt or other fabric (1 per child)
- yarn pieces

What to Do

Put the supplies out, together with a sample worm puppet. Invite the children to use the materials to create their own worm puppets.

Independent Play Ideas

1. Leave a worm jar out for observation.
2. Create a craft station for creating worms from a variety of materials: old stockings, clay, pipe cleaners, paper towel tubes, and more.

Snack

FROSTING WORMS

What You Need
- a batch of brownies
- pink frosting
- a icing bag or several zip-top baggies with one corner cut off
- waxed paper

What to Do

To prepare, put a small amount of icing in an icing bag or the zip-top bags. Give each child a square of wax paper and a brownie. Have them use the bag to squeeze a frosting worm onto their brownie "soil." You may want to practice on the wax paper first. Enjoy!

Book Ideas

CHILDREN'S FICTION

Big Fat Worm, by Nancy van Laan, Alfred A. Knopf, 1987 – simple text tells the chain of events set off when a bird finds a big fat worm and other animals threaten prey; appropriate for young children.

Crow Moon, Worm Moon, by James Stofield, Macmillan, 1990 – a read-aloud poem about spring and its animals, including worms, with beautiful watercolors.

National Worm Day, by James Stevenson, Greenwillow Books, 1990 – three funny animal stories, one is about a new worm holiday.

The Outside Inn, by George Ella Lyon, Orchard Books, 1991 – a funny rhyming book suggests various wiggly, muddy meals; great illustrations.

CHILDREN'S NONFICTION

An Earthworm's Life, by John Himmelman, Grolier, 2000 – simple text and pictures, describes the daily activities and life cycle of the earthworm.

Wonderful Worms, by Linda Glaser, Millbrook, 1992 – a nicely illustrated, appealing book with minimal text, describes the values of worms, and appendix provides answers to many questions about worms.

RESOURCE BOOKS FOR ADULTS AND CHILDREN

The Wonderful World of Wigglers, by Julia Hand and Common Roots, Food Works, 1995 – an excellent activity and information resource, geared for elementary age children but much of it is adaptable to younger children.

Wormology, by Michael Elsohn Ross, Lerner, 1996 – a good introduction to worms, with suggestions for child directed experiments to learn about worm behavior.

Worms, by Theresa Greenaway, Raintree Steck-Vaughn, 1999 – nicely detailed text and clear diagrams help children to learn about worms and how to observe them.

Wiggly Worms

We have been investigating earthworms: learning about their bodies, what they eat, and how they move. We have even been conducting worm experiments.

Continue the Learning at Home

Scientists classify earthworms as segmented worms because their bodies are divided into a series of sections. Color the worm below. Cut the worm out and use it to measure a variety of objects around your home. What is larger than the worm? Shorter? How many segments long is your finger? How many segments wide is a doorknob? Can you think of other items that you could use as measuring tools? (paper clips, blocks, pencils, etc.)

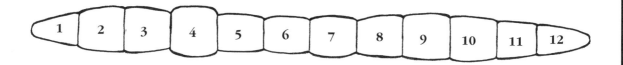

More Fun with Worms

Go on a nighttime worm search! Choose an evening when it is raining lightly. Bring a flashlight with you (using a red cellophane cover over your light will help preserve your night vision). How many worms did you find?

Produced and copyrighted by Vermont Institute of Natural Science, 2005.

CONNECTIONS TO NATURE

Connections to Nature

Like an enormous spider web, nature connects us all. Large animals eat small creatures; small creatures feed on insects; insects rely on plants; and plants, ultimately, need the sun and rain to sustain themselves. Connected to all these elements of nature, of course, are people.

In their daily lives, young children frequently experience vital connections with nature, though they may not often be aware of them. Snack time provides opportunities to get to know more about the food we eat: where it comes from and how it grows. A sunny day is a perfect time to witness the sun's light and warmth and to make connections about plant growth, to learn about the seasons, and to reflect on our own need for sunshine. Even a tiny mouse scurrying across the kitchen floor can remind us that human structures are forever connected to the natural world in which they exist. While discovering the strands that connect all of nature, young children grow to appreciate their own important role in the web of life.

Within the Connections to Nature theme are wonderful opportunities to explore both the common (like apples or the sun) and the more unusual (like ice or food chains). As children engage in the connection activities they will become familiar with the ways food is grown and processed, humane ways to handle even pesky critters, and the importance of every part of nature's web.

All about Apples

Focus: Apples have many characteristics (color, shape) and properties (such as floating). There are many different varieties of apples and many different ways to enjoy them.

Objective: To observe, investigate, and appreciate apples from their skins to their cores.

Extra Information for Adult Leaders

DIGGING IN...

When you bite into an apple, you are tasting thousands of years of history. From ancient Rome to colonial North America, the apple has been celebrated in legend, folklore, and song. The apples of today are all quite different from their wild ancestors, believed to have originated in Kazakhstan. It is thought that people traveling the silk route through Asia and Europe brought the best of Kazakhstan's apples to eat along the way. As they tossed the cores, the seeds fell and sprouted into young trees. Apple seeds, however, do not produce trees that bear fruit similar to their parent tree. The new apple trees were an unreliable source of edible fruit, and their apples were primarily used for hard cider and feed for livestock.

It wasn't until the Chinese developed the art of grafting that the apple tree became a major source of fruit for human consumption. Grafting involves two separate trees: the **rootstock** – a tree the size and shape the orchardist desires, and the **scion** – a stem from a tree bearing the type of fruit the orchardist wishes to propagate. The bark on a branch of the rootstock is cut and the scion inserted into the incision, ensuring that the **cambium,** or growth layers (located just under the bark), of both are touching. The orchardist then binds the two branches until they have grown together. If done correctly, the graft will soon bear fruit. It is even possible to graft two different types of scions to the same rootstock, creating a tree that bears two types of fruit, such as apples and pears.

People in England, Europe, and Asia used grafting techniques to produce numerous apple varieties that thrived in their respective climates. When settlers first came to America, however, the trees they brought with them did not survive the early frosts, and most of the old varieties were lost. The survivors bred with wild American crab apples, enabling them to cope with the new soils and climate found in the New World. New apple varieties were developed, producing trees that were uniquely suited to North America.

Apples, of course, have not only become a North American crop, they've also become part of the folklore. In the early 1800s, Massachusetts-born John Chapman made an annual trek to western Pennsylvania, where he gathered seeds from the fragrant piles of pressed apples he found behind cider mills. He traveled by dugout canoe down the Ohio River and its tributaries, planting apple nurseries as he went. Johnny Appleseed worked his way across the wilderness several years ahead of the western expansion, and by the 1830s operated dozens of nurseries from western Pennsylvania, through Ohio, and into Indiana. Although we envision Johnny Appleseed planting apples to eat, it wasn't until the Women's Temperance Union Movement that sweet apples were bred and promoted as a healthy snack. Johnny Appleseed was welcomed into communities because his trees bore fruit for the production of hard cider and to feed livestock.

Pollination is critical for the production of apple fruit. The more seeds that successfully develop within the apple (the maximum number of seeds for most varieties is ten), the larger and better-developed the fruit. In fact, **flowers** that have not been pollinated well enough produce fruit will fall off the tree before they are fully developed.

To attract pollinators, the apple tree produces fragrant pink blossoms that face outward, exposing

apple blossom

their reproductive parts to potential pollinators, most frequently bees. After fertilization, the flowers fade to white, the petals fall off, and the seeds and fruit begin to develop. The leaves are the food factory for the tree, providing energy for the apples to develop and the tree to grow. Soon after the flowers begin to emerge, the smaller shoot buds at the tips of the twigs push the bud scales open and new branches and leaves emerge. A mature

apple tree can produce between 50,000 to 100,000 leaves.

Apples are now a staple in the American diet. They are nutritious, they keep well through the winter, and they can be used as a dessert, in sauces, chutneys and jellies, or pressed into cider. Their story goes far beyond the bag of fruit that can be picked up at any grocery store. They are part of the world's agricultural and natural heritage and are a curiosity to explore with our minds and our taste buds!

Indoor Activities

FIND THE APPLE

Objective:	*To practice using our various senses to find apples.*
Materials:	• red apples (3 or 4) • 1 each of 3 different kinds of apples (at least 1 green or yellow) • 4 red objects (ball, bean bag, etc.) • 4 roundish, apple-size objects (tennis ball, peach, plum, etc.) • 4 fruits and/or veggies, preferably with strong scents • 4 small yogurt cups – with holes punched in lids • 4 fruits or veggies with textures similar to an apple (could be same as above) • blindfolds (1 per child) • cutting board and knife

Activity:	Investigate apples using four of the five senses.
	1. **Sight:**
	  • Line up the red objects (including an apple) on a table or floor.
	  • "Reading" from left to write, ask a child to tell you which place the apple is in. (Example: "The apple's in place # 3.")
	  • Shuffle the objects, and ask another child to do the same.
	  • Talk about the basic appearance of an apple (shape, color, size). Also mention that apples are not always red. Show the children a green apple and yellow apple, if available.
	2. **Touch:**
	  • Seat the children in a circle on the floor. Blindfold them. (Or alternately, seat them in a tight circle, with backs to center, so they can pass objects behind their backs. Or place each object in its own paper bag to pass.)
	  • One at a time, pass the roundish objects around the circle, allowing the children to feel them carefully (including the apple).
	  • After each object has made its way around the circle, ask the children to guess what the object was. Was it an apple?
	  • Talk about the unique shape and feel of the apple (including the bumps at the bottom, stem, etc.)

3. **Smell:**
   - Beforehand, cut several strongly scented fruits and vegetables into small pieces.
   - Place each item in a yogurt cup with a perforated lid.
   - Pass the containers around the circle, one at a time.
   - After it has made it all the way around the circle, ask the children to guess what the object was. Was it an apple?
   - Talk about the unique aroma of an apple. If you like, you might also compare the aromas of different apple varieties.

4. **Taste:**
   - Cut several fruits and/or vegetables (including an apple) into bite size pieces.
   - Have the children close their eyes and put out one hand, palm side up.
   - Give each child a small taste of one of the foods. Is it the apple? What is it?
   - Talk about the special taste of raw apples.

Talk about the many different ways apples can be experienced through sight, taste, touch, and smell. Which was the children's favorite way?

APPLE FAVORITES

Objective: | *To compare the appearances of different varieties of apples and to discuss favorites.*

Materials: |
- bushel of a variety of apples (different colors, too)
- cutting board and knife
- chart making supplies

Activity: |
1. Place the bushel of mixed apples in the center of the circle. Pour them onto the floor.
2. Ask the children to sort the apples according to appearance and then ask them, "How are the apples similar? Different?"
3. Try tasting each variety of apple. Which do you like best? You might create a chart or graph, illustrating which apples the children like best.

Talk about where the many varieties of apples came from. Apple growers create new varieties of apples by combining parts of existing trees – say, grafting the crown of a sweet fruited tree onto the rootstock of a winter hardy tree. Also, certain apples have preferred characteristics, such as better lasting ability or becoming soft in a pie.

APPLE MAGIC

Objective: *To notice that apples float and to learn why.*

Materials:
- large bowl of water
- apple
- carrot
- other fruits or vegetables (tomato, garlic, onion, peach, etc.)

Activity:
1. Set up the large bowl of water.
2. Ask one child to put the apple into the water. What happens?
3. Ask another child to put the carrot into the water. What happens?
4. Now provide a variety of other items. Ask the children to predict whether they think the object will sink or float, then test their prediction.

Talk about what the floating objects have in common – they all have tiny air spaces inside. Why would this be good for apples? (So they might float on a stream or river to a new location, where the seeds might sprout and grow.)

• •

HOW DO APPLES GROW?

Objective: *To learn the details about how apples grow.*

Materials:
- *The Seasons of Arnold's Apple Tree* by Gail Gibbons
- bee (on page 208) and apple blossom (on page 207) illustrations
- craft sticks
- tape
- apple
- 50 paper leaves (apple tree leaves)

Activity:
1. To prepare, cut out the bee and apple blossom illustrations and attach craft sticks to make them into puppets.
2. Read *The Seasons of Arnold's Apple Tree* aloud to the children. Take time to stop and discuss the story.
3. Using the puppets, invite the children to act out pollination.
4. Ask the children to count out 50 leaves, then place them next to the apple. That's how many leaves it takes to make enough food to grow one apple.

Talk about the astounding number of leaves an apple tree must have to grow a good crop of apples. Also talk about the other events in the life of an apple and apple tree.

APPLE PARTS

Objective: *To let the children look closely at the parts of a single apple.*

Materials:
- apples – 2 per pair of children
- cutting board and knife
- illustration of an apple cross section, with labels for stem, leaf, core, flesh, skin, and seeds

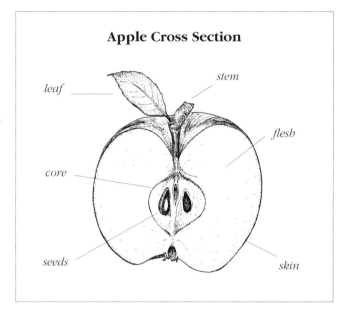

Apple Cross Section

leaf — stem — flesh — core — seeds — skin

Activity:
1. Have the children find partners. Provide each pair with an apple, cut in half lengthwise.
2. Ask the children to compare their apple halves to the drawing. Notice and talk about the parts they can see.
3. Now provide each pair with another half of an apple, this time cut horizontally. What apple parts can the children see now?

Talk about the functions of the various parts (leaves manufacture food; stem holds fruit on tree; core is a strong center support and growth area; flesh attracts animals to eat and disperse the seeds; skin is attractive and protects inside flesh; seeds allow new tree to begin).

APPLE SEEDS

Objective: *To investigate apple seeds.*

Materials:
- apples (variety)
- cutting board and knife
- magnifying lenses
- other fruit and vegetable seeds

Activity:
1. Ask the children to predict how many seeds they'll find inside a particular apple. Cut the apple open and count the seeds together. Repeat with different apple varieties. Do all the apples look similar inside, even if they look different outside?
2. Have the children closely examine the apple seeds with magnifying lenses. Note shape, size, color, etc. Compare the seeds of different apples.
3. Finally, ask the children to compare apple seeds to other fruit and vegetable seeds.

Talk about how apple seeds are also known as **pips.** Discuss the purpose of seeds, as well as how they might be dispersed to new areas and what they need to grow into apple trees.

Outdoor Activities

SEARCHING FOR APPLES

What You Need
- a place where the children can find some apples, either an area with wild apple trees or a local apple orchard that accommodates field trips
- bags

What to Do

Take the children to pick some apples. Learn about the the history of the area and share it with the children. How long have apples been grown here? Has the land been used for anything else? Help the children pick some apples.

Take some time to look at the apples you have picked. Can the children see any signs that an animal may have been munching on one or two of them? Do any have dents or scratches from when they were bumped as they grew? Check the ground for any apples that have been nibbled on. Finally, take the picked apples home to process into applesauce or apple butter.

A note to teachers: It may be wise to scout the area ahead of time, to make sure that wasps have not become active in apples that have fallen to the ground.

• •

APPLE TOSS

What You Need
- laundry or bushel basket
- lots of old or wild apples

What to Do

Play a game of tossing apples into a laundry or bushel basket, gradually moving the basket further and further away. How far can the children toss an apple accurately?

• •

APPLE PASS

What You Need
- old or wild apples (at least 1 per group of 3 children)
- 4 lengths of rope

What to Do

Play this game in a grassy area. Help the children to form teams of three people. Designate the playing area by stretching a rope on either end, plus two more ropes equally spaced between them. Child #1 stands on the first rope; child #2 near the second; and child #3 near the third. (The last rope is vacant.) Give an apple to child #1 and help her to hold it between her knees or in any way except in her hands or mouth. Now, very carefully, she walks toward child #2 and the rope. Child #1 passes the apple to child #2 who then continues toward child #3 in the same fashion. Child #3 completes the relay.

WHAT COLOR IS YOUR APPLE?

What You Need
- pre-cut lots of 6-8 inch paper apples in many colors
- tape

What to Do
Play this game in pairs. Without letting the children see, the adult tapes a colored apple onto each child's back. At the "go" signal, the children move around in pairs, each person trying to spy their partner's colored apple. If they can guess the correct color, they win. The game can be played in two other ways: Provide two copies of each color apple. Each child is given a color, then have the children walk around to find the child with the same color apple. Another way to play is to not tell the children the color of their apples. One at a time the children turn their back to the other children, showing them the color of their apple. Then, turning back to the group, the person is given clues about the apple he is holding until he guesses the color, then another child takes a turn.

Language Activity / Song

(To the tune of "Peanut, Peanut Butter")

Apple, Apple Orchard
Cider!
Apple, Apple Orchard
Cider!

First you take the apples
and you pick them, you pick them.   *[pick apples]*
Then you take the apples
and you wash them, you wash them!   *[wash apples]*

Apple, Apple Orchard
Cider!
Apple, Apple Orchard
Cider!

Next you take the apples
and you press them, you press them.   *[press apples]*
Then you take the cider
and you drink it, you drink it!   *[drink]*

Apple, Apple Orchard
Cider!
Apple, Apple Orchard
Cider!

YUM!

We Care about . . . Apples

As you have fun playing games with apples, remind the children that, although we are borrowing the apples from nature, they are not toys (especially not objects to be thrown at each other!). Make a point of returning the apple to nature when you are done playing. If you are playing outdoors by an apple tree, return the apples to the foot of the tree.

If you have a compost bin accessible, compost the apples and apple scraps when you are finished.

If neither option is available, take the time to sing out a big "Thank you, Apple Tree" to remind the children where today's topic came from.

Crafts and Projects

APPLE PRINTS

What You Need
- apples (precut into halves, crosswise and lengthwise)
- paper
- paint
- brushes or rollers
- sponge

What to Do
Help the children to apply paint to the apples (using the brushes and/or paint-soaked sponge), then press them facedown onto the paper to make lovely prints. (You might choose to use just the core for printing, so the remainder of the fruit can be used later for cooking.) Also, try cutting notches in the apples before printing, so the children will be able to grasp them more securely.

APPLE RINGS

What You Need
- apples – cored, then sliced thinly by an adult
- 12-inch pieces of string or yarn (1 per child)

What to Do
Tie an apple ring to the end of each piece of string or yarn. Distribute the strings to the children and have them string apple rings on to it. When finished, hang the strings in a sunny, airy place to dry. Taste the chewy dried applies when they are ready. Or, alternately, create mobiles or wreaths with the dried apple slices.

Independent Play Ideas
1. Provide plenty of apples for sorting, counting, grouping, and weighing.
2. Provide plenty of wild apples, plus some toothpicks or craft sticks. Allow the children to build structures with the apples and sticks.

Snacks

TASTING APPLES

What You Need
- apples prepared in various ways and ready for tasting – raw, steamed, mashed into apple sauce, dried, baked, caramel dipped, apple chips, cider
- appropriate utensils and dishes for serving the apples to the children

What to Do
Have the children taste and talk about the various forms of apples. Which do they like best? Ask the children which preparation would be best if they were taking the apples on a long hike, if they love sweet things.

• •

APPLE MATH

What You Need
- one-half apple per child
- knife
- paper plates

What to Do
To prepare, cut each apple into quarters and core. Give each child two matching quarters. Encourage the children to put their quarters together. What did they make? (half of an apple). Go around to each child and cut their quarters in half. How many pieces do they have? Again, try to assemble half an apple with the pieces. Eat one piece. How many pieces are left? Keep eating until you reach zero.

• •

APPLE DIPPERS

What You Need
- one-half apple per child
- variety of dips (peanut butter, caramel, honey, apple butter, cinnamon sugar)
- knife
- cutting surface
- spoons for serving
- plates (1 per child)

What to Do
Cut each apple into slices or chunks. Allow the children to choose from a variety of dips to enjoy with their apple. Which apple-dip combination do the children like best?

Book Ideas

CHILDREN'S FICTION

Apples, Apples, Apples, by Nancy Elizabeth Wallace, Scholastic, 2000 – an informative yet simple book about the value of apples and how they grow.

Apple Farmer Annie, by Monica Wellington, Dutton, 2001 – tells about a woman who happily grows apples, prepares lots of apple dishes, and sells them at a city market, simple and very attractive.

The Apple Pie Tree, by Zoe Hall, Blue Sky Press, 1996 – a visually appealing story about two girls who observe an apple tree, pick the apples, and finally bake an apple pie.

The Seasons of Arnold's Apple Tree, by Gail Gibbons, Scholastic, 1995 – A pleasant story about a boy and his apple tree and the many changes in the tree through the seasons.

Ten Red Apples, by Pat Hutchins, Greenwillow Books, 2000 – this rhyming book counts down the apples as eaten by a host of animals.

CHILDREN'S NONFICTION

An Apple a Day, by Melvin Berger, Newbridge, 1993 – uses great photos and minimal text, describes apples – how they form, grow, get picked, processed, and enjoyed.

I Am an Apple, by Gene Marzollo, Scholastic, 1997 – a nice and simple book for young children.

RESOURCE BOOKS FOR ADULTS AND CHILDREN

How Do Apples Grow?, by Betsy Maestro, Scholastic, 1992 – a nice, thorough description of the complete cycle of an apple flower to apple to seed and beyond.

Flowers & Fruits (Plants and Plant Life, Book 2), by Jill Bailey, Grolier Educational, 2001 – one of a series of plant resource books for older children, in-depth information about the biology of flowers and fruits.

The Apple Grower: A Guide for the Organic Orchardist, by Michael Phillips, Chelsea Green, 1998 – handbook for adults about organic apple growing.

ALL ABOUT APPLES

We've been using our senses to observe, investigate, and appreciate apples inside and out.

Continue the Learning at Home

Cut out the apple pattern. Fold the apple along the dotted line, so the seeds are on the inside. Color the outside of the apple red and the seeds inside black. When you are finished creating your apple, use it to act out the poem below:

Inside an Apple

Here is my apple,   *[hold the folded apple in your palms]*
red and round.

Open it up and   *[open the apple]*
look what I've found.

Seeds in the center,   *[point to the seeds]*
black against white.

They make a small star.

Mmmm! Take a bite!   *[pretend to bite the apple]*

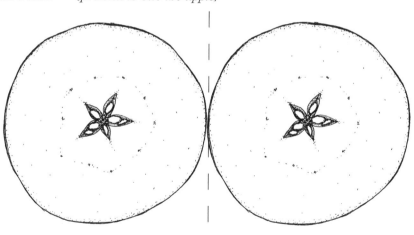

More Fun with Apples

Read an apple story together. Titles you might enjoy are *Apple Farmer Annie* by Monica Wellington and *The Seasons of Arnold's Apple Tree* by Gail Gibbons.

Produced and copyrighted by Vermont Institute of Natural Science, 2005.

Food for All

Focus: During this workshop, children will explore the plant and animal origins of their foods and the special features that help wild animals to hunt and to avoid being eaten by other animals.

Objective: To identify the plant or animal origins of familiar foods, to experience some of the connections between animals and their food sources, and to learn how teeth can be important to an animal's survival.

Extra Information for Adult Leaders

Food is important for survival, both at home and in the wild. Children know this on a very basic level – through the feelings in their stomachs. Their stomachs tell them when they are hungry, when they need food. Animals know this too. Animals who do not find sufficient food are more susceptible to disease, **predation**, and, ultimately, starvation, than other, healthier animals. Finding food becomes especially important during pregnancy and when an animal is raising its young. A pregnant (or laying) animal needs to feed both herself and her developing young. This represents a tremendous energy demand. For animals that take care of their young, the demand for food continues until the young are capable of feeding themselves.

Winter, and the months preceding it, can also represent a tremendous amount of stress for animals. Before winter, animals often fatten themselves up or store food so that they can survive the lean months ahead, **migrate** to places where food is more plentiful, or **hibernate** or become **dormant** to save their energy. Animals can get their energy from two sources: plants or other animals. Animals that eat only plants are **herbivores.** Those that eat only meat (other animals) are **carnivores**. Animals that eat both plants and animals are **omnivores**.

Animals find food in many different ways. Some use their keen sense of smell to locate food, while others use their sense of hearing, and still others are equipped with sharp sight. Of course, most animals use a combination of senses to find food. An animal's mouth represents a specialized tool for processing and often accessing food. Insects have special mouth parts for

DIGGING IN...

chewing, sucking, or biting, and birds have specialized beaks (see "Growing Up a Bird" unit in Growth and Change for beak activities). For mammals, it is their teeth that are specialized for various tasks such as cutting, grinding, and chewing.

Getting enough energy can also be challenging to plants. They can wither if they are shaded by other plants. During times of stress, plants often produce smaller fruit or fewer seeds than at times when energy is plentiful. Plants that have lost too many leaves to hungry omnivores or herbivores can also weaken and die. Many plants have developed defenses against animals, such as thorns or spines, poisonous leaves, or sticky sap.

Although it is not always easy to observe animals eating, signs of feeding can be found everywhere. Signs of herbivore or omnivore activity can include nibbled leaves, pinecone scales, nipped stems or branches, or scraped bark. Signs of predation can include tufts of fur or loose feathers, running tracks, or bones. Even an untrained observer, once aware of the signs, can find many indications of animal activity in their environment.

Indoor Activities

GARDEN OR COW?

Objective: *To sort some familiar foods according to their origins - garden or cow?*

Materials:
- a variety of real foods, approximately half beef and dairy products (like hamburger, steak, milk, cheese, yogurt) and half garden produce (cucumber, carrots, broccoli)
- processed plant foods, like crackers or cereal
- cloth or paper bag to hide each of the food items separately

Activity:
1. Place each food item in a separate bag.
2. Gather the children in a circle. Explain that you've placed a variety of foods people eat inside the bags.
3. Pull an item from one of the bags and show it to the children.
4. The children must decide: does this food come from a cow or from a garden? If the children choose cow, have them raise their hands to their mouths and "mooo" loudly. If the children think the food comes from a garden, they should pretend to hoe a garden.
5. Begin with just the direct meat items and the garden produce. Later, show the milk or cheese and explain that those items also come from cows. Finally, show the children the processed foods. Explain that these, too, come from plants.

Talk about the ways that the processed foods have been changed somehow from their natural form – for example, heated, or ground, or mixed with water or other foods. Still, none of them would be possible without plants and animals. Where do these plants and animals get their energy to grow? (plants from sunlight; animals from the plants and animals they eat.)

LET'S LOOK AT OUR LUNCH BOXES

Objective: *To think about the origins of the foods in our lunch boxes.*

Materials:
- children's lunch boxes
- paper plates (2 per child)
- crayons or markers
- 3 paper plates, 1 labeled for each category: plant, animal, and plant and animal

Activity:
1. Ask the children to tell which foods in their lunch boxes come from plants and which from animals.
2. Encourage the children to draw two of their favorite foods, one per paper plate. (You may want to label the drawings.)
3. At the end of the week, show the children the three labeled plates: plant, animal, and plant and animal. Ask the children to sort their food drawings into the three groups, and post the results around the room.

Talk about which foods the children seem to eat more of – those from plants or those from animals? Are there any vegetarians in your group?

ANIMALS EATING CHARADES

Objective:	To imitate animals as they eat. (see "Animal Eating Charades Cards" on page 226)
Materials:	• illustration of woodpecker pecking for insects • illustration of squirrel eating nuts • illustration of fox pouncing • illustration of bear rolling log for insects • illustration of deer browsing • illustration of caterpillar eating leaf • 6 large index cards or cardstock • glue or tape (for teacher)
Activity:	1. To prepare, mount each illustration on a large index card. 2. Form the children into pairs or small groups, giving each a card. 3. Tell the children to look at the cards and consider how they might act out that scene. 4. Take turns performing the scenes on the cards, asking the other children to guess what animal is being portrayed and its activities.

Talk about which animals ate plants and which ones ate animals. Introduce the terms "hunter" and "hunted" (or **predator** and **prey**).

RABBIT, RABBIT, FOX!

Objective:	*To play a game and have some fun.*
Materials:	• illustration of a rabbit • illustration of a fox
Activity:	1. Seat the children in a circle on the floor. 2. Show them the pictures of the fox and the rabbit. Ask, "Who eats who?" ("So the fox is the hunter – or predator – and the rabbit is the hunted – or prey.") 3. Now tell the children that they're going to play a game very similar to "duck, duck, goose," but called "rabbit, rabbit, fox." 4. One child (the rabbit) walks slowly around the outside of the circle, gently tapping the head of each child as he says, "rabbit," "rabbit," .... Then the "rabbit" child taps someone and says "fox!" The fox jumps up and chases the rabbit around the outside of the circle, trying to tag him before he jumps into the seat that the fox formerly occupied. 5. Repeat with new foxes and rabbits until all of the children have had a turn.

Talk about the fact that foxes do, in fact, chase rabbits. Foxes try to surprise the rabbits, then they try to outrun and catch them. Lots of rabbits get away. Ask the children, "If you were a small rabbit trying to outrun and maybe hide from a fox, where might you go?"

A PEEK AT TEETH

Objective: *To observe different types of teeth and to learn about how teeth help animals eat food.*

Materials:
- hand mirrors, 1 per child
- beaver incisor illustration
- deer molar illustration
- dog molar illustration
- canine illustration

Activity:

1. Have the children look at their teeth in the mirror. Count teeth as a group. Can the children find little teeth? Big teeth? Sharp teeth? Bumpy teeth?

2. Show the children the beaver tooth sketch. Do they have any teeth that are as long as the beaver's? As sharp? The beaver uses it teeth to gnaw on wood. The **incisors** sharpen themselves and grow for the beaver's entire life. Animals also use incisors for cutting and biting. Our incisors are the paired front teeth on top and bottom.

3. Show the children a dog **molar.** Do they have a tooth that looks similar to this molar? Dogs and other carnivores use their large, sharp, bumpy molars to grasp, gnaw, cut, and tear food.

4. Show the children the picture of a deer molar. Deer have molars, just like people, but they look very different than ours. Both molars (deer and human) are use for grinding food. It is the same kind of tooth, but the surface is different.

5. Lastly, show the children a **canine**. Many animals that eat meat have these sharp teeth for biting, puncturing, and holding. Can the children spot their canines? (the third tooth from the center)

Talk about how animals who eat plants have flat teeth and animals who eat meat have sharp teeth. Animals who eat both plants and animals have sharp teeth in the front of their mouths and flat teeth in the back of their mouths. What kind of teeth do we have? (Sharp and flat: people eat both plants and animals). Many mammals use their teeth as their knives and forks, so they have many jobs.

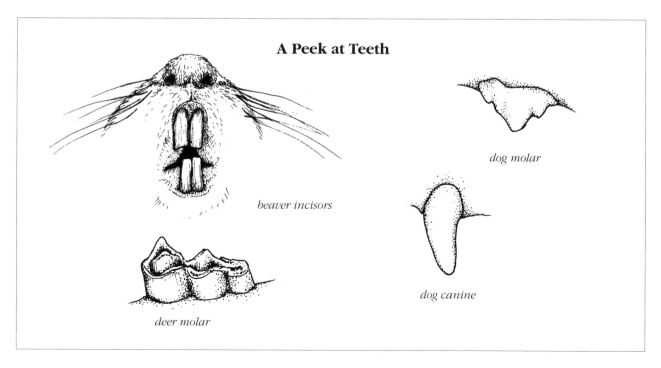

A Peek at Teeth

beaver incisors

dog molar

dog canine

deer molar

Outdoor Activities

SIGNS OF EATING

What to Do

Walk through the nearby woods, fields, or neighborhood, searching for signs that animals have been eating. Evidence of a recent meal could include chewed acorns, feathers, stripped tree bark, broken bird seeds, egg shells, and more. (see *"Small Wonders* at Home" on page 228).

HUNGRY BOBCATS

What You Need

- many mouse cutouts (see mouse illustration in "Mighty Mice" unit on page 252)
- bobcat illustration

What to Do

Before the children arrive, copy and cut out (or create) a number of mice (at least three per child). (If you have more life-like rubber mice, even better.) Hide the mice outside in the bushes, tall grass, and other places mice might be. Bring the children outside, and show them the picture of the bobcat. Tell them they are going to pretend to be hungry bobcats, searching for yummy mice to eat. Go!

bobcat

POPCORN, BUNNIES, AND FOXES GAME

What You Need

- popcorn
- paper bunny ears
- red crepe paper
- an old blanket (optional)
- cones or plates to mark boundaries (optional)
- fox illustration (optional)

What to Do

Beforehand, scatter some popcorn in your playing area (size will depend on the number of children playing). Designate a safety area (maybe with an old blanket). Prepare several sets of bunny ears from paper, as well as some fox tails from red crepe paper. Finally, you'll need several paper bags (one for each of your bunnies).

Choose about 3/4 of the children to be bunnies; give them ears. The remaining children will be foxes; give them tails.

Explain to the children that when the game begins, the bunnies will enter the playing field first, and they will try to collect as much popcorn in their bags as they can. After a ten-second head start, the foxes will come in and try to tag the bunnies. The bunnies, however, can run to the "berry patch" (blanket) safety spot for a moment. If a bunny is tagged, then she becomes a fox – and must go to the adult to replace her ears with a red tail.

Sometime before all the bunnies are gone, call "stop" and count how many bunnies and foxes are left. Scatter more popcorn and play again, if you like.

Language Activity / Song

(To the tune of "If You're Happy and You Know It")

If you're hungry and you know it, clap your hands.	*[clap twice]*
If you're hungry and you know it, clap your hands.	*[clap twice]*
If you're hungry and you know it, and you really want to show it,	
If you're hungry and you know it, clap your hands.	*[clap twice]*

Repeat with other movements, like "gnaw a carrot," or "scratch your tummy," etc.

Crafts and Projects

FEED ME!

What You Need
- paper plates (1 per child)
- hole punch
- yarn
- plastic darning needles
- scissors
- crayons or markers
- tape

What to Do

To prepare, fold each plate in half and cut a hole in the center. Have each child draw a face around the hole, using it as the mouth. Encourage the children to draw pictures of foods around the edge of the plate. You can label the drawings as the children work on them. Help each child punch a hole next to each food item using the hole punch. Finally, help each child use the needle and yarn to connect the food items to the mouth.

• •

FOOD MOBILE

What You Need
- clothing hangers (1 per child)
- pipe cleaners – cut in half
- fox illustration (1 per child)
- mouse illustrations (2 per child) (see "Mighty Mice" unit)
- corn kernal illustrations (4 per child)
- hole punch
- scissors
- crayons or markers

corn kernal

What to Do

To prepare, cut around fox, mouse, and corn sketches for younger students. Provide each child with a set of sketches to color. When they finish coloring the sketches, help each child punch a hole at the top of each of their pictures. Use the pipe cleaners to attach the drawings to the hanger in the following manner: fox at the hook, mice at the corners, corn along the bottom of the hanger.

Snacks

WHICH FOODS NEED TO BE EATEN WITH TEETH?

What You Need
- a few "chewing and biting foods," such as carrots, apples, or crackers
- a few soft foods, such as pudding, applesauce, or gelatin
- spoons, if needed

What to Do

Serve the children a combination of "chewing and biting" foods and soft foods. As the children enjoy their snack, talk about how some foods require lots of biting and chewing, while other foods do not. Which are the children's favorites?

• •

FOODS FROM OTHER LANDS

What You Need
- a few exotic plant foods, like mango, kiwi, couscous, etc., ready to be looked at whole, then served to the children

What to Do

Taste some foods that are not native to North America. Mangos, for example, are native to southern Asia. Kiwi fruit originated in China, but is now grown in many places, including New Zealand, California, Chile, Spain, and Australia. Couscous is a type of pasta that comes from North Africa. Mention that, just as foods from other lands are unusual to us, some of the foods we think of as common are unusual in other parts of the world.

We Care about . . . Food for All

Human food helps children grow and lead healthy lives. That food, however, can lead to problems when it is consumed by animals. The food that people consider healthy and/or enjoyable rarely contains the nutrition that animals require. Consumption of human food can actually sicken wild animals. Too, a reliance on human food sources can attract animals to areas with dangerous traffic or result in problem animal behavior, such as destroying property or bothering people. A good rule of thumb is to be careful stewards when eating out-of-doors. Don't share snacks with animals and clean up everything before you move on to an activity. Remember, you are not providing animals a treat when you leave human food for them. You may be hurting them.

Book Ideas

CHILDREN'S FICTION

Dinnertime!, by Sue Williams, Harcourt 2001 – a hungry fox perpetually chases the fat rabbits in this rhyming tale.

Fox Went Out on a Chilly Night, by Peter Spier, Dell, 1993 – a wonderful story and song about a fox catching food for his family.

The Little Red Hen, by Paul Galdone, Houghton Mifflin, 1998 – a classic tale about a hen who, step by step, makes bread but fails to find any friends to help her with the work involved.

The Little Red Hen Makes a Pizza, by Philemon Sturges, Dutton Children's Books, 1999 – a cute and funny variation on the classic, with the friends ultimately pitching in to help.

The Mitten, by Jan Brett, Putnam Sons, 1993 – a building story, where a series of animals climb into a lost mitten.

Rosie's Walk, by Pat Hutchins, Alladin, 1968 – the story of a hen chased by a fox.

CHILDREN'S NONFICTION

Dinnertime for Animals, by Jane R. McCauley, National Geographic Society, 1991 – dedicated to what and how animals eat; from nursing mothers to predation, storing food, and using tools.

When Hunger Calls, by Bert Kitchen, Candlewick Press, 1994 – each page describes the predatory behavior of a different animal, great illustrations.

RESOURCE BOOKS FOR ADULTS AND CHILDREN

Foodworks: Over 100 linked science activities and fascinating facts that explore the magic of food, Addison-Wesley, 1987 – deals with food and the human body.

Who Eats What?: Food Chains and Food Webs, by Patricia Lauber, HarperCollins, 1995 – conveys the ecological concept of how plants, animals, and people are linked.

Independent Play Ideas

1. Put out lots of animal toys, so the children can act out their eating habits.
2. Leave out the cards created for the "Animal Eating Charades" activity to spark interest in role playing activities.
3. Put out a variety of play food and two boxes for sorting. Label one box with a drawing of a plant and one box with a drawing of an animal. Allow the children to sort the foods into the plant and animal boxes.

ANIMAL EATING CHARADE CARDS

bear rolling log

deer browsing

caterpillar eating leaf

ANIMAL EATING CHARADE CARDS

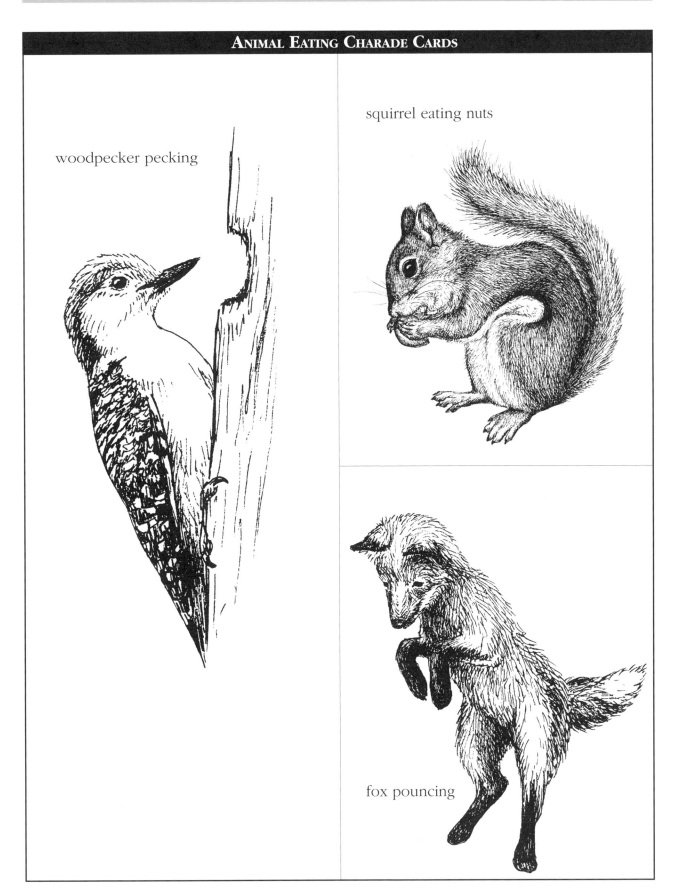

woodpecker pecking

squirrel eating nuts

fox pouncing

FOOD FOR ALL

We have been learning about different types of foods (those from animals and those from plants) and how animals eat them.

Continue the Learning at Home

Talk a walk through nearby woods, fields, park, or neighborhood, and search for signs that an animal has recently had a meal. Clues you might notice are chewed nuts or acorns, nibbled mushrooms, broken shells of bird seed, or leaves that have been munched on. The illustrations below may help you in your quest.

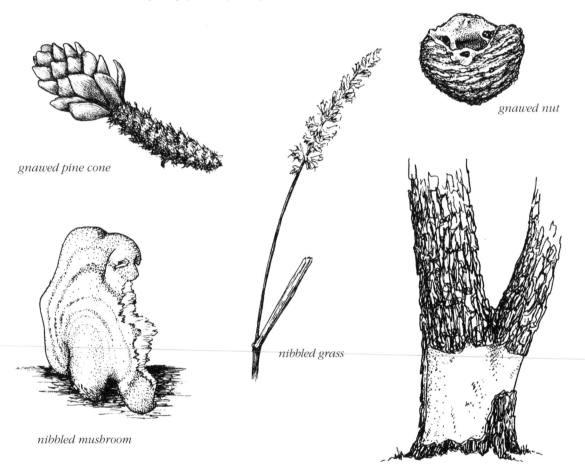

gnawed pine cone

gnawed nut

nibbled grass

nibbled mushroom

stripped bark

More Fun with Food

Plan a family trip to a dairy farm or other food producing/processing facility.

Produced and copyrighted by Vermont Institute of Natural Science, 2005.

Wild about Water

Focus: Water can occur in three states: solid, liquid, and gas. Each state has its own unique properties.

Objective: To experience water in its many states: liquid, solid, and gas, and to understand the cleaning and dissolving powers of water.

Extra Information for Adult Leaders

Water can be found on earth in three states: solid (ice), liquid, and gas. Water is essential for life on earth and exists in a finite supply. Ninety-seven percent of the earth's water supply is salty, with fresh water composing the remaining three percent. Two thirds of the fresh water supply is locked in glaciers and polar ice caps. The remaining portion of the fresh water supply is divided between groundwater, the soil, bodies of water, the atmosphere, and the bodies of plants and animals.

Water is circulated between the atmosphere and the earth's surface in a process known as the **water cycle**. In the water cycle, **condensation** moves water vapor from the atmosphere to the earth's surface. Condensation occurs as droplets in water vapor gather around tiny particles called **condensation nuclei** (condensation does not occur without these nuclei). Tiny droplets or crystals that are too small to be influenced by **gravity** form clouds. When the condensing water droplets become large enough, they fall to the earth's surface as rain, snow, sleet, or hail. Condensation may also occur closer to the earth's surface in the form of fog or dew.

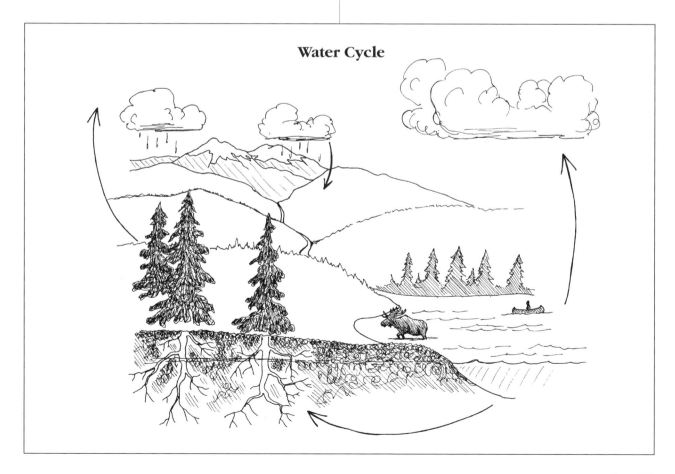

Water Cycle

Evaporation, sublimation, and transpiration move water from the surface of the earth to the atmosphere. **Evaporation** occurs when liquid water turns into water vapor; **sublimation** is the vaporization of solid water. **Transpiration** involves the release of water from **stomata**, or holes, in a plant's leaf. About ten percent of the moisture found in the atmosphere originates from transpiration. Although they do not necessarily intend to be, plants are very efficient at moving water from the soil to the atmosphere. A large oak tree can **transpire** 40,000 gallons of water a year.

Before being evaporated, sublimated, or transpired, water that falls on the earth's surface may become part of a lake or stream or the ocean; be absorbed by the soil, a plant, or an animal; become part of the groundwater supply; be frozen in an ice cap; emerge at a spring; or any combination of these.

Interestingly, as water moves, it dissolves minerals and salts from the surfaces it contacts. As it evaporates, it leaves those salts behind. For example, when water evaporates from the ocean, it leaves its minerals and salts behind, creating a salty body of water. Because

water only flows into, not out of, the ocean, the salts left behind by evaporation cannot be washed away, and they become concentrated.

Water has several interesting properties. It is a powerful **solvent**, dissolving more substances than any other liquid on earth. Water is also sticky, bonding to itself (**cohesion**) and to many surfaces (**adhesion**). You can see cohesion as surface tension when you fill a glass to the rim with water: a domed surface will form over the top before the water spills over. When you empty the glass, the water sticks to the sides until it is eventually pulled down by gravity. This adhesive property of water helps it move up **veins** in trees and in the capillaries of our bodies. Perhaps one of water's most unique properties is its ability to float as a solid. Water expands as it freezes, creating a solid that is less dense than the liquid (liquids typically become more dense as they enter the solid phase). Water's many unique properties and importance to the survival of life on earth make it an important subject to learn about and a fun substance to experiment with.

Indoor Activities

RECOGNIZING WATER

Objective:	*To use our senses to recognize water.*
Materials:	• 2 clear plastic cups or jars – 1 filled with water, the other white vinegar
Activity:	Tell the children that you've filled one cup with water, the other with something else. Can they tell which cup has the water in it? How do they know?
	Talk about the fact that water is a colorless, odorless, tasteless liquid.

WATER CAN MIX

Objective:	*To learn how to use water to dissolve and reconstitute.*
Materials:	• source of water
	• clear plastic cups (1 per child)
	• clear glass jars (jelly type work well) (1 per child)
	• spoons (1 per child)
	• tea kettle or pot for heating water
	• powdered lemonade mix
	• dried fruit
	• powdered soup or cocoa mix

- white sugar
- paper and pencil for recording

Activity:

1. Provide cold water, clear cups, spoons, lemonade mix, and soup or cocoa mix.

2. Read aloud the mixing instructions for each item. Then assist the children as they mix the appropriate amounts of powder and COLD water. Ask the children to observe what happens to the powder. Is it entirely dissolved?

3. Ask the children to add cold water to half the dried fruit. What happens? Does it become soft?

4. Repeat the two experiments using the same amounts of powder and HOT water. Compare to the results with the cold water.

5. Now give each child a cup of cold water. Instruct them to add one spoonful of sugar at a time, then stir until dissolved (invisible). Add another spoonful, again stirring to dissolve. Stop when you can no longer dissolve all the sugar. Record the amount of sugar added.

6. Repeat this process but with HOT water. How many teaspoons of sugar can be dissolved now? Why?

Talk about how powders (solids) can be mixed into (dissolved in) water but only to a certain point. At some point, they won't dissolve any more (the saturation point). Warm or hot water will dissolve more solids than cold water. Also discuss the convenience of using water to reconstitute dried foods and beverages. (They're smaller, lighter, require less packaging, etc.) However, dried foods and drinks can be trouble, too. What would happen if you mixed a drink or food with dirty water?

• •

WATER CAN CLEAN

Objective: *To witness the cleaning powers of water.*

Materials:
- several cloths for cleaning – some dry and some wet (1 of each per child)

Activity:
1. Give the children the dry cloths and ask them to clean a dirty table.
2. Now give them dampened cloths to use. Which worked better? Why?

Talk about water's power to dissolve, or break up, dirt and other solids.

• •

WATER CAN FLOAT THINGS

Objective: *To experiment with water's ability to keep things afloat (buoyancy).*

Materials:
- several plastic dish basins half-filled with water (1 basin per 2 to 3 children)
- aluminum foil squares (10 or so inches per side) – 2 per child
- pennies – 10 per child
- toy boats
- toy animals and people
- large sheet of paper
- marker
- tape

Activity:
1. To prepare, set up several work stations with basins of water.
2. Ask the children to use the flat aluminum pieces to build boats.
3. Once they're successful, they could try adding weight (the pennies) and see what happens.

4. After a bit more time for experimentation, invite the children to share information and their findings. Create a chart with two columns, one for the boats and one for the number of pennies the boats held. Test each child's boat, then add it to the chart by placing the boat in the "boat" column and writing the number of pennies it held in the pennies column. Ask the children which boat held the most pennies. Why?

5. For younger children, you might simply collect toy boats to compare their floating abilities. If possible, add toy animals or people to the boats and see if they still float.

Talk about the similarities in the most successful boat shapes (flat bottom, etc.). Was it important how you added the pennies to the boat?

SINK OR FLOAT?

Objective: To predict which items will float and which will sink.

Materials:
- several dish basins half-filled with water
- a collection of objects to test (wooden block, crayon, lemon, cotton ball, twist tie, etc.)

Activity:
1. Show the children the objects. Have them predict which will float and which will sink, then test the predictions.
2. Ask the children to collect some additional classroom or household objects. Some of the children will predict the objects will float, and others will predict they will sink. Test the predictions in the water and classify the objects based on whether or not they float.

Talk about the fact that objects float because they weigh less than the water that is pushing upward beneath them.

STATES OF WATER

Objective: *To compare water in its various states (liquid, solid, gas).*

Materials:
- water in a large container (a water table is perfect)
- tools for pouring, filling, sprinkling
- 2 identical plastic containers for freezing some of the water
- cooking or tea pot

Activity:
1. First let the children play with the water as they like.
2. When they're through, have them help you to put some of their play water into one plastic container. Place the container outside or in a freezer. (To speed things along, it's best if you've already pre-frozen another, identical container of water.)
3. Look at the ice. How is it similar and different than the water?
4. Take some of the water from the table and put it in a pan or tea pot. Boil the water until steam rises. Notice the steam. Where did the steam come from?

Talk about the three states of water – liquid, solid, gas.

HELP FROM THE WIND

Objective:	*To show how wind speeds evaporation.*
Materials:	• at least 2 cloth handkerchiefs, 1 wet and 1 dry • clothesline and clothespins to hold cloths • cardboard piece
Activity:	1. Use the clothespins to hang the two cloth pieces from the line (indoors or out). 2. Ask the children to take turns fanning the cloth on the right until it feels dry to the touch. Where did the water in the cloth go? Does the left cloth (the one without any fanning) feel dry, too?

Talk about how wind evaporates water and helps things to dry out. Even though we can't see it, the water in the cloth evaporates into water vapor in the air.

TRAVELING DROPS

Objective:	*To observe water in motion*
Materials:	• sheets of wax paper (1 per child) • straws (1 per child) • tape • cups of water • eyedroppers (1 per child or pair) • paper towels • food coloring (optional)
Activity:	1. Give each child a sheet of wax paper. You may want to tape the sheets to the table if they are curling up. Provide access to an eyedropper and water (add a drop of food coloring to the water, if desired). 2. Have the children use the eyedropper to place drops of water on their wax paper. Blow gently on the drops with a straw. Blow hard. (Warn the children not to blow on each other!)

Talk about what happens to small drops when they touch each other. What happens to large drops when you blow hard on them?

WATER DOWNHILL

Objective:	*To experiment dropping water onto different surfaces.*
Materials:	• several clipboards • tape • eye droppers • gallon-size plastic bags • cups of water • paper towels or rags • blocks or other props • variety of surfaces (construction paper, paper towel, waxed paper, foam sheet, coarse and fine sandpaper sheets, plastic wrap)
Activity:	1. To prepare, place each clipboard in a plastic bag to protect it from the water. (You may want to tape the bag in place). 2. Working in small groups, have the children choose a surface (for example, sandpaper) to attach to the clipboard. Once the surface has been attached, prop one end of the clipboard up on a block or other item to create a ramp. 3. Ask the children what they think will happen when they squeeze a drop of water onto the surface. Test their ideas. 4. As a group, try several different surfaces, keeping paper towels or rags handy to keep your work area from getting soggy.

Talk about the results of your experiments. Some surfaces absorb water, while others allow it to slip off. Did you test the children's ideas while the clipboard was lying down, as well as inclined?

• •

A SPONGE CLOUD

Objective:	*To simulate precipitation from a cloud.*
Materials:	• sponge, cut into cloud shape • eyedroppers or spoons (1 per child or pair) • cup of water (1 per child or pair) • basin or bowl
Activity:	1. Hold the sponge cloud by the edges above a basin or bowl. 2. Have the children add one eyedropper or teaspoon full of water at a time to the cloud. 3. Count the number of eyedroppers/spoons of water it takes until the cloud "rains".

Talk about how the sponge is like a cloud, collecting more and more water (vapor, in the cloud's case), until it becomes saturated and drips (rains). If the cloud is very cold, what comes out of it? (snow, sleet)

We Care about...
Water

Water is an important resource that exists in a finite supply. Teach children to care for their water supplies by using water responsibly (such as turning off the tap when finished). Teach children to never dump fluids or throw trash into storm drains because storm drains connect to water supplies. Children should also be taught to dispose of waste properly, as much litter also ends up blowing or washing into streams, lakes, and the ocean.

Outdoor Activities

RAIN DROP WALK

What to Do

On a rainy day (or just after a rainstorm) take a walk around your neighborhood. Is there any water flowing? Where have puddles formed? Where does the rainwater go? How does the air feel? How does the ground feel? Has any soil been washed away?

ICE STRUCTURES

What You Need
- plastic containers of various shapes and sizes (yogurt containers, buckets, ice cube trays, etc.)
- water source
- food coloring

What to Do

Fill the containers with colored water and freeze them outdoors in winter or in a freezer. Allow the ice to sit in a warm room (or sunny spot) for a few moments for easier removal, then have the children create colorful ice structures with the colored ice.

ICE AND SALT SCULPTURES

What You Need
- large plastic bowl
- large shallow pan
- spray bottle
- salt
- water source

What to Do

Freeze a large plastic bowl full of water. Turn it upside down in a larger shallow pan. Provide child with a plant mister (set on "spray") full of lukewarm SALT water. Let the child use the salty water spray to melt the ice, forming all kinds of "valleys" and fissures.

PAINTING WITH WATER

What You Need
- buckets
- house painting brushes and/or paint rollers

What to Do

On a warm day, provide buckets of water and house painting brushes for the children. Invite them to paint the sidewalks, building, etc., with water.

Language Activity / Poem

Dark clouds
streak the sky.

All waits.
Anticipates.

The air is heavy.
A leaf stirs.　　　　　　　　　　*[rub hands together]*
Slow rain pats the ground.　　　*[snap fingers slowly]*

Large drops　　　　　　　　　*[being snapping faster]*
Splash my nose.
Dot my clothes.
Wet my toes.

Drops patter　　　　　　　　　*[begin clapping]*
Fall faster
Puddles gather,
Overflow.　　　　　　　　　　*[pound floor with feet]*

Slowly, the rain　　　　　　　　*[stop stomping, begin clapping]*
lightens　　　　　　　　　　　*[begin clapping slower]*
until . . .　　　　　　　　　　*[and slower]*

Slow rain pats the ground . . .　*[stop clapping and begin snapping]*
and then,
only a cool breeze stirs.　　　　*[rub hands together]*

Independent Play Idea

On different days, fill your water table with water, ice,
and snow. Provide tools to manipulate the various forms
of water. Do different tools work better with snow . . .
with ice . . . with water? If you don't have a water table,
a supervised exploration station can be created using a
basin or other shallow tub. Be sure to protect the floor
beneath from spills!

Crafts and Projects

CLOUD PICTURES

What You Need
- large sheet of white paper (1 per child)
- tempera paints
- paint brushes
- light gray, blue, and/or pink paper
- glue
- spray bottles

What to Do
Provide each child with a large sheet of white paper and some tempera paints. Paint outdoor scenes. After the paintings are dry, give each child a couple of pieces of light gray or blue or even pink paper. Tear this paper into clouds and glue in place on the large paintings. Finally, provide spray bottles (set on "mist"), and let the children offer "rain" for their pictures. Watch what happens to the paints.

• •

BLOW PICTURES

What You Need
- tempera paints
- eye dropper (1 per color)
- straw (1 per child)
- white paper (1 sheet per child)

What to Do
Dilute tempera paints in water until quite runny and provide an eye dropper with each color. Give each child a straw and white paper. Have the children drip a few drops of colored paint-water on their papers, then blow these colors around with their straws.

Snack

A MEAL WITH WATER

What You Need
- variety of foods that require water for mixing
- bowls
- spoons
- water source
- materials for eating and serving

What to Do
Create a multi-item snack, using foods that require water for mixing.

Book Ideas

CHILDREN'S FICTION

Bringing the Rain to Kapiti Plain, by Verna Aardema, Dial Books, 1981 – an African folktale about a dry plain environment in need of water and how the people bring it rain.

Hey, Frog!, by Piet Grobler, Front Street & Lemniscaat, 2002 – a frog drinks up all the water on the savannah, a lighthearted look at water rights – funky illustrations!

Pond Year, by Kathryn Lasky, Candlewick Press, 1995 – appealing story of two young girls exploring a wetland near their homes throughout the seasons.

The King's Fountain, by Lloyd Alexander, Dutton, 1971 – a story about a rich king wants to build a fountain that will cut off the water supply of the common people and the man who convinces him not to, raises many ethical questions.

Who Sank the Boat?, by Pamela Allen, Coward-McCann, 1983 – a funny tale about animals loading into a boat until it no longer floats.

CHILDREN'S NONFICTION

A Drop of Water, by Walter Wick, Scholastic, 1997 – extraordinary photography and easy-to-understand explanations of various properties of water (from surface tension to evaporation).

I Am Water, by Jean Marzollo, Scholastic, 1996 – a fine introduction to water and where it's found, especially good for two- and three-year-olds.

In a Small, Small Pond, by Denise Fleming, Holt, 1993 – brief, lively text describes the activities typical of pond animals throughout the year.

The Magic School Bus at the Water Works, Scholastic, 1986 – Miss Frizzle and her gang learn about the water cycle.

Water, by Andrienne Soutter-Perrot, Creative Editions, 1993 – a superbly simple, yet very appealing book about water – where it is, the water cycle, and why clean water is important.

Wet World, by Norma Simon, Candlewick, 1997 – an inviting book about weather and how it makes one feel.

RESOURCE BOOKS FOR ADULTS AND CHILDREN

Water, by Kim Taylor, John Wiley and Sons, 1992 – a scientific reference for older kids, explains air moisture, surface tension, bubbles, and more.

Where Does Water Come From?, by C. Vance Cast, Barrons, 1992 – Clever Calvin takes readers on a fact-filled journey that explores the water cycle, a municipal water system, and more!

WILD ABOUT WATER

We have been investigating the properties of water and its many states: solid, liquid, and gas.

Continue the Learning at Home

Gather together a variety of small, clear containers and a selection of liquids (milk, water, oil, vinegar). Create a workspace that can withstand spills (lay down newspaper and cover with paper towels). Next, pour the liquids into the clear containers (one type of liquid in each container). Add a drop of food coloring to each. Observe. Stir if you wish. Try adding salt and/or sugar to a new set of liquids. What happens when you mix? Test what happens when you add drops of food coloring to these new liquids. You may even want to test what happens when you freeze the different liquids.

More Fun With Water

Take time to investigate how water travels through your home and your neighborhood. How does water enter your home? Where is it heated? Do you have a water meter? Where can you see pipes? Where does water go when it lands on the roof? On the driveway? When your streets are flooded?

Produced and copyrighted by Vermont Institute of Natural Science, 2005.

Animal Tracks

Focus: As they move, animals leave clues about their activities. The tracks and other evidence they leave behind can tell us a lot about what they were doing. By learning how to recognize these tracks, we can learn more about the habits and kinds of animals that are active in the environment.

Objective: To help children become more aware of the tracks and evidence left by wild animals.

Extra Information for Adult Leaders

Do you enjoy a good mystery? Well, learning to read animal tracks is a lot like that. You begin by sorting out the characters, searching for clues about their activities and identities. Then you follow the plot – what happened? Where did it happen? Finally, you put all those clues together and you figure out "who done it and why"!

One of the most important things to take note of when you discover a set of tracks is the **habitat** – the type of environment you are in. For example, you're not likely to find muskrat or beaver tracks far from water. Forests are favored habitats for squirrels, while fields are where you'd expect to find mice. By noting habitat, you can narrow your choices considerably.

Next, you can consider the relative size of the animal. Are the footprints you discovered large or small? As you'd logically assume, larger animals usually have larger feet; while smaller animals have smaller feet. In fact, sometimes footprint size is the most reliable way to tell one animal track from another. For example, coyotes and foxes are both members of the **canid** or dog family. All canids have very similar shaped feet, and, thus, leave nearly identical footprints – except for size! Amongst the **ungulate** or hoofed animal group, similar comparisons can be found. White tailed deer tracks are usually about three inches long, while moose prints may be nearly twice that length!

Related to the size of the footprint is the degree to which it sinks into the soil or snow, an indicator of the weight of the animal creating the tracks. A tiny animal, such as a mouse, will barely mark the surface of most substrates. A heavy deer or moose will sink deep into the snow.

Close examination of the individual footprint can also help to identify the track-maker. One important thing to notice is the number and placement of the toes. Certain animal groups, like the **felids** or cats, always have the same number of toes (four, in the case of cats). A cat's toes are arranged in a curving arc above the heel pad. Because they are able to retract their claws (in order to maintain sharpness), cat tracks rarely show claw marks. Wild and domestic dogs, on the other hand, also have four toes; but the claw marks are usually quite obvious.

Some animals, such as **rodents** (including squirrels, mice, and beavers), have a different number of toes on their front and back feet. If you examine a gray squirrel's footprints, for example, you'll find four toe impressions on the front foot and five on the back. You'll also notice that the back foot is larger, and differently shaped, than the front.

It's quite rare, though, to find a clear, easy-to-read individual animal footprint. More often, the footprints are obscured by blowing wind, melting snow, rain, or other weathering factors. Don't get discouraged if you can't discern the precise number of toes or see the claw marks. You can also learn about track-makers by their **track pattern**: the way the feet fall as the animal moves. Certain animals leave a characteristic series of footprints that can help you to distinguish one type of animal from another.

Deer, moose, coyotes, foxes, and bobcats are known as **walkers** (or **trotters**). As these animals travel, they usually place their hind feet in the prints made by their front feet (left hind foot falling into the depression made by the left front foot). The result is a nearly straight line of tracks. The red fox, for example, quite often leaves an almost perfectly straight line of small tracks. However, if the animal is running, the pattern tends to be more broken, often showing four feet closely placed, then another four further down the trail.

DIGGING IN...

Other animals are known as **gallopers** or **hoppers**. Some notable gallopers include rabbits, hares, squirrels, and mice. These creatures typically push off with their front feet, causing their bodies to become airborne for a moment, before their back feet land around the outside and a little bit further forward than their front feet. The track pattern will show hind footprints actually in front of the front feet. Seeing these track patterns and knowing the swift animals that leave them, you can imagine the quick critter in mid-leap!

Equally quick, but leaving different track patterns, are the **bounders**. Bounders place their front feet next to each other, and then leap forward so that their two back feet fall into the prints just vacated by the front feet. These long-bodied, slinky-like animals include weasels, otters, skunks, and mink.

Finally, not nearly so swift or agile are the **waddlers**. The waddlers are the chubby animals – raccoons and porcupines, for example. As they move forward, waddlers leave a trail of big and little tracks, with their larger hind feet planted next to their smaller front feet. This movement can be quite similar to the way a human baby crawls.

When tracking animals, just like when reading a good mystery book, it's imperative to be alert and to consider all the clues given to you. Habitat, size, and depth of footprint, shape, and features of the footprint, pattern of movement, stride and straddle are all important clues to discovering what animals passed before you and exactly what they were doing.

bobcat track (actual size is 2 inches by 2 inches)

Indoor Activities

MAKING TRACKS

Objective: *To make tracks with our own feet.*

Materials:
- large sheets (or roll) of newsprint paper (several yards long) – 1 per child
- aluminum lasagna-type pan
- washable paint – spread in a thin layer in the bottom of the aluminum pan
- plastic tarp (or lots of newspaper) to protect the floor
- dish pan filled with warm soapy water
- towels
- a chair
- white cardstock paper (8.5 x 11 inches) – 1 page per child

Activity:
1. Set up your floor protection. Then stretch a sheet of paper out flat. At one end, place the paint pan. At the other end, place the soapy water and towel, and a chair.
2. Work with one child at a time. Help the child to remove her shoes and socks, then roll her pants up to her knees.
3. Help the child to carefully step into the thin layer of paint. (Too much paint or the wrong paint consistency will make track-making more difficult.)
4. First help the child to make one nice, clear footprint on one page of cardstock paper.
5. Now have the child walk slowly along the length of the newsprint paper, leaving both left and right footprints.
6. Use the soapy water and towels to help the child clean her feet afterwards.
7. Repeat for all the children – and the teacher, too!

Talk about the footprints – called "tracks" – that were made. Can the children tell which way the person was walking? Notice how the paint color fades from one end of the paper to the other. What else do you notice about the tracks?

BIG FEET, LITTLE FEET

fox track (actual size is 2.5 inches by 1.75 inches)

Objective: *To compare foot sizes.*

Materials:
- individual footprints, made during the previous activity
- bobcat track
- fox track
- mouse track
- gray squirrel track
- grouse track
- deer track
- moose track
- ruler and animal tracks field guide (optional)

Activity:
1. Gather the children in a circle. In the center, place all the footprint pages made earlier.
2. Have the children work together to put the footprints in order according to size (smallest to biggest).
3. Ask the children to find the toes on the footprints. How many are there on each foot? Are they all the same size? Compare the prints to the children's actual feet.
4. Look at the wild animal footprints. Have the children count the number of toes on each one. Also notice toenail (claw) marks.
5. Show the deer and moose tracks to the children. Explain that these two mystery animals walk on just two toes (shown in the print). What animals do they think might've made these tracks?
6. Compare the size of the deer and moose tracks. If appropriate, ask the children to measure the tracks – length and width. Show the children how those measurements (track length and width) are always noted in animal track field guides.

Talk about the correlation between the size of the footprint and the size of the actual animal (the bigger the print, the bigger the animal). Also the heavier the animal, the deeper its track will be in soft ground, mud, or snow. You can talk about how some animals leave claw marks (like the fox), while others don't (like the bobcat). Bobcats, like all cats, have retractable claws, so they won't get too worn.

• •

LEFT AND RIGHT FEET

Objective: *To notice that wild animals, like people, have left and right feet.*

Materials:
- dry newsprint tracks (from the "Making Tracks" activity)
- rope
- bobcat track
- fox track
- mouse track
- gray squirrel track
- grouse track
- deer track
- moose track

squirrel track (actual size is: front – 1.5 inches by 1 inches; rear – 2 inches by 1 inch)

Activity:

1. Lay out at least one of the Making Tracks papers.
2. Give the rope to two children. Ask them to stretch the rope down the middle line of the tracks, so the left feet are on one side and the right feet are on the other.
3. Review left and right feet. Have the children take turns walking on the tracks and noticing that their left feet are stepping on one side of the rope, while their right feet are on the other.
4. Look again at the wild animal tracks. Help the children to find the left and right feet.

Talk about how, aside from humans, virtually all the animals we might find tracks from walk on four feet. So they have both left and right, and front and back, feet. The exception is birds. How many feet do birds have?

• •

GET MOVING, ANIMALS!

Objective:

To pretend to be animals moving through snow and also to notice how tracks can tell us about how an animal moves.

Materials:

- chart of animal movement patterns (see next page)
- illustrations or magazine pictures of the animals described in the movement chart
- red and blue construction paper – cut into circles (red for front feet, blue for back feet)
- masking or duct tape

Activity:

1. Using the animal movement patterns chart as your guide, tape the construction paper circles to the floor in the three movement patterns – walk, bound, and hop. (Space them appropriately, so the children will be able to reach them.)
2. Now, one at a time, invite the children to practice moving along each of the track patterns, placing their hands on the red circles and their feet on the blue circles.
3. After the children have tried one pattern (say, hopping), show them a picture of a wild animal that moves that way.
4. Repeat with the other movement patterns and animal pictures.
5. Option for younger children – Simply demonstrate each of the three movement patterns (walking, hopping, and bounding). Play "follow the leader" so the children can try the movements, too.

Talk about the bodies of the animals in relation to how they move. For instance, a rabbit has long and powerful back legs to help it hop. A deer's long and slim legs step into the snow as it walks. A mink's body is "slinky" shaped, so it can bound easily.

deer track (actual size is 3.5 inches by 2.5 inches)

WHO WENT THERE?

Objective: *To follow pretend tracks to find an animal picture.*

Materials:
- balls of 4 or 5 different colored yarns
- animal pictures or illustrations (at least 5)
- "start here" cards

Activity:

1. Prepare the tracking area by weaving the yarns through the room (going under tables, around play equipment, intersecting with other yarns, etc.). At one end of each color yarn, place a card that says "start here." At the other end, place an animal picture.
2. Choose as many children as you have yarns. Match each child with one yarn – "Delia, you'll follow the yellow yarn. Mark, you'll follow the blue yarn."
3. Each child should begin at the "start here" card.
4. Then, pretending they're following animal footprints, the children carefully trace their yarn paths until they find their animal pictures.
5. Review by asking, "What animal did the yellow yarn lead to?"

Animal Movement Patterns

Hoppers:
rabbits, squirrels, mice

Walkers:
deer, fox, cats

Bounders:
weasels, mink

Talk about how animal tracking is done in much the same way. Instead of following yarn paths, we follow footprints (tracks) left on the ground. If we're lucky, we might even find a real animal waiting at the end of the track trail! There are other clues and evidence that animals leave behind. Looking for signs of nibbling, gnawing, claw marks, droppings, and other clues can tell us even more about the animals' activities.

deer browsed twig

ANIMAL FEET

Objective: *To practice matching animals with their footprints and to practice group decision making.*

Materials:
- bobcat track
- fox track
- mouse track
- gray squirrel track
- grouse track
- deer track
- moose track
- grouse illustration
- deer illustration (see page 243)
- moose illustration
- bobcat illustration (see "Food for All" unit on page 222)
- fox illustration (see "Food for All" unit on page 220)
- mouse illustration (see "Mighty Mice" unit on page 252)
- gray squirrel illustration (see "Chipmunks and Their Cousins" unit on page 128)
- glue, scissors, and cardboard or cardstock paper

*grouse and grouse track
(actual size is 2 inches long)*

Activity:

1. Prepare the "animal tracks" sketches into separate cards (by photocopying and gluing them onto cardstock paper). Do not label them.

2. Gather the children in a circle and look at the animal pictures together. Make sure everyone knows all the animals.

3. Give one animal picture to each child (or pair of children). Then group the children into two teams.

4. Place the animal track sketch cards at the other end of the room.

5. At your signal, choose one child (or pair) from each team to walk (or hop or bound) to the other end of the room, where the animal track sketches are. The child should look at the track sketches and choose the one that he thinks belongs to his animal. (For example, he would choose the hoof print if he's got a picture of a deer.)

6. The child then brings both the animal picture and the track sketch back to his group. He asks the children in the group if they agree with his choice. If there is some disagreement, then the children need to reach some kind of decision anyway. (The child may return to the track pile and bring another track choice back to his group.)

7. Continue until all the track sketches have been chosen.

8. Review the choices made.

Talk about the differences between the various feet. How might having claws help a fox? What do the children notice about the size of the mouse's feet? Which animals have similar feet?

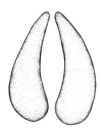

*moose and
moose track
(actual size is 7 inches
by 5 inches)*

STORY IN THE SNOW

Objective: *To observe and then retell a story of tracks in the snow.*

Materials:
- old window shade (or a 4-foot length of paper)
- thin permanent markers – several colors
- story in the snow illustration below

Activity:

1. The story in the snow illustration reveals clues about the activities of several animals.

2. With the children gathered around so everyone can see, draw this same scene on window shade. The children should observe carefully as you tell the story and draw the corresponding animal tracks.

3. You might tell a story like this:
   - First, I'll show you the location where our story takes place. (Draw the trees and swing set.) This is the story of several animals in someone's backyard.
   - The people who live here like to watch birds, so they put up a bird feeder on a post. (Draw the feeder.)
   - Many birds came to visit. The birds dropped lots of seeds on the ground. (Draw the birds and the seeds below.)
   - A squirrel smelled the birdseed and came to eat some of the fallen seeds. (Draw the squirrel's tracks leading from the tree, to the birdseed, and back to the tree.)
   - A mouse also smelled the birdseed and popped out of its hole in the snow, over near the swing set. The mouse ran to the birdfeeder. (Draw the mouse's tracks.)
   - After filling its little belly with seeds, the mouse walked – a bit more slowly now – back toward its tunnel near the swing set. (Draw the tracks to midway between the tree and swing set.)
   - Suddenly, a red fox appeared! The fox ran to the mouse, quickly snatched it up into its mouth and ran away! (Draw the fox tracks.)

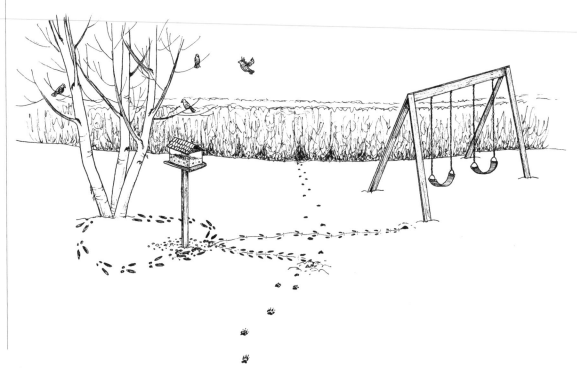

4. Now, using the window shade sketch as their guide, ask the children to retell the story in the snow. What happened first? Next? Was it a happy ending? (For the fox it was!)

Talk about good clues to use when tracking or following stories in the snow. Notice the habitat (the backyard in this story). Would a beaver be found there? Notice the size of the tracks. Notice tail or claw marks. Notice the direction of the tracks. Where do the children think the animal was going? What do they think the animal was doing?

Outdoor Activities

ANIMAL TRACKS SEARCH

What You Need
- several spray bottles with colored water (one per two children) or small flags made by tying a ribbon to a dowel

What to Do
Take a walk outside on a snowy or muddy day and look for animal tracks. Help the children to find partners. Give each pair a water bottle if looking for tracks in the snow or flag if looking for tracks in mud. Encourage the children to use their water bottles or flags to mark any animal tracks they find. Then the other children can look closely, too.

ANIMAL ACTIVITIES

What You Need
- peanut shells (or other evidence of eating)
- yellow colored water in bottle

What to Do
Before the children arrive, walk a short distance through the snow (perhaps around the building). Leaving space between them, set out clues to represent several essential animal activities:
- sleeping area: lay your body down in the snow and form a "bed"
- eating area: leave some peanut shells behind
- potty area: spray a bit of yellow water on the snow
- play area: run around a bit, leaving lots of tracks

Talk about some of the things that all animals must do – eat, sleep, go potty, and play (or move about, especially in cold weather). Challenge the children to follow your tracks and see if they can decide what might've happened in each place.

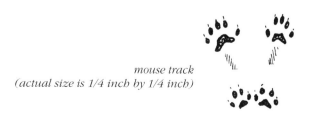

mouse track
(actual size is 1/4 inch by 1/4 inch)

STRIDE RIGHT

What You Need
- yardstick to measure the distance between footprints on "stride" (optional)

What to Do
Find some unmarked snow. Side by side, being careful not to step on each other's tracks, ask the children to slowly walk through the snow. Look back at the tracks, and especially notice the short distance between one footprint and the next.

Find another fresh snow area. Have the children run, using giant steps, to move through the snow. Look back at the tracks, and notice the longer distance between footprints now.

Talk about trying to follow some wild animal tracks. Can you find places where the animal was walking? Running? Sliding? Lying down?

Language Activity / Rhyme

Let's go walking in the snow. Walking, walking, on tiptoe.
Lift your one foot way up high – then the other, to keep it dry.
All around the yard we skip. Watch your step, or you might slip.

Crafts and Projects

TRACK STAMPS

What You Need
- sponges or erasers or potatoes to cut into animal track-shaped stamps
- paper
- washable ink pads

What to Do
Prepare the track stamps ahead of time. Using the ink pads and stamps, the children can create designs, stories, or other ways to display the animal tracks.

• •

TRACK CASTS

What You Need
- shallow pan of loose, moist sand
- plaster of paris
- plastic cup
- stick or spoon
- water
- an old toothbrush
- paint and brushes

Independent Play Idea
Provide a variety of animal clues – acorns chewed by squirrels, empty sunflower seeds, beaver stick, insect holes in wood – for the children to examine.

What to Do

Help one child to carefully step (barefooted) into the sand, forming a footprint in the sand. Now fill the cup halfway with plaster. Slowly add water, stirring, until the mixture is thin enough to pour but not too runny either. (You might need to practice a bit.) Pour the plaster mixture into the footprint in the sand. Let it harden for about ten minutes. Remove the track cast from the sand; brush it off with an old toothbrush; then have the child paint it.

Snack

TRACK CRACKERS

What You Need

- graham crackers
- white cake frosting
- plastic bowls
- raisins
- plastic knives
- napkins

What to Do

Give each child a napkin, graham cracker square, and plastic knife. Sharing a bowl of frosting with a neighbor, the child should use the knife to spread an even layer of frosting on her cracker. Then give each child a few raisins and ask her to place her raisins on the frosted cracker, so they look like animal tracks crossing the snow.

We Care about . . . Animal Tracks

Winter's a tough time for most animals in the north country. It's cold and dark, there's not much food, and animals have to use a lot of energy just to stay alive. During particularly difficult (cold) times, many animals seek out shelter. Deer gather together, sheltered from the wind and heaviest snows, in deer yards. Raccoons and skunks enter hollow trees or crawl under fallen logs. Bats congregate in comparatively warmer rock caves. One way you can help animals survive the most difficult times of winter is to stay away from their winter shelters. If you are following tracks and happen to find an animal's shelter, observe it from a distance and then walk away and take care to avoid it in the future.

Book Ideas

CHILDREN'S FICTION

Around the Pond: Who's Been Here?, by Lindsay Barrett George, Greenwillow Books, 1996 – a beautifully illustrated book that tells the story of two children who find clues about the animals that live nearby.

Big Tracks, Little Tracks, by Millicent Selsam, Scholastic, 1995 – an engaging book that challenges children to become nature detectives, gathering clues and evidence to decide which animals have passed by them.

In the Snow: Who's Been Here?, by Lindsay Barrett George, Greenwillow Books, 1996 – presents animal clues found by two children and invites the reader to guess which animals left them.

In the Woods: Who's Been Here?, by Lindsay Barrett George, Greenwillow Books, 1996 – another in the "Who's Been Here?" series.

Whose Tracks Are These?, by Jim Nail, Roberts Rinehart, 1994 – a guessing book, offering progressively more obvious clues about animals' identities.

CHILDREN'S NONFICTION

Crinkleroot's Book of Animal Tracking, by Jim Arnosky, Bradbury Press, 1979 – an exciting look at tracking, packed with natural history about animals.

How to Be a Nature Detective, by Millicent E. Selsam, HarperCollins, 1996 – a colorful primer on tracking.

RESOURCE BOOKS FOR ADULTS AND CHILDREN

Tracking & the Art of Seeing, by Paul Rezendes, Camden House, 1992 – a wonderful guide to tracking appropriate for adults, organized by animal families.

Tracks in the Wild, by Betsy Bowen, Little, Brown & Co, 1993 – lovely woodcut illustrations and detailed information about many northern animals and their tracks.

Tracks, Scats and Signs, by Leslie Dendy, Northword Press, 1995 – useful for adults and children, discusses several forms of animal signs you might discover.

ANIMAL TRACKS

We've been learning about the clues that many animals leave behind – animal tracks. We've noticed things like number of toes, left and right feet, claw marks and the patterns the feet make in the snow or soil.

Continue the Learning at Home

Take a walk with your child around your neighborhood, searching for footprints, nibbled nuts, and other signs of animals (including pets). When you return to your home, take a few minutes to review the animal signs you discovered AND where you found them (in Mr. Jones' front yard, beneath the big tree in the park, etc.). Get out some paper and crayons and draw a very simple map with your child. You might even use a key to indicate the location of certain findings (especially those you found in several locations).

On another day, take your map and walk the same route again. Are there recent animal signs in the same places? Did you find anything new?

Option: Borrow one of the following books from your library: *In the Snow: Who's Been Here?* or *In the Woods: Who's Been Here?*, both written by Lindsay Barrett George. Compare your map to the one inside the front cover of either book.

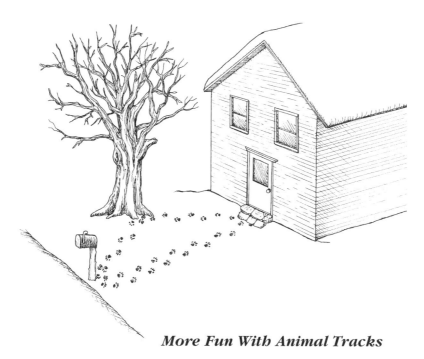

More Fun With Animal Tracks

Using washable ink pads, help your child to make lines of thumbprints across a paper. Pretend these marks are the heel pads of some animals walking in the snow. Provide washable markers, so your child can add toes to these "footprints" or "tracks."

Produced and copyrighted by Vermont Institute of Natural Science, 2005.

Mighty Mice

Focus: Mice are widespread and highly adaptable animals that are a prey species for many animals.

Objective: To learn about the typical foods, behaviors, senses, and habits of mice.

Extra Information for Adult Leaders

DIGGING IN...

Just about everyone has struggled to remove a population of mice from their home at one time or another. Although we may not see these **nocturnal** creatures when they are in our midst, evidence of their activities is often widespread. Chewed packaging, missing food, shredded paper, and droppings all serve as signs that mice are active in an area. As mice are a very **fecund** species, controlling them can become an involved project.

House mice are not native to North America. Rather, they were accidentally introduced on the ships of the early colonists. The adaptable mouse adjusted well to its new surroundings and began reproducing at its usual high rate, eventually expanding its range to include the continental United States and Canada. There are several native North American species of mice, including the deer mouse, harvest mouse, and white-footed mouse, to name only a few.

The deer mouse, one of the most widespread native mice, is brown with a white belly. Like all mice, they are nocturnal, but will become active during the day if stressed by snowfall or a food shortage. Deer mice eat fruits (including a variety of berries) and seeds (from shrubs and wildflowers), as well as insects in the summer. They add nuts to their diet throughout the cooler months of the year. Insects fill out the mouse diet when they are available. It is not uncommon for deer mice to climb trees and shrubs in search of food.

In addition to eating seeds, mice are also notorious for nibbling on tree bark, shoots, and buds, especially during difficult winters. Mice also **cache** seeds and nuts (they often partially shell the nuts before storage). Caches can be buried or stashed in natural holes or cracks. One mouse can store up to eight quarts of food in a cache.

Mouse nests can be found anywhere there is an accessible cavity, such as under a log, in an abandoned burrow (deer mice do not dig their own burrows), even in an abandoned bird nest, or a bird house. Mice build their nests out of soft materials, including bark, cattail fluff, hair, moss, and grass leaves. Mouse nests look like balls and have one opening that the mouse closes when inside. Be careful to avoid touching mouse nests (especially if you are not wearing gloves): mice defecate and often urinate in and around them. In fact, the best way to avoid disease transmission from mouse droppings is to use a wet cloth to pick up any mouse materials and to then disinfect the area.

Deer mice breed throughout the spring and summer, sometimes as many as four times during the year. A deer mouse litter typically has three to five babies, or pups, that spend their first two weeks blind, deaf, and helpless. A typical house mouse has litters of up to ten pups at a time and breeds throughout the year. Mice, like all **mammals**, produce milk to feed their young. This period of time is an especially stressful one for the female mouse, as she requires two to three times as much food as usual to produce milk for her pups. One reason mice reproduce in such large numbers is that their probability of survival is very low. While they may be a pest to humans, mice benefit many predators, including foxes and many owl species, by serving as a dependable food source.

Indoor Activities

WHAT BIG EYES YOU HAVE!

Objective: *To compare the vision of an animal with small eyes to one with big eyes.*

Materials:
- mouse illustration
- egg cartons, cut into 6 parts, each with 2 adjacent sections
- hole punch
- string or yarn
- sharply pointed scissors or craft knife

Activity:
1. Have the children look at the mouse picture and point out special things they notice about the mouse's body, including the large eyes.
2. Help the children to prepare several sets of "glasses." To make the glasses, cut the egg cartons into sections of two cups each. Then use the hole punch to make holes on the outside of each cup; tie 12-inch yarn pieces here (so the glasses can be tied around head). Finally, on half the glasses, poke a small hole in the center of each "eye piece." On the other half, make a large hole in each eye piece.
3. Have the children try on the two versions – explaining that the small hole represents the sight of, say, a mole (who rarely comes above ground to look around), while the large hole represents the big eyes of a mouse (who relies on excellent eyesight to survive).
4. Ask the children which pair of eye glasses allows more light to enter the eye? Why is it good (helpful) for the mouse to have such big eyes?

Talk about the reasons mice need such big eyes. Most importantly, mice are active at night time, when there's not much light available for seeing. Large eyes allow more light to enter the eye, allowing animals to see more clearly at night. Because mice mostly eat small seeds in the wild, they need to be able to see in order to find their food. Also, having large eyes helps mice to see dangerous hunters before they get too close. Finally, mice have large eyes positioned on the sides of their heads (not the front), so they can see danger approaching.

WHAT BIG EARS YOU HAVE!

Objective: *To use our hearing to identify a variety of common sounds.*

Materials:
- sheet or blanket, tacked or held up to form a wall in front of the children
- variety of common noise-producing objects (bouncing ball, comb, stapler, straw blowing bubbles under water, bell, whistle, etc.)
- mouse illustration (optional)

Activity:
1. Seat the children in front of the blanket "wall." Hide the noise-producing objects behind the wall and station yourself there.
2. Peeking over the wall, explain to the children that they will soon hear several familiar sounds. Rather than yelling out when they recognize a sound, the children should wait until you make each sound three times, then identify it. Everybody should be quiet and listen.
3. One by one, make the sounds and see if the children can recognize them. (For younger children, you might want to show the children all the sound-makers first, then make the sounds behind the curtain and see who can identify them.)

4. Repeat part or all of this activity after showing the children how they might cup their hands behind their ears to make the sounds seem louder.

Talk about how a mouse's ears are large and cup-shaped. The sound waves produced by even the smallest of sounds are "caught" by the mouse's big ears and bounced into the ear, so the mouse can hear even very quiet sounds. Mice, too, are very quiet as they move because if they made too much noise they couldn't hear other noises. Has anybody ever heard the expression "quiet as a mouse"?

SOUND-PICTURE PAIRS

Objective: *To encourage the children to select visual images to match the sounds they hear.*

Materials:
- tape recorder
- prerecorded tape
- bingo boards with symbols of the sounds recorded on the tape (1 board per child)
- markers for boards (beans or pennies work well)
- photos of the children (optional)

Activity:
1. Prepare the cassette tape by recording common sounds heard in and around your child care setting (toaster, hammer, washing machine, door closing, etc.). Use drawings or photos to create corresponding visual images of sound-makers.
2. Mount the pictures (in different arrangements) on cardboard to create bingo boards for the children.
3. Provide each child (or pair) with a picture board and place markers (pennies).
4. Play the tape for the children, and direct them to place a marker on the pictures representing the sounds they hear. Who can cover their board first?
5. Variation: Prepare a tape with the sound of each child's voice. Prepare boards with the photos of the children. Ask the children to recognize the sounds of their friends' voices.

Talk about the sounds we hear around us. What other sounds could the children recognize? What kinds of sounds might a mouse hear at night in your house? In the forest?

WHY THE WHISKERS?

Objective: *To demonstrate the importance of a mouse's whiskers.*

Materials:
- clay or craft dough
- pipe cleaners
- variety of tubes, bottles, and other "tunnels" or "openings"

Activity:
1. To prepare, create small life-size mice with pipe cleaner tails and whiskers from clay or craft dough. (The whiskers, when spread out, should be approximately the same size as the widest part of the mouse's body.)
2. Explain to the children that the mouse's whiskers are kind of like its fingers – the mouse can feel with them even in the dark. Also the whiskers help the mouse to judge whether its body can fit through a certain opening or tunnel.
3. Give each child or pair of children a mouse (or construct them together).

4. Challenge the children to test the various tubes, bottles, etc. with their mice. (If the mouse's whiskers wiggle or bend when its head is pushed into the opening, then it's too tight.)

Talk about what might happen to a mouse if it ignored the "whisker warning" and tried to squeeze into a too-small tunnel. (It might get stuck and not be able to wiggle free!)

FOLLOW THAT TRAIL

Objective: *To recognize and match scents.*

Materials:
- 10 or more plastic film canisters (each with a small hole poked in the lid)
- strong smelling items, such as coffee grounds, cinnamon, peppermint, and parsley

Activity:
1. Prepare the film canisters by putting a bit of each scented item in two of the film canisters (two coffee, two peanut butter, etc).
2. In small groups, tell the children to take a small sniff of each item (through the hole in the lid). Then challenge them find the second canister with that same smell.
3. Continue until matches have been found for all the scents.
4. Ask the children if they can identify any of the smells? Take a look at each item.

Talk about how mice use scent and smell to survive. A mouse leaves a faint scent trail from an oil on the bottom of its feet as it walks. This allows other mice to follow it. Mice also use urine to scent mark their territories. Finally, mice use their sense of smell to find food.

MOVING MICE

Objective: *To try moving like a mouse.*

Materials:
- mouse track pattern illustration
- construction paper – cut into 8 large ovals and 8 small circles and 4 long thin strips

Activity:
1. Study the mouse track pattern, or better yet, look at some real mouse tracks. Especially notice that the mouse moves by putting its front feet together, then galloping forward so its back feet come around and land in front of the others. The tail often drags.
2. Place the construction paper tracks on the ground to duplicate the pattern.
3. Have the children try to move like mice, galloping.

(enlarged)

Talk about the fact that mice often need to move quickly to escape danger. When mice are really moving, their front and back feet tracks are far apart. Smaller mice (like white-footed and deer mice) leave prints close together, while larger jumping mice leave prints farther apart – reflecting their ability to leap.

MOUSE DRESS UP

Objective:	*To pretend to be a mouse, with a long tail and whiskers.*
Materials:	• used brown paper grocery bags (1 or 2 per child)
	• cloth strips (3 feet long by 3 inches wide)
	• stapler
	• pipe cleaners
	• scotch or masking tape
Activity:	1. Help the children to tear the bags so they're flat.
	2. Starting at one corner, twist the bags into tail-like snakes. Leave one end open, so you can staple the cloth strip to it midway.
	3. Tie the cloth strip around the child's waist, allowing the long tail to hang down in back.
	4. For each child, twist together several pipe cleaners and tape them to his upper lip as whiskers (or attach them to a string which you tie around the child's head).
	5. Have the children pretend to be mice running about exploring their environment.

Talk about what it might feel like to be a mouse.

● ●

HIDING MICE

Objective:	*To pretend to be mouse hunters.*
Materials:	• aluminum foil pieces – shaped into pretend mice
Activity:	1. Beforehand, hide lots of foil "mice" in your room or outdoors.
	2. Gather the children and tell them they're going to pretend to be "mouse hunters." Ask each child to tell you the kind of mouse-hunting animal he wants to be.
	3. Let the children (animals) search for the hidden mice. Count how many mice each child found.

Talk about how the mouse's small size is one of the things that helps it to avoid being caught by its enemies. The tiny mouse can hide in small places and often isn't seen by its hunters. Also, mice are mostly brown and gray, ideal for woodland and field camouflage.

● ●

MOUSE MATH

Objective:	*To appreciate how quickly mice can reproduce.*
Materials:	• copies of mouse drawings – copied onto stiff paper (at least 70 total)
	• blocks
	• calendar
Activity:	1. Read the following script, placing paper mice on the table or floor as you speak.

Once upon a time, one New Year's Day, two mice were born into different families. One was a boy mouse. The other was a girl mouse. In late February, when these two mice were just two months old, they met and the girl mouse became pregnant. Four weeks later, she gave birth to eight babies. Again, the mice mated and produced eight more baby mice.

This happened again, every month, another eight baby mice were born to this couple. By the end of the year, the two mice had produced more than 80 babies!

Also, as their babies grew into adult mice, they, too, mated and gave birth to many baby mice. In just one year, those two mice and their babies produced many hundred babies!

2. Now look at a calendar with the children and explain that the mice in the story have a new litter of baby mice at the end of each month, beginning in March. That's ten litters of eight babies each.

3. Challenge the children to build a block tower ten stories tall, with eight blocks on each layer. Add two final blocks to the top (those represent the original parent mice).

Talk about the fact that this might be a real-life story. Real mice, in the wild, can have many hundreds of babies during their lifetimes. However, because there are so many dangers for mice, only a small number of these mice survive to mate and produce young.

• •

HOME SWEET HOME

Objective: *To learn about what mice eat and why they like to come into people's houses.*

Materials:
- seeds, nuts, dog or cat food, noodles, apple, and any other mouse foods you can find
- mouse chewed bag or container, if you have one
- carrot sticks (1 per child)

Activity:
1. Show the children the mouse food. Which ones are also people food? How do you think mice get dog food or noodles?
2. Show the children the chewed bag or container.
3. Explain that mice are able to chew through even hard materials, thanks to their very sharp and always growing front teeth (incisors). When a mouse eats, it uses those front incisor teeth to nip off the food, then its tongue passes the food to its back molar teeth, where the mouse grinds the food into little bits for swallowing.
4. Try eating your carrot stick as a mouse would.
5. Explain that one reason why mice like to come into people's houses is that there's almost always good food available. Also, the mice find the other two things they need – warmth and shelter from enemies and rain or snow.
6. Take a walk around your building and search for good homes for mice – places where the mice would be warm and sheltered and find some food.

Talk about how barns and houses are perfect places for mice to spend the winter. They can easily find food, shelter, and warmth there. Mice are **rodents**. The word "rodent" comes from "rodere," meaning "to gnaw." If a mouse didn't chew hard things to wear down its **incisor** teeth, they'd grow two inches each year.

Outdoor Activities

MOUSE TUNNELS IN THE SNOW

What to Do

Take a walk outdoors and search for tunnels made in the snow by mice and their cousins, voles. Put your ear to the snow. Can you hear the mice under there? Carefully follow alongside a tunnel to see how far it might go. Look for places where the mouse comes up for fresh air.

• •

MOUSE TRACKS

What You Need
- garbage can lid
- flour
- seeds and/or peanut butter
- flat plate

What to Do

Place a garbage can lid outside (upside down) and dust it with flour. Put a bit of peanut butter and seeds on a flat plate in the center of the garbage can lid. Leave this "trap" outside overnight. In the morning, check the flour for footprint tracks from visiting mice.

• •

SHY AND TIMID SAVES THE DAY

What You Need
- nuts or seeds
- playing area with places to hide (under or behind equipment, behind trees)

What to Do

1. Place the nuts or seeds in a small pile in the center of the playing area.
2. Have each child find a good hiding place near the outskirts of the playing area. The children should pretend to be shy and timid mice.
3. When you motion with your finger, the mice can slowly, quietly creep out of their hiding spots, toward the seeds.
4. However, when they hear you make a squeaking (danger) noise, then they must quickly scurry back to their hiding places.

Talk about the things the shy mice might be afraid of – owls, snakes, cats, hawks, coyotes, dogs, foxes, etc. Mice have lots and lots of predators who want to eat them, so they must be very careful. What would happen if a mouse ignored the sound and stayed out in the open?

Language Activity / Rhyme

Hickory dickory dock,
The mouse ran up the clock,
The clock struck one,
The mouse ran down,
Hickory dickory dock.

Crafts and Projects

CLAY MICE

What You Need
- bakeable clay
- pieces of felt
- strong craft glue
- wiggle eyes (1 pair per child)
- small pieces of yarn (1 per child)

What to Do

To prepare, cut out a pair of small mouse ears from felt for each child. Give each child a piece of hardening clay to use to shape a mouse. Glue on eyes, tail, and whiskers, if you like.

We Care about . . .
Mice

Especially during difficult winters, mice can create a lot of damage, indoors and outdoors. It is tempting to attempt to poison the mice before they create major damage, but rodent poisons can move beyond mice, working their way into the bodies of animals who happen upon a dead mouse and eat it. This, in turn, can affect the animal's health. Trapping, whenever possible, represents the best solution to any mice problems you may experience.

To avoid having to trap mice in the first place, remind the children in your care to be careful about cleaning up food materials. If mice are a concern, store snack materials in airtight plastic containers and cover any materials that might be used to build a nest. There is a possibility that the mice will move on if there is no food incentive in the area to entice them to stay. Mice can also cause problems outdoors, especially to young trees. Damage can be prevented by wrapping hardware cloth (wire mesh with quarter- to half-inch holes) around the tree base to prevent mice from accessing it under the snow. It is best if you can bury the bottom two inches of the wire mesh in the soil to prevent mice from accessing the bark underground.

ASSEMBLY MICE

What You Need
- brown or gray construction paper
- construction paper (variety of colors)
- glue
- scissors (for teacher)

What to Do
To prepare, precut from construction paper the following shapes for each child: one large oval (body), one large circle (head), two medium circles (ears), two small circles (eyes), four medium triangles (feet), one small triangle (nose/mouth), eight lines (whiskers), one long squiggly line (tail).

Provide background paper and glue and ask each child to assemble a mouse.

• •

WALNUT MICE

What You Need
- walnuts
- white, pink, and brown construction paper
- pencils
- glue
- yarn

What to Do
Prepare the walnuts by carefully breaking them in half, so you have a clean-edged half shell. The children will trace around the shell, and you will cut out the shapes. The children can then glue the pieces of construction paper to the bottom of the shell. Cut out ears from pink construction paper and whiskers and eyes from white. Using liquid white glue, glue these in place on the shell. Add a yarn tail.

• •

HEART MICE

What You Need
- construction paper
- scissors
- yarn

What to Do
Give a small piece of construction paper to each child, directing him to fold the paper in half. Then use scissors to cut the papers into heart shapes. Glue a yarn tail to the bottom of the heart, then glue the two sides of the heart together, creating a teardrop shape. Then add eyes, ears and whiskers.

Independent Play Ideas
1. If you have or can borrow a live mouse, let the children observe its activities.
2. Put out pint and quart containers and a variety of seeds in a tub. Let the children play in the seeds and practice measuring.

Snack

PIZZA MICE

What You Need
- English muffins
- pizza sauce
- cheese
- pepperoni
- green pepper
- knife
- cutting surface
- oven
- baking sheet

What to Do

To prepare, cut the pepper into thin strips, then invite the children to help you make English muffin pizzas, adding pepperoni and pepper strips for ears and whiskers.

Book Ideas

CHILDREN'S FICTION

One Dark Night, by Lisa Wheeler, Harcourt, 2003 – rhyming story of a mouse and mole's fear-filled trip through the marsh.

Seven Blind Mice, by Ed Young, Philomel Books, 1992 – the classic tale of seven mice who each explore and describe a different part of an elephant, and finally put together their observations to conclude that they've explored an elephant.

Town Mouse, Country Mouse, by Jan Brett, G.P. Putnam's Sons, 1994 – two mice learn to appreciate their own homes when they change places, gorgeous, intricate illustrations.

Two Tiny Mice, by Alan Baker, Scholastic, 1990 – a simply written and nicely illustrated description of the various animals two mice see in the course of a single day.

What Does Violet See?: Raindrops and Puddles, by Julie Aigner, Clark, 2002 – follows a young mouse who takes a walk, exploring the world around her.

CHILDREN'S NONFICTION

A Bed for Winter, by Karen Wallace, Dorling Kindersley, 2000 – a door mouse searches for a place to hibernate for the winter.

A Mouse's Life, by John Himmelman, Children's Press, 2000 – describes the life of a white-footed mouse, including its food, daily activities, and predators, includes a piece about a child who captures a wild mouse, then returns it to the outdoors.

Where's Mouse?, by Alan Baker, Kingfisher Books, 1992 – a unique and visually appealing book, pages fold out to show the mouse's habitat both above and below ground.

RESOURCE BOOKS FOR ADULTS AND CHILDREN

A Look Through the Mouse Hole, by Heiderose and Andreas Fischer-Nagel, Carolrhoda Books, 1989 – a family of mice who lives in a basement compared to outdoor mice.

Mice, All about Them, by Alvin Silverstein, Lippincott, 1980 – examines the habitats, and habits of mice, including how human culture portrays them in folktales.

MIGHTY MICE

We have been learning about mice and the various adaptations that help them survive in their environment.

Continue the Learning at Home

Take turns creating a story about a mouse and fox. Use the illustrations below to help develop your story.

More Fun with Mice

Read a story about mice together, such as *Town Mouse, Country Mouse* by Jan Brett.

Produced and copyrighted by Vermont Institute of Natural Science, 2005.

Circle of the Sun

Focus: The Sun's heat and light powers life on Earth. The Sun's presence is felt in many ways in our environment: through the warmth of a Sun beam, in the bright colors of a sunset, in the glow of the Moon at night, and in shadows.

Objective: To appreciate the many ways the Sun affects our world through the day/night cycle influencing our feelings, warming the Earth, and casting shadows.

Extra Information for Adult Leaders

Though it is a mind-boggling 93 million miles away, the Sun is the closest star to our planet and the centerpiece of our solar system. The next closest star is 270,000 times as far away. The conversion of **matter** into energy by **nuclear fusion** at the Sun's core produces energy that emanates from the Sun's surface and is received as light and heat by the Earth. It takes about eight minutes for sunlight to reach the Earth. If the Sun were any closer to Earth, the Earth could be too hot to maintain a water cycle or atmosphere; too far away and the Earth's surface might be covered with ice.

The Sun's **mass** produces a field of **gravity** that pulls the planets in our solar system around and around in a yearly **orbit**, or path around the Sun. Each planet **revolves** around the Sun in a counterclockwise direction, and each planet orbits at a different rate in relation to their distance from the Sun. Planets closer to the Sun, such as Mercury, Venus, Earth, and Mars (in order of proximity), revolve more quickly than those further away. It takes tiny Mercury only 88 Earth days to revolve around the Sun, whereas the distant, giant gas ball planet Saturn takes 30 Earth years to complete an orbit. The Earth makes one complete revolution around the Sun every 365.24 days. This is why every four years we build a leap year into the calendar. If we didn't, over time our calendar and the seasons would no longer correspond.

At the same time the Earth is orbiting the Sun, it is also **rotating** counterclockwise on its **axis**, an imaginary line that extends through the Earth between the North and South Poles. It takes the Earth 24 hours to complete one full rotation. As the Earth spins, different places on its surface face the Sun, and we experience the Sun "rising" in the eastern sky and

DIGGING IN...

"setting" in the western sky. The Moon and constellations move across the night sky as the night progresses. The Earth completes a full rotation in 24 hours, resulting in some parts of the Earth experiencing full daylight while other parts are in the depth of night.

Just as planets are flung into orbit around the Sun due to its gravitational pull, satellite objects, including the Earth's moon, orbit around planets due to the planet's gravitational pull. Unlike a star, the Moon does not produce its own light, rather, it reflects light from the Sun. We always observe the same side of the Moon because it rotates on its axis at about the same rate it rotates around the Earth, a little more than 29.5 days.

The rhythm of day and night affects animal behavior. There are three main time periods that animals are active: **diurnal** animals are active during the day; **nocturnal** move about at night, and **crepuscular** utilize the in-between times of dawn and dusk. There are many reasons why animals are active during a specific time period. Some animals exploit resources that are available only at a certain time of day. Others might be active at a certain time to avoid predation. Animals that utilize the same food resources are often active at different times of the day, maximizing their access to the resource (for example some hawks prey on small mammals during the day, while owls prey on them at night). Nocturnal animals include foxes, bats, owls, moths, fireflies, mice, and raccoons. Diurnal animals include squirrels, chipmunks, chickadees, woodpeckers, and snakes. Crepuscular animals include deer and snowshoe hare.

Next time you are outside, notice which animals you see active. As you observe, you should begin to notice patterns of activity. Too, reflect on how the Sun affects your mood and behavior. What other Sun rhythms do you and the children have?

Indoor Activities

WE KNOW THE SUN AND MOON

Objective: *To describe the appearance of the Sun and the Moon.*

Materials:
- yellow and orange construction paper, precut into circles and long, skinny triangles (or rectangles)
- white construction paper cut into a variety of circles and crescents (phases of the Moon)
- large black and blue (or white) background papers (1 per child)
- glue with dishes and brushes
- reflector and a flashlight (optional)

Activity:
1. Provide the children with the cut paper shapes, background papers, and glue. Ask them to make a Sun picture and a Moon picture from the materials provided.
2. Ask the children open-ended questions about their pictures: "Which picture is the Sun/Moon?" "What shapes did you use in your picture?" "Why?" "What color did you use as your background?"
3. Some children may get creative with their pictures, placing the Sun and Moon together on one paper, putting rays on their Moon, or placing two Moons or Suns on a page. Don't worry too much about correcting this creativity, but do be sure to ask the children questions about the real Sun and Moon: "When do we see the Sun/Moon?" "How many Suns/Moons do we have?" (If the children do not know the answers to these questions, go outside and find the Sun and have them find the Moon at home if it is not visible the day you are looking) "Does the Moon change shape?" "How does sunlight feel?" and so on.

Talk about the parts of the Sun, especially the rays. Explain to the children that the Sun is actually a very, very bright star. The Sun's rays are the light that comes from that star. The Earth receives light from the Sun. We see the Sun during the day, and the Moon usually at night... although there are days when you and the children will spot the Moon in the sky with the Sun. Unlike the Sun, the Moon is not a star. It does not give off its own light, rather, it reflects light from the Sun. (You may wish to demonstrate reflection by showing the children a reflector, and then shining a light on it. The flashlight's light makes the reflector bright, just as the Sun's light makes the Moon bright.)

DAY AND NIGHT

Objective: *To demonstrate that day and night occur because the Earth spins.*

Materials:
- large yellow ball (Sun) (can be made from a painted foam ball)
- small blue ball (Earth) (can be made from a painted foam ball)
- picture of the Sun (optional)

Activity:
1. Have the children join hands in a circle, with the Sun in the middle. Drop hands and have everybody sit down, cross-legged.
2. Ask the children the difference between day and night. Have they ever seen a sunset? A sunrise? Ask them to describe them.
3. Use the balls to demonstrate how day and night are caused by the Earth spinning (rotating) on its axis. Sometimes we face toward the Sun (day) and sometimes we face away from the Sun (night).

4. Demonstrate this by having the children stand facing the Sun. This is day. Now, have them turn their backs to the Sun (if possible, have the children turn in a counterclockwise direction). Turn out the lights. Now it is night.

5. Turn back toward the Sun, completing the circle, and turn the classroom lights on. Tell the children they have begun a new day.

6. Practice day and night several more times.

Talk about the way the Earth rotates. Each day, the Earth turns or rotates fully, making one full day.

COMPLETING A YEAR

Objective: *To learn that a year is considered to be one revolution around the Sun.*

Materials:
- large yellow ball (Sun) (can be made from a painted foam ball)
- small blue ball (Earth) (can be made from a painted foam ball)

Activity:

1. Use the balls to demonstrate how the Earth orbits, or circles, the Sun. It takes one year to complete an orbit.

2. Hand the Earth ball to one of the children and place the Sun ball in the center of the circle. Have the child holding the Earth walk the circle around the other children and round the Sun. Talk to the group about how walking one full circle equals one time around the Sun or one year.

3. Ask one child how old she is. Explain that she has "circled the Sun" that same number of times. (A four-year-old has been around the Sun four times.)

4. One at a time, ask the children to say how old they are, then encourage them to hold the Earth ball and walk around the circle (Sun) the number of times that match their age.

Talk about the way that the Earth revolves. Each year, the Earth makes a full circle around the Sun, making one full year.

SHADOW PLAY

Objective: *To practice using light to create shadows.*

Materials:
- light colored paper (or table top)
- flashlights (1 per child)
- collection of small toys – animal, people, etc.
- pencils (optional)

Activity:

1. Darken the room as much as possible.

2. Let each child select a small toy from the collection provided.

3. Give each child a flashlight.

4. Encourage the children to use the flashlights to create shadows of their small toys.

5. Challenge them to vary the shadows cast by asking questions like: "What happens to the shadow when you hold the light on the other side of the toy?" and "What happens to the shadow when you hold the light directly above the toy?"

6. Allow the children to exchange the toys and make different shadows.

7. They might also use pencils to trace the shadows onto paper. Then, later, match the traced shadows to the real objects.

Talk about how the shadows change shape and size, depending on where you hold the flashlight. Connect the flashlight and shadows with the Sun and the shadows it casts outdoors.

NIGHT AND DAY – "NOCTURNAL AND DIURNAL"

Objective: *To learn a couple of new words that describe when animals are most active - night or day.*

Activity:

1. Tell the children that the word ecologists use to describe animals who are the most active during the night is nocturnal. Can they think of any nocturnal animals? (cat, fox, bat, owl, moth, firefly, mouse, raccoon, etc.)
2. Tell the children that the word ecologists use to describe animals who are most active during the day is diurnal. Can they think of any diurnal animals? (dog, squirrel, chipmunk, chickadee, woodpecker, snake, etc.)

Talk about the advantages of being a diurnal animal – easier to see food (animal or plant), warmer, easier to move around. Also talk about the advantages of being a nocturnal animal – small creatures can hide in darkness, skin stays moist (important for frogs and salamanders), can avoid competition with other hunters. For example, hawks take the day shift; owls take the night.

NIGHT ANIMALS BINGO

Objective: *To learn some fun and interesting facts about some nocturnal animals.*

Materials:
- night animals bingo cards (1 per child or pair; located at end of unit)
- pennies, paper squares or other bingo markers
- night animals bingo clues (located at end of unit)

Activity:

1. Prepare the bingo cards by making copies of the card at the end of the unit. Cut out the squares and then rearrange them to make several different cards for the children to play with.
2. One at a time, read the animal clues. Ask the children to raise their hands and guess what animal you might be describing.
3. Confirm the correct answer and help the children to mark their cards, where appropriate.
4. Continue until someone gets "bingo."

Talk about the special things that many of these nocturnal animals have in common – dark coloring, big eyes, quiet behavior, etc.

ANIMAL SLEEPERS

Objective: | *To compare the different body positions that animals take when they sleep.*

Activity: | Use the following list (plus your ideas) to compare and imitate the different body positions that animals take to sleep –

- bat – upside down, with wings wrapped around like a blanket
- fox – curled up, with tail wrapped around
- horse – standing up, with head drooping (for brief rests)
- sheep – lying down, with feet tucked under body
- birds – standing on branch
- mice – lying down, surrounded by leaves and other bedding
- turtle – burrowed down into the mud

Talk about how all animals, whether nocturnal or diurnal, need a safe and comfortable place to sleep.

Outdoor Activities

SHADOW DANCING

What You Need
- a tape player that can be used outdoors
- music of your choice

What to Do
On a sunny day, take the children outside to dance with their "shadow dance partners" (their shadows). Try playing different kinds of music and asking the children to vary their dances accordingly.

SHADOW TAG

What to Do
Play an old favorite! Play a rousing game of tag, but instead of tagging someone, just touch his shadow.

TREE AND OTHER SHADOWS

What You Need
- lots of colored wooden popsicle (craft) sticks

What to Do
On a sunny day, ask the children to use a popsicle stick (stuck into the ground) to mark the top of a tree's shadow. After one hour, mark the top of the tree's shadow again. Repeat after another hour. Why is the tree's shadow moving?

Have the children find other objects that cast larger shadows (bird bath, swing set, etc.) Provide lots of popsicle sticks, so the children can mark the edges of the shadows. If you like, you can ask the children to use just one color to mark the object's shadow, then to return in an hour to mark the shadow with a new color.

Talk about how the Sun is responsible for the shadows cast. The Sun rises each morning in the east (point east) and sets in the west (point west). Shadows are smallest when the Sun's directly overhead.

THE WARMING POWER OF THE SUN

What You Need
- large and dark colored rocks – 2 per child (if necessary, paint them)
- large plastic cups filled with cold water – 2 per child
- thermometer (optional)
- a very sunny day

What to Do
Give each child two dark rocks. Instruct them to place one in the sun and the other in the shade. Now give the children the water cups and ask them to do the same with those.

Wait several hours. Then ask the children to feel the two rocks. Which is warmer? Why? Now feel the water. Which cup is warmer? If you like, you can measure the water's temperature in each location.

SHADY PATCH, SUNNY PATCH

What You Need
- carpet squares or towels (optional)

What to Do
Find a grassy area that has both sun and shadows. Begin in the shadows. Sit where all the children can see you. Encourage them to stretch out their arms in the shade. How does it feel? Then have them close their eyes and open them. Now, move to the sun. (To aid the transition, you may want to mark out a circle or semi-circle with carpet squares or towels in advance). Sit where all the children can see you. Encourage them to stretch out their arms. Do they feel the sun on their arms, on their clothing? Encourage the children to stretch out in the sun and close their eyes. Can they "see" the sun through their eyelids? Where do the children prefer to sit – in the sun or in the shade?

Language Activity / Rhyme

Sunbeam, Sunbeam, shining down,
How many _____ have you found?   *[noses, hands, etc. – avoid eyes and mouth]*
One, two, three, four...   *[count the number of noses, hands, etc. in the circle as you go around]*

Each time you complete the rhyme, go around the circle, placing a dab of "sunbeam" (children's cosmetic glitter or glitter gel) on each body part identified in the poem.

Crafts and Projects

SUNSHINE STREAMERS

What You Need
- 8 to 12 inch size embroidery or other hoops – 1 per child
- yellow, gold, and white colored ribbons (precut into 6-foot lengths)

What to Do

Help the children to fold each ribbon in half, then to attach it (using a half-hitch knot) to the circular hoop. Leave just enough space for a hand to hold the hoop. Then have the children go outdoors with their "Sun circles" and run so the ribbons trail behind (like sunrays).

• •

MANY COLORED SUNS

What You Need
- yellow construction paper – precut into 10-inch-diameter circles and long, thin triangles
- waxed paper
- colored tissue paper
- glue
- scissors

What to Do

Prepare the waxed paper by cutting it into 10-inch circles. Provide many colors of tissue paper for the children. Have them tear the paper into small pieces, which they then glue, in a slightly overlapping fashion, over the entire waxed paper circle. Next, glue the yellow circle around the outside of the colored circle. Finally, add triangular sunrays.

We Care about . . . the Sun

As the children are out exploring and enjoying the sun, remember that it is never too early to begin teaching about sun safety. Encourage families to apply sunscreen to their young children before they arrive on days with outdoor programming and encourage families to provide their children hats to wear when playing and exploring out-of-doors. Model this good behavior yourself, as the teacher.

NIGHT PICTURES

What You Need
- black construction paper (1 sheet per child)
- light colored chalk

What to Do
Use chalk to draw nighttime pictures on the black paper.

Snacks

SUN FRUIT

What You Need
- canned pineapple rings (1 per child)
- canned pineapple chunks (about 10 per child)
- canned peach halves (about 1 per child)
- knife
- plates (1 per child)
- spoons (1 per child)
- napkins or paper towels

What to Do
Prepare by cutting the peach halves into long, thin slices. Place a pineapple ring in the center of the children's plates and give them a pile of pineapple chunks and a pile of peach sticks. Encourage the children to turn their pineapple ring into the Sun by arranging the pineapple and peach shapes around it. After appropriate admiration of each of the Suns, allow the children to eat their masterpieces!

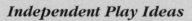

MOON COOKIES

What You Need
- sugar cookie dough
- baking sheet
- access to an oven

What to Do
Give each child a piece of cookie dough. Have them pat it into a Moon shape (either round or one of the phases). Bake and enjoy a Moon snack.

Independent Play Ideas

1. Provide flashlights and new objects for the children to use to make shadows.
2. Set up a shadow screen (a white sheet hung or stretched with a lamp behind) and let the children create shadow dramas for each other (the light should be supervised).

Book Ideas

CHILDREN'S FICTION

Gift of the Sun, by Dianne Stewart, Farrar, Straus, & Giroux, 1996 – an amusing South African tale about a man who tries to raise all sorts of animals and who always bring mischief to his family.

Like Butter on Pancakes, by Jonathan London, Viking, 1995 – describes a day with the activities graced by the Sun.

Sun Up, Sun Down, by Gail Gibbons, Harcourt Brace Jovanovich, 1983 – a young girl discovers the properties of the Sun and the many ways it affects life on Earth.

The Sun Is My Favorite Star, by Frank Asch, Gulliver Books, 2000 – celebrates the many ways life on Earth relies upon the Sun.

The Sunflower House, by Eve Bunting, Voyager Books, 1999 – a young boy tells in verse the story of the sunflower seeds he planted in a circle.

Who Gets the Sun Out of Bed?, by Nancy White Carlstrom, Little Brown, 1992 – a nicely illustrated rhythmically written book about winter's darkness.

What Can You Do in the Sun?, by Anna Grossnickle Hines, Greenwillow Books, 1999 – a board book that shows how a person can enjoy and interact with sunlight.

CHILDREN'S NONFICTION

Sunlight and Shadows, by John and Cathleen Polgreen, Doubleday, 1967 – written for older children but sections of this simply worded book can be used to describe shadows, the Sun's effect on weather and seasons, etc.

Night Creatures, Scholastic, 1994 – an introduction to some of the many nocturnal animals.

RESOURCE BOOKS FOR ADULTS AND CHILDREN

Light, by Kim Taylor, John Wiley and Sons, 1992 – photos and ideas for experiments, explanations of topics in sunlight such as eyes, shadows, and light in the sky.

Our Solar System, by Seymour Simon, Morrow Junior Books, 1992 – a science reference about the players in our solar system.

Sunshine Makes the Seasons, by Franklyn Branley, Thomas Crowell, 1974 – a good reference for adults and older children, explains the Sun's influence on seasons in a clear and simple way.

Keepers of the Night, by Michael Caduto and Joseph Bruchac, Fulcrum Press, 1994 – a combination of Native American stories and activities focused on the night world (most for older children).

The Night Book, by Pamela Hickman, Kids Can Press, 1999 – an excellent resource book for teaching about night, with clear explanations and illustrations.

CIRCLE OF THE SUN

We have been learning about day and night and the Sun and Moon. Our lessons have included shadow play, comparing the temperature of sunny and shady spots, and learning more about night animals.

Continue the Learning at Home

Take your child outside to discover some of the differences between day and night. Use the scavenger hunt below as a guide. Complete the first half during the day and the second half at night.

Day/Night Scavenger Hunt

Close your eyes. Now, keeping your eyes closed, point to the Sun.

Find your shadow. Wave to it. Does it wave back?

Find a big shadow. Stand inside it.

Watch the Sun set.

Find an animal that is active during the day

Find something that's been bleached by the Sun.

Listen for special night noises.

How many can you count?

Point to the stars.

Find the Moon.

Find a shadow cast by the Moon

Take time to sniff the night air.

Do you notice any special nighttime scents?

Produced and copyrighted by Vermont Institute of Natural Science, 2005.

Nocturnal Animals Bingo Card

Produced and copyrighted by Vermont Institute of Natural Science, 2005.

NIGHT ANIMALS BINGO CLUES

red fox: I run quickly across fields, searching for mice and other small animals to eat. I'm very quiet and sly, so I'm not often noticed as I go about my night rounds. My fur is reddish, and I look like a small dog. Every once in awhile, I sneak into a chicken coop for a tasty hen.

skunk: I eat just about anything I can find – including bird eggs, worms, and apples. I'm easily seen at night because I have a big white stripe down my back. When I'm frightened, I raise my tail and spray a foul smelling liquid.

frog: In the early spring, at night, I call "peep, peep, peep" from my pond so I can find a mate. I eat flies and other insects that I catch with my sticky tongue. I move by hopping.

spider: During the night, I'm busy spinning a web to catch tasty flies and other insects for my meals. I have eight legs. Some people are frightened of me.

owl: I'm active at night and rest during the day. When I'm hungry, I fly quietly looking for mice to eat. I grab mice with my sharp claws (called talons) and bring them back to my nest or branch to eat them. Sometimes I call "whooo."

bat: I'm a nighttime flyer, catching my insect meals on the wing. When I'm sleepy, during the day, I hang upside down to rest. Some people say I look like a mouse with wings.

worm: I like nighttime best because the hot sun of daytime makes my skin dry out. In the cool evenings, I like to wiggle through the dirt. Sometimes people put me on hooks when they go fishing.

mouse: I'm a furry little critter who comes out at night. I scurry around, looking for seeds, crackers, and other tasty foods. I like to come into people's houses in the winter time. I have a long tail, whiskers, and big ears.

bobcat: At night, I can be found quietly running around the forests, catching mice, and other small animals. I'm a wild cousin of your pet cat.

toad: I use the stretchy skin beneath my mouth to send out loud calls to my friends. Like my cousin the frog, I hop about mostly at night looking for insects. My skin has bumps on it, and I'm a good friend to have in your garden.

firefly: Because I'm so small, it's hard for me to find my mate at night. But I have a special trick – in the darkness of evening, the back of my body flashes light so my friends can find me. I'm sometimes called a lightning bug.

shrew: I'm mostly a night animal. I look a lot like a mouse, but I'm not. My pointy nose lets me poke into small tunnels in the ground, searching for worms, bugs, and other tasty foods.

slug: Some people think I'm yucky, just because my skin is slippery and slimy. In the cool night hours, I like to chew on plant leaves. But when the hot sun comes out in the morning, I hide under rocks and logs, or in other shady spots.

moth: Unlike my butterfly cousins, I like to fly around at night. I drink the sweet nectar from flowers. During the day, my brown and dull colors help me to hide on tree trunks and other places.

opossum: Although I look like a rat, I'm not. I'm a cousin of the kangaroo, and I have a pouch for my babies, too. I'm active at night, and I use my tail to hang from branches while I nibble apples and other fruits.

raccoon: I prowl around forests and neighborhoods at night. I like to eat all kinds of things – from wild apples to dog food left on somebody's porch. My black mask and striped tail make me easy to recognize.

Get Growing!

Focus: Plants need water, sunlight, air, and nutrients to grow. A seed is the beginning of most plants. There are six basic plant parts – roots, stems, leaves, flowers, fruits, and seeds.

Objective: To learn how seeds grow and to learn about the roles of different plant parts.

Extra Information for Adult Leaders

Plants need water, sunlight, air, and nutrients to grow and reproduce. Without reproduction, plants, and all other life, would cease to exist. For many plants, the first steps to successful reproduction involve fertilization and seed creation, followed by seed dispersal in an attempt to ensure that at least one seed will land in an area that will provide the proper balance of moisture, sunlight, temperature, and minerals for germination and growth. In addition to those plants that reproduce by seeds, there are some (for example, ferns) that reproduce from **spores** or, more rarely, by cloning (for example, moss).

Plants use a variety of strategies to ensure that at least some of their offspring mature and reproduce. Some plants produce tremendous numbers of seeds or spores, increasing the likelihood that at least one will survive and end up in a suitable location. Other plants put energy into wrapping their seeds in fleshy fruits that attract animals who move the seeds as they consume the fruit and excrete the seeds. Some seeds are designed to fly, other seeds are designed to float, and still others are designed to hitch a ride on a passing animal. The strategies for moving seeds are many and varied.

Seeds help increase the odds of successful germination by providing a small amount of stored energy to support the **seedling** until its leaves grow enough to produce energy on their own. Seeds contain a plant embryo and the **endosperm**, a food supply. In addition a seed is covered by a seed coat, which helps protect the embryo from disease and injury and from drying out. When the seed **germinates**, or begins to grow, the first thing to grow is the root, followed by a shoot composed of the leaves and stem.

Springtime, when everything begins to turn green and sprout, is the perfect time to explore plants and how they grow.

DIGGING IN...

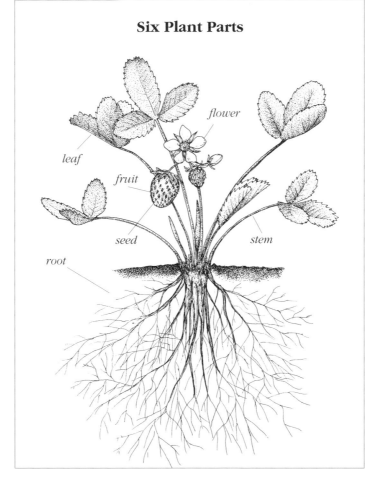

Six Plant Parts

flower

leaf

fruit

seed

stem

root

Indoor Activities

DANDY DANDELIONS

Objective: *To look closely at each and every part of a dandelion plant.*

Materials:
- *The Dandelion Seed* by Joseph Anthony
- several, live dandelion plants, with roots intact, some with flowers, some with ripened seed heads
- milkweed seed pod (optional)
- magnifying lenses

Activity:
1. First, read *The Dandelion Seed* aloud. Encourage the children to talk about the many places the dandelion seed traveled. Do they think this is a realistic story?
2. Now, in pairs, have the children closely examine the real dandelion plants. Help the children to use descriptive terms like "roots," "stem," "leaves," and "flower." Notice similarities and differences among the plants.
3. Finally, give the children several dandelion plants that have already gone to seed (fluffy seed heads). Use the magnifying lenses to examine the seed heads. Outdoors, invite the children to blow the seeds aloft.
4. Extension: Have the children look at the milkweed seed pod. How are the milkweed seeds similar to the dandelion's?

Talk about the end of the story, where the seed reaches the soil and soon sprouts into a new plant. To sprout properly, a seed needs water, soil, and sunlight to continue to grow. Also, talk about how the dandelion seed travels on the wind (like a parachute). If the seed did not travel, it might be unable to compete with the larger, more established plants nearby.

. . . .

START WITH A SEED

Objective: *To collect, count, and compare seeds from some of the foods children eat.*

Materials:
- seeds
- envelopes
- magnifying lenses

Activity:
1. With their parents' help, ask the children to collect as many seeds as they can from the fruits they eat for one week. Parents can help their children to collect, wash, dry, and store the seeds in labeled envelopes (example: "apple seeds").
2. At the end of the week, gather together to share the seeds. You might do some of the following:
   - look closely at the seeds collected
   - count the total number of seeds collected
   - count the number of seeds you've collected from each fruit type
   - compare the sizes, colors, and other characteristics of the seeds
   - list the names of all who've eaten apples (pears, cucumbers, etc.)
   - draw some of the seeds
   - weigh the seeds
   - try sprouting and growing a few of the seeds

Talk about the seeds you've collected and how, if conditions are just right, they might each grow into a new plant capable of producing many fruits, each with many seeds.

SEED SPROUTS

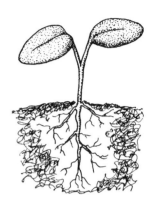

Objective: *To sprout some edible seeds, then enjoy eating them.*

Materials:
- quart jar (1 or more)
- loosely woven cloth piece (to cover the top of the jar)
- rubber band (to hold cloth over jar opening)
- alfalfa, mung bean, sunflower or other seeds suitable for *sprouting*

Activity:
1. Place 2 to 3 tablespoons of seeds in the jar. Add water to cover them completely. Let it sit for about 24 hours.
2. Cover the jar opening with cloth piece, and strain out water.
3. Rinse seeds again with fresh water, then strain again. Lie the jar on its side.
4. Continue rinsing and straining daily until sprouts are enough to eat. Rinse thoroughly before eating. Serve on cucumber sandwiches or any way the children like. (You can also purchase sprouted seeds.)

Talk about the speed with which the seeds sprout. Look closely at the tiny seeds, as well as the sprouts.

WHERE DID IT GROW?

Objective: *To compare where some of our common vegetables grow – above or below ground.*

Materials:
- samples of several vegetables (potato, carrot, radish, lettuce, cucumber, tomato)
- paper or felt board depicting above and beneath the soil level
- paper or felt pieces depicting several vegetables that grow above and below ground
- book *Tops and Bottoms* by Janet Stevens

Activity:
1. Begin by reading *Tops and Bottoms*. Look at the drawings. Review some of the "tops" vegetables – the ones that grow above ground. Also review some of the "bottoms" vegetables – the ones that grow below ground.
2. Now look at the vegetables you've gathered. Ask the children, where do each of these grow – above or below ground?
3. Think of some other vegetables and fruits – where do they grow?
4. Use the felt or paper visual aids to supplement your discussion.

Talk about who likes to eat each vegetable or fruit. The vegetables that grow underground are the roots of the plants. Like all roots, their job is to gather water and nutrients from the soil and to store energy for the plant (in the form of root mass).

SIX PLANT PARTS

Objective: | *To introduce the six basic plant parts.*

Materials:
- strawberry plant illustration (see page 275)
- samples of foods people eat that come from each of the six plant parts (carrot, celery, lettuce, broccoli, apple, sunflower seeds)
- magazine photos of a variety of plant foods
- plant part category cards (see page 285)

Activity:
1. Show the strawberry plant illustration to the children, pointing out the six parts of the plant, as well as their functions:
   - Roots soak up water and nutrients from underground.
   - Stems (trunk) hold up/supports the rest of the plant.
   - Leaves collect sunlight to produce food (sugars) for the plant's growth.
   - Flowers attract insects and other pollinators to produce seeds.
   - Fruits hold the seeds.
   - Seeds allow for a new plant to grow.
2. Explain to the children that most of the foods we eat come from these plant parts. Show the category cards, and see if the children can tell you which plant parts they represent. Using the category cards sort the vegetables and fruits.
3. Using the magazine pictures and category cards, continue to examine the plant origins of the foods we eat and sort them into plant part categories.

Talk about other foods we eat and where they come from.

• •

CELERY'S A STEM

Objective: | *To conduct a very simple experiment to show how celery stalks (stems) carry water to the leaves.*

Materials:
- 2 or 3 celery stalks with leaves (or white carnation or Queen Anne's lace flower)
- sharp knife
- 1 jar per stem
- water
- food coloring (1 color per stem)

Activity:
1. Cut the base off of each plant stem used.
2. Fill one jar with plain water.
3. Mix a different color water in each remaining jar.
4. Place one stem in each jar.
5. Let sit for at least 24 hours.
6. Allow the children to examine the changes that have occurred in each stem and leaves/flowers. You may want to cut the stems lengthwise to allow the children to examine the inside.

Talk about how the stem has pulled the colored water up to the leaves and flowers, changing their appearance. Ask the children why the stem in the clear water still looks the same (the water was not colored). Add color, wait a day, and see what happens. (You may want to cut the bottom of the stem off again to ensure the water will flow freely into the stem.)

BEAN SPROUT

Objective: | *To study a seed as it sprouts and grows into a plant.*

Materials: |
- plastic, zip-top baggies (1 per child)
- bean seeds
- paper towels
- water sprayer bottle
- duct tape
- soil and small planting containers (optional)

Activity: |
1. Provide a baggie, paper towel, and bean seed for each child.
2. Ask the children to dampen their paper towels, wrap them around the bean seed, then place them inside the baggies. (Do not seal the bag.)
3. Place the baggies in a warm, relatively dark place until they sprout.
4. After the seeds have sprouted, continue to keep them damp, but tape the baggies to a sunny window. (Also, allow the sprouting bean stem to escape from the paper towel and baggie, as it grows.)
5. Help the children to watch and care for their seeds daily.
6. Extension: Plant the sprouts in pots with soil and keep watered.

Talk about the changes the bean seed goes through as it grows.

WHAT DO PLANTS NEED?

Objective: | *To learn about the things plants need to grow (sun, air, water) and to find out what happens when one or more of these important things is missing.*

Materials: |
- 4 small paper cups or an egg carton cut into cups
- potting soil
- water sprayer bottle
- packet of marigold or radish seeds

Activity: |
1. Number the cups and help the children to prepare and care for the seeds in each cup as follows:

   Cup #1 (no soil) – Put two seeds in an empty cup. Water the seeds by spraying them twice daily. Place the cup on a sunny windowsill.

   Cup #2 (no water) – Fill the cup with potting soil, bury two seeds in the soil. Place on a sunny windowsill. Do not water.

   Cup #3 (no sun) – Fill the cup with potting soil, bury two seeds in the soil. Give the seeds water by spraying them twice daily. Place the cup in a dark cupboard or closet.

   Cup #4 (has everything) – Fill the cup with potting soil, bury two seeds in the soil. Give the seeds water by spraying them twice daily. Place the cup on a sunny windowsill.
2. Encourage the children to observe and care for the seeds daily.
3. After two weeks, compare the four different cups.
4. Extension: Transfer the plants to the outdoors. If you've grown marigolds, let them flower and produce seeds. Save the seeds to plant again next spring.

Talk about how seeds need several things to grow big. While seeds can sprout in darkness, the young leaves soon need sunlight to grow. The roots need nutrients from the soil. The seed needs water to sprout, and the plant needs water to continue growing.

Outdoor Activities

PLANTS ALL AROUND US

What to Do

Take the children for a walk outdoors. Spend your time and attention looking – really looking – at the plants around you. Where are the leaves on a pine tree? What do the flowers look like before they bloom? What do the roots of a wildflower look like?

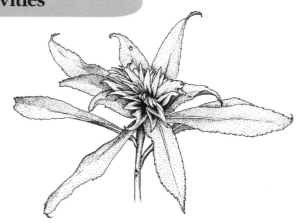

GRASS PATTERNS

What You Need
- hard, heavy paper
- scissors
- weights, such as rocks

What to Do

Cut some geometric shapes from hard, heavy paper (10 or so inches across). Put them outside on some green grass. Weight them down with a rock and keep them in place for several days. Check to see what has happened to the grass beneath, now that it's not getting any sunlight.

CHANGING TREES

What to Do

In the early spring (March and April), choose a shrub or low-branching tree to observe carefully with the children. Notice how the flower and leaf buds swell over time, how the leaves unfurl, what happens to the flowers after they bloom, and more.

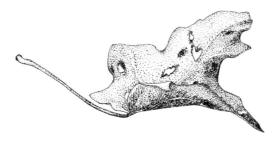

We Care about . . . Growing Plants

When young plants are newly sprouted, they are very tender. Teach children to avoid stepping on newly-planted grass and to stay on designated pathways where appropriate. If possible, plant your classroom plants outside of the schoolyard and allow the children to participate in their care.

Language Activity / Rhyme

Seeds in a row,   *[spread fingers on left hand, pretend to plant seeds between]*
How do they grow?
Roots grow down   *[point down between two fingers]*
Stems grow up.   *[point up between two fingers]*
Leaves sprout.   *[hold closed fists together then open them]*
Flowers come out.

Crafts and Projects

GROWING GRASS PATTERNS

What You Need
- bowls (1 per child)
- potting soil
- cups for scooping soil
- small (3 or 5 oz) cups (1 per child)
- grass seed
- popsicle sticks (1 per child)
- spray bottles filled with water
- permanent marker (to label bowls)

What to Do

Give each child a bowl labeled with their name. Help the children fill their bowls with potting soil. Once full, encourage the children to gently pat their soil smooth, then to use the wide side of their popsicle sticks to draw a simple pattern in the soil. This could be a shape, a squiggly line, dots, a letter. It may help to demonstrate an example to the children.

Once the drawing is complete, give each child a cup containing grass seed. Have the children carefully drop pinches of grass seed into the patterns they have created. Finally, sprinkle enough dirt to cover the seed over each bowl. Spray water over the soil and put the bowls in a sunny spot. Continue to keep the soil moist by spraying it every day or every few days. Watch for the seeds to sprout, then admire the patterns the children have created in the soil.

BEAN MOSAIC

What You Need
- variety of beans and seeds of different colors
- shoebox lid or stiff cardboard piece
- paint or paper (if necessary to cover up writing)
- glue

What to Do

Provide children with a variety of beans and seeds of different colors, shapes, and sizes. Give each child a shoebox lid (or other stiff cardboard piece). Cover any printing with paint or paper. Then use glue to create a mosaic picture with the beans.

BEAN MARACAS

What You Need
- paper towel rolls
- tape
- beans
- paint, cloth, and/or paper

What to Do
Put some beans inside a paper towel roll and cover the ends with tape. Decorate with paint, cloth, or otherwise. Shake and make some music!

SUNFLOWERS

What You Need
- paper plates (1 per child)
- yellow paint
- paint brushes
- scissors
- sunflower seeds
- glue
- green construction paper
- green tongue depressor (1 per child)

What to Do
Paint a paper plate yellow. Cut notches around the outside to form the petals. In the center, glue sunflower seeds. Add a green tongue depressor for the stem. Leaves may be made from green construction paper.

PLANT PAINT BRUSHES

What You Need
- flower heads (marigolds and dandelions work well)
- plant leaves
- tempera paints
- paper (at least 1 sheet per child)

What to Do
Collect leaves and flower heads from flowers past their prime. Marigolds and dandelions work well. Mix up some tempera paints and have the children use the plant parts as paint brushes.

Snack

PLANT PARTS FINGER SALAD

What You Need
- large lettuce leaves
- thin celery sticks
- thin carrot rounds
- cut tomato pieces and/or cucumber pieces
- small chunks of broccoli
- raisins
- paper plates (1 per type of plant and 1 per child)
- cutting board and knife (for cutting)
- 1 or 2 types of thick salad dressing for dipping, Russian or Ranch (optional)

What to Do

Wash and prepare each fruit/vegetable and put it onto separate plates. Let children help where possible. Gather the children together and help them identify each plant part represented (leaf-lettuce, celery-stem, carrots-roots, tomato/cucumber-fruit and seeds, broccoli-flowers, raisins-fruit). Next, allow each child to take a plate and to create their own "finger salad." Put a piece of lettuce on the bottom of the plate and scoops of various ingredients on top (encourage the children to try at least one new vegetable). If desired, give each child a scoop of thick salad dressing on the side of their plates for dipping. Ask the children about the vegetables they are tasting. How's that stem? How about those cucumber seeds?

Independent Play Ideas

1. Fill your sand table (or other large container) with potting soil. Provide plastic flowers for the children to "plant" there.

2. Provide lots of seeds for the children to pour, sift, layer into plastic jars, etc.

3. Leave plant part category cards out for children to use to categorize play food (see end of unit).

Book Ideas

CHILDREN'S FICTION

Eve and Smitty, by Michelle Edwards, Lothrop, Lee, & Shepard, 1994 – a charming and quirky story about two friends with different styles but similar interests in gardening.

Flower Garden, by Eve Bunting, Voyager Books, 1994 – a lovely story about a child and father who purchase and plant a window box garden for the child's mother.

One Bean, by Anne Rockwell, Walker & Company, 1998 – two children plant a bean seed and watch it grow to produce flowers and, ultimately, another bean.

The Apple Pie Tree, by Zoe Hall, The Blue Sky Press, 1996 – an attractive book about an apple tree and how it changes through the seasons.

The Carrot Seed, by Ruth Krauss, HarperCollins, 1945 – a classic story about a boy who awaits the sprouting of his carrot seed, despite the doubts of his family.

The Dandelion Seed, by Joseph Anthony, Dawn Publications, 1997 – an imaginative and beautiful tale about a dandelion seed's travels.

Tops and Bottoms, by Janet Stevens, Harcourt Brace, 1995 – an amusing story about a tricky rabbit who takes advantage of some available garden space to grow a variety of vegetables.

CHILDREN'S NONFICTION

Eyewitness Books: Plant, by David Burnie, Alfred A. Knopf, 1989 – extraordinary photos, a fine introduction to the lives of plants.

Pumpkin Pumpkin, by Jeanne Titherington, Scholastic, 1986 – with minimal words, this story follows the life cycle of a pumpkin, from seed to pumpkin and seed again.

The Tiny Seed, by Eric Carle, Picture Book Studio, 1987 – a simple description of a plant through the year's seasons.

RESOURCE BOOKS FOR ADULTS AND CHILDREN

Dig and Sow! How Do Plants Grow?, by Janice Lobb, Kingfisher, 2000 – a fun reference book answers all kinds of questions about plants and includes experiments, even jokes!

Growing Radishes and Carrots, by Faye Bolton and Dave Snowball, Bookshelf Publishing, 1986 – a cute little book that describes the steps required to grow radishes and carrots, includes "pop up" carrots and radishes.

How a Seed Grows, by Helene Jordan, Scholastic, 1992 – introduces the purpose and variety of seeds, then gives step-by-step instructions for growing bean seeds

The Marshall Cavendish Science Project Book of Plants, by Steve Parker, Marshall Cavendish, 1989 – a good plant and experiment reference book for teachers.

The Plant-and-Grow Project Book, by Ulla Dietl, Sterling, 1992 – full of project ideas for bottle gardens, lemon plants, even banana trees.

Plant Parts Category Cards

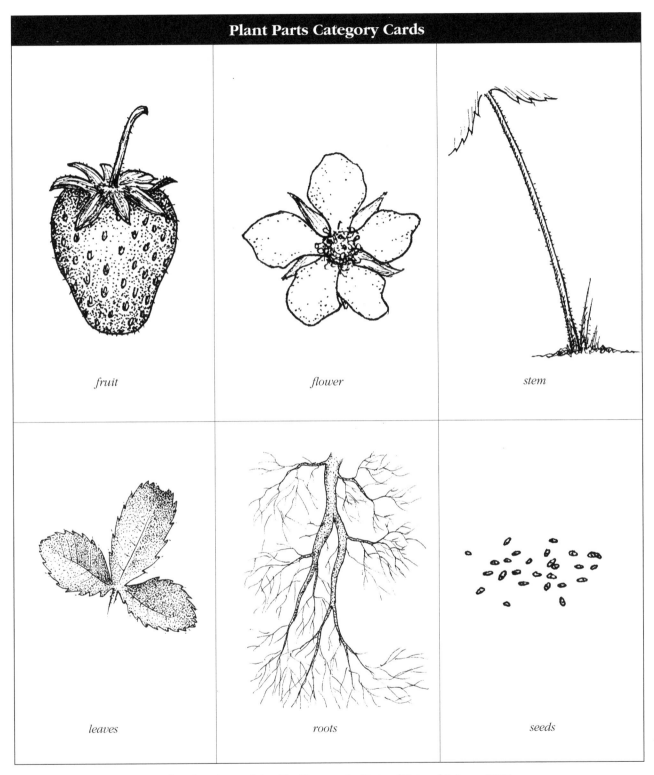

fruit

flower

stem

leaves

roots

seeds

Produced and copyrighted by Vermont Institute of Natural Science, 2005.

Small Wonders at Home

GET GROWING

We have been learning about how seeds grow and the roles of different plant parts.

Continue the Learning at Home

Help your child cut out the cards below and put them in order. Take time to ask questions and to talk about what you see in the different pictures.

Sunflower Sequencing Cards

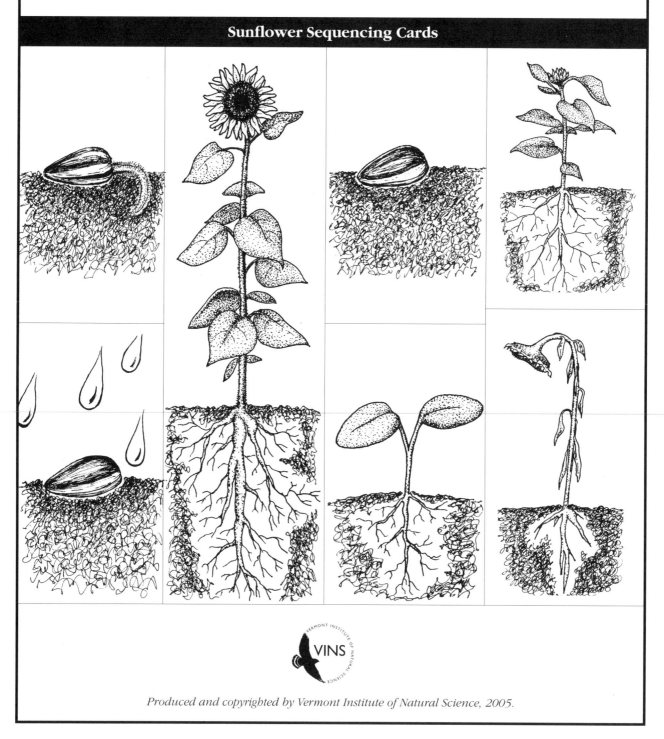

Produced and copyrighted by Vermont Institute of Natural Science, 2005.

Nature and Us

Focus: Virtually everything we use in our everyday lives is connected to nature in one way or another. Responsible use of our natural resources is important for everyone, including young children.

Objective: To increase children's awareness of simple things they can do to care for nature and to increase their awareness of how nature is a part of their lives.

Extra Information for Adult Leaders

Everything we use in our daily lives, and everything we produce, comes from the earth and has to end up someplace on the earth. People have always relied upon the earth for food, fiber, fuel, and shelter, and we have always produced waste. For thousands of years, Native Americans living along the Atlantic coast feasted on seafood found in mudflats and tide pools and tossed clam and mussel shells into piles called **middens** that we now unearth as evidence of their seasonal camps. We are not the first to produce waste or the first to affect our surroundings by living our daily lives.

However, the quantity of earth's resources that humans in the developed world consume today far surpasses what humans have consumed at any other time in history. Learning the origins of items we need or want and how these items are made is interesting and informs our choices as consumers. Understanding how to reduce our use of resources and how to properly manage materials we no longer want or can no longer use is a worthy lesson in citizenship, no matter what a person's age.

Humans and all other species depend upon the earth's natural processes and materials, or **natural resources**. Plants and animals that we harvest are considered in the group of **renewable resources**. Though a resource might be renewable, it may lose productivity and health if over-consumed. For example, forests provide habitat for animals, as well as trees for people to turn into paper, homes, and other wood products. Even rubber, cinnamon, and some pharmaceuticals originate in the forest. Forests that are entirely cleared, or divided by roads and development, will no longer provide natural habitat for wildlife. It is important to harvest and use renewable resources wisely with the best practices known to limit negative effects and ensure future yields.

DIGGING IN...

Nonrenewable resources are resources that took millions or billions of years to produce. These include fossil fuels, metallic minerals such as iron or copper, and nonmetallic minerals such as clay, sand, or phosphorous. Once a nonrenewable resource is used, it cannot be regenerated. Sand, deposited on lake or ocean beaches or from glacial deposits, is mined and then heated to extremely high temperatures and manufactured into glass for windows or bottles. These bottles can be recycled and manufactured into a similar or different product, but they will never again be sand. Similarly, iron ore can be removed from the earth and **smelted** in plants that use enormous amounts of energy to separate the high quality ore from the remains or tailings. The ore is then used to make products we use every day, such as bicycles, cars, and planes. These items can again be recycled but not replanted or turned back into ore – not, at least, in a time frame comprehensible to the human mind.

When we finish eating a meal, we often need to throw out the left over scraps of food. If the milk carton has been emptied or paper towels or napkins used, they must be disposed of too. Where do these things go?

Food products can, and should, be **composted.** Nearly 75% of a typical American's household food waste is easily composted. Composting is simple, cheap, and good for the environment. It can be easily done in a backyard bin. A well made compost pile contains a combination of organic materials that are high in carbon, such as leaves or sawdust, and materials high in nitrogen, such as table scraps and lawn clippings.

Waste that can't be composted can still be handled responsibly. Some items, such as wood, cloth and paper, are **biodegradable** and break down over time but are not good to put into a compost bin. Many plastics, metals, glass, and paper can be recycled into items that are useful once again. Items that may

have come to the end of their original use, such as magazines, the odd sock or button, can be reused as craft items, containers, or construction materials.

Young children can do a lot to care for the world around them. They can start by becoming aware of how to care for their indoor and outdoor spaces. Teaching about the origins of natural resources and the waste stream are excellent opportunities for practicing earth-friendly actions. Encourage the children to recycle and purchase items that have been recycled, are recyclable, or have minimal packaging. Your local solid waste district can help provide you with information and resources for setting up recycling and compost programs in your classroom and at home.

Indoor Activities

CARING FOR OUR SPACE

Objective: *To become aware of how important it is to care for our special places.*

Activity:
1. Find a space within your school that can be left messy overnight. It could be a craft room, the play area, or the entire classroom.
2. Toward the end of the day, allow children to go about their usual activities but do not say anything about cleaning up.
3. After they leave the school, leave the scraps of paper on the floor, misplaced toys out, etc.
4. The following day, as the students come into the classroom, gather them together.
5. Ask them "What happened to our room!?"

Talk about how the classroom is a special place for the children. As a group, you all work together to pick up things and put them away to make the room nice for the next day. If we do not care for our special places, pretty soon, they will no longer be nice places to play in. As a group clean up the area before beginning the day. Talk about where the different things "go." (Paper into recycling, toys on shelves, etc.) Everything has a place.

• •

WHAT DO WE THROW AWAY?

Objective: *To become more aware of the garbage we each create daily and to encourage recycling.*

Materials:
• trash bags (at least 2)
• tarp or blanket
• plastic baggies for leftover food

Activity:
1. One morning, tell the group that you are going to save all the trash the children throw away. Set aside one spot for "clean waste" and one spot for "germy waste" (tissues and used paper towels – these will not be used in the activity). Even save leftovers from snack but seal them in plastic bags to avoid creating a big mess. (Extension: You may wish to add some of the waste you create while at home, to add some variety to what the children examine, or you

may want to send each child home with a garbage bag and a set of instructions to continue to collect waste from home and bring it back the next day.)

2. The next day, pile all the trash together in a pile on the tarp.

3. Take a look at your garbage. Ask the children if they know where their trash and garbage goes after they put it in the wastebasket. (Depending on your community, your waste is probably dealt with by some combination of landfilling, incineration, composting, and/or recycling.)

4. Ask the children what they can do to make the pile smaller. What items can be used to create something new (crafts, building materials, and so-on)? Pile these pieces together and set the pile aside.

5. Check with your local solid waste district about which items can be recycled in your area. Not all items – even ones with a recycling symbol – will be accepted everywhere. Show children the recycling symbol on the items. Join the children in hunting for and setting aside materials that can be recycled in a second pile.

6. If a composting facility is available, set aside plant-based food materials in a third pile.

7. Take a look at your pile of throw-aways. Point out that our "dump" has become smaller now.

Talk about the ways the children have decreased the amount of waste they throw away. The children can reduce their waste by using only what they need: using one paper towel to dry their hands, saving scraps of paper for future art projects, or choosing items with minimal packaging or use reusable containers for packaging rather than throw-aways. The children can remember to separate items that their community recycles, and they can reuse items for future projects.

COMPOST JAR

Objective: *To watch, first-hand, how waste decays.*

Materials:
- a large, clear jar with a screw-on lid (food service operations are a good source of large jars)
- biodegradable waste items, such as paper and snack scraps
- nonbiodegradable waste items, such as plastic wrappers and crushed aluminum cans

Activity:
1. With the children, squash and jam as much waste as possible into the jar. Make sure a variety of biodegradable and non-biodegradable items are visible through the side of the jar.

2. Tightly screw the lid on the jar and set it somewhere where the children can easily view the jar but where it can sit undisturbed.

3. Observe what happens over a period of weeks – or even for the rest of the year!

Talk about the progression of decay that you observe. The food items will decay first, changing color as they mold, and finally leaving a space where they once were in the jar. The metal and plastic items, however, will remain pretty much unchanged, just as they remain in nature for a long, long time (an aluminum can takes over 100 years to decompose; a plastic cup can take more than 50 years to decompose).

SAND TO GLASS

Objective: *To learn about how glass is made.*

Materials:
- book *From Sand to Glass* by Gerry Ellis
- several glass items of assorted colors (to sort into colors)

Activity:
1. As a group, sort the glass into colors. What is the group's favorite color of glass? Ask the children if they know where glass comes from.
2. Read the book *From Sand to Glass* to the children and discuss the process of turning sand into glass. (If you can, it would be wonderful to visit a glass blower!)
3. Ask the children, "Where does glass come from?" (sand) Where have the children found sand before? (beaches, streams) If the sandbox is mentioned, you can talk about how people make sandboxes by using sand from places like beaches to fill the sandbox.
4. Ask the children if glass looks like sand. (no) What did the people do to change the sand into glass? (made it very hot and melted it)

Talk about how sand is a "natural resource," a material that comes from nature that people can change and use to make new things. Once sand is turned into glass, it cannot be made into sand again, but old glass can be melted and turned into new glass.

THERE'S NATURE IN THERE!

Objective: *To learn that there is nature in many items we use every day.*

Materials:
- matching cards on page 291 and 292 (1 for each picture)
  - tree – book (red border)
  - sand – glass bottle (blue border)
  - iron ore – tricycle (yellow border)
  - sheep – sweater (orange border)
- markers to add borders to the matching cards

Activity:
1. To prepare, cut out the matching cards and add the corresponding colored border.
2. Gather the children into a circle.
3. Spread the set of cards in the center of the circle.
4. Ask the children if they can find items that are made by people. (book, bottle, can, sweater)
5. Can they find items that are found in nature? (tree, sand, iron ore, sheep)
6. Now have the children help you match the cards according to their colored borders.
7. Finally, take a tour around your room and find other items that come from nature. As you find the items, name their source. (For example, if the children point to glass in the window, say "sand.")

Talk about how each of the "people-made" materials came from a natural resource.

There's Nature in There

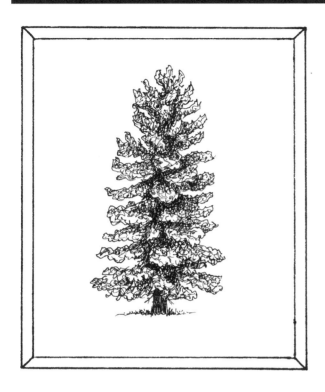

Elmer's Guide to
Animal Tracks

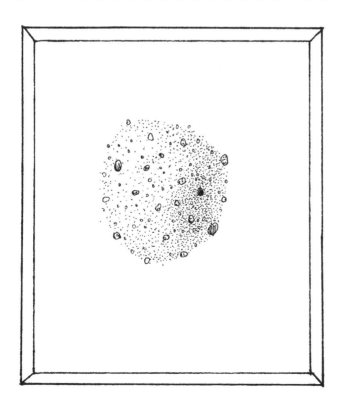

Apple Cider Vi

Produced and copyrighted by Vermont Institute of Natural Science, 2005.

There's Nature in There

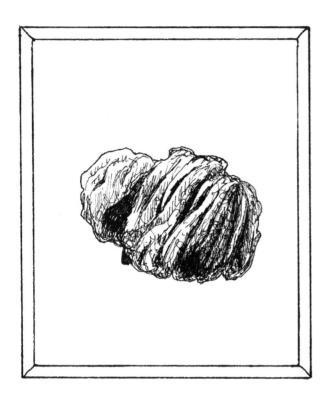

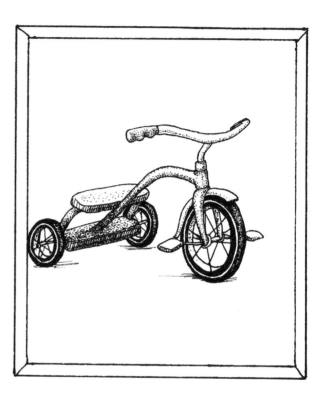

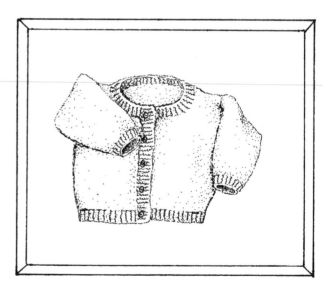

Produced and copyrighted by Vermont Institute of Natural Science, 2005.

USE THEM AGAIN!

Objective: *To recognize earth-friendly alternatives to throw-aways.*

Materials:
- paper napkin and cloth napkin
- paper towels and cloth rag
- foam cup and ceramic/plastic cup
- paper lunch bag and reusable lunch bag/box
- individually wrapped crackers and crackers in reusable container
- juice box and juice in reusable bottle

Activity:
1. Explain to the children that one way they can produce less trash is to reuse items over and over again.
2. On one side of the room (or outdoors), place all the single-use items. On the other side, place the reusable alternatives.
3. Working in pairs, have the children first choose one single-use item, then go to the other side of the room to find its earth-friendly alternative choice.
4. Finish by asking the children to share what they've chosen.

Talk about the natural resources required to produce the single-use items (trees, oil, metal, etc.). Make a pile of the paper products, foam cup, cracker wrapper, and juice box. Look at all the waste the children have saved by choosing things they can use over and over!

THAT'S NOT JUNK!

Objective: *To establish a special place in the room where parents and children can sort and save discarded materials to reuse for future art projects, science experiments, etc.*

Materials:
- variety of shoeboxes
- samples of items to be collected and reused for projects (examples: magazine pictures, packing peanuts, ribbon, paper towel rolls, scraps of cloth, plastic containers, egg cartons, old greeting cards).
- crayons and markers
- paints, glitter glue, additional decorative materials (optional)
- strong craft glue
- scissors

Activity:
1. Tell the group that the class is going to start collecting materials to use for class projects and individual creations.
2. Show them examples of the types of craft materials you will be collecting. Talk about the different ways you could re-use the materials, turning them into something new.
3. In small groups, decorate one shoe box for each type of material that you will be collecting. Be sure to incorporate the material to be collected in your decoration. For example, if you are collecting paper tubes, decorate pieces of tube and glue them onto the outside of the box. The magazine box will have magazine pictures on the outside, ribbon box ribbons, and so-on.
4. Place the finished boxes on a shelf that is accessible to the children.
5. Send a note home with the children, explaining to their families the types of re-usable materials you will be collecting for projects.
6. When a child brings material from home to school, allow them to sort the materials into the appropriate boxes.

Talk about how instead of throwing some materials away, we can use them again to create new things. One person's "trash" can be another's "treasure." Think of creative ways to reuse trash items.

Outdoor Activities

NATURE CHAINS

What You Need
- several plastic darning needles
- yarn
- access to leaves and other natural materials for decorating
- pipe cleaners
- scissors
- hot glue or other strong craft glue
- a sheltered place outdoors, or a corner of the room to hang the chain

What to Do
In your school yard, a nearby natural area, or park, have the children pick up some of the prettiest things from nature. Don't forget to follow park rules for collecting! If the school yard has limited access to natural items, have children collect them from home the day before the activity or augment your supply with some leaves, seeds, pinecones, and sticks from home. As the children bring their "finds" back to you, help them string the leaves together using the needle and yarn. (It works well to make a stitch across the face of each leaf). Attach items that do not thread well (sticks, pinecones, acorns) with a pipe cleaner hook or a bit of glue. Finally, hang your chain in a corner of your room or a sheltered place outdoors.

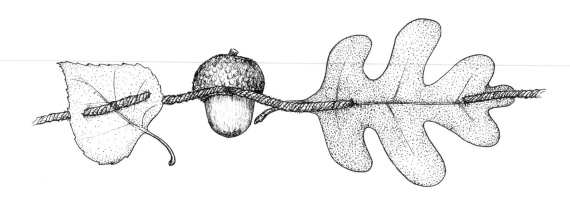

COMPOST IT AWAY!

What You Need
- a collection of plant-based food waste (banana peels, apple cores, bread crusts, etc.)
- some noncompostable items like a tin can, a plastic bag, or a foam cup
- a couple of plastic onion bags

What to Do
Find a cool, shady place. Dig several holes there. Now place the food waste items in one onion bag; the tin can, baggie, and cup in the other. Tell the children that you're going to bury these items in the dirt, keep them moist and shaded, and dig them up and check them again in two weeks. What do the children predict will happen to these items? Have the children cover the bags with dirt, water them lightly each day, and finally check them in two weeks. Make connections to composting food waste and how other materials can stay around for a long time. Even food should not be just thrown out onto the ground. It should be put in a special place for composting because people food is often not good for animals to eat.

• •

WHAT DOESN'T BELONG HERE?

What You Need
- 10 small household items (pencil, spoon, comb, wrapper, tissues, lollipop stick, popsicle stick, etc.)
- path or area to distribute items

What to Do
Prepare for this activity by selecting ten small household items (pencil, spoon, comb, etc.). In a nearby natural area, find a short path and place the items within eyesight of the path – left and right, on the ground, in low branches, etc.

Now challenge the children to walk the trail, searching for items that don't belong there. If you're in a group, encourage the children to silently count the items as they spot them but do not say anything aloud and do not pick up the items.

When everyone's finished, go back over the trail and pick up the items. Ask the children if they belong in nature. (No.) Why? (These are items that people made and that people should take care of.)

Language Activity / Poem

I once had a lollipop
and took a lick
and a lick and a lick
until I found the stick.

I thought to myself,
"Oh No! I don't know!
Where, on earth, does my
sticky stick go?"

I tried my pocket
but that wouldn't do.
My quarter became
All covered in goo.

I tried to give it
to my friend named Stan
but he wouldn't take it –
and I understand.

Another person's stick
that has already been licked
is definitely not
a very nice gift.

The only choice left
was to come up with a plan
I looked all around for
a nice garbage can.

Left. Right.
Up. Down.
Sure enough a can
was found.

Into the can
I placed my stick
I didn't even take
one final lick.

Crafts and Projects

FAVORITE NATURE ACTIVITIES

What You Need
- paper (at least 1 sheet per child)
- drawing materials
- construction paper (variety of colors)
- glue or glue sticks

What to Do

Gather the children together. Ask the group about some of their favorite things to do in nature. These could be stomping in puddles, listening to birds, camping with family, walking in the park. Have each child draw a picture of one of their favorite nature activities. Label each child's picture as they finish and frame the drawing with construction paper in the child's choice of color. When the pictures are finished, hang them near your nature chain (see the activity, "Nature Chains" on page 294).

NAPKINS TO USE AGAIN AND AGAIN

What You Need
- scraps of cotton fabric
- fabric paint
- paint brushes
- paint trays

What to Do

Using scrap pieces of cotton fabric, make your own reusable cloth napkins. Mark each napkin with the child's initials.

We Care about . . . Our World

Many communities, cities, and even some states have a green-up day – a day to gather volunteers to help make public areas more beautiful. This can include picking up litter from roadsides or parks, raking leaves, painting, or even planting **bulbs** or flowers. The best green-up days are community events, with time allowed for social gatherings around a coffee break or picnic lunch. Think about how you can have a green-up day at your school or involve your school and families in a community effort. Young children, if supervised, can help pick up litter, help put plants in the ground, and even paint. Be sure everyone washes their hands when the tasks are finished. As an alternative, you could gather students and families to help prepare the school yard for winter and plant spring bulbs (daffodil bulbs work well, as they are hardy and unattractive to rodents, who might otherwise eat them). The children will love anticipating their efforts through the winter and seeing the results in the spring. With a little coordination, families can even get involved with caring for or "adopting" sections of a garden or an individual planter. Don't forget to allow a time for celebration during your green-up event.

TOAD HOMES

What You Need
- old plastic flowerpots with holes in the bottom (1 per child)
- saw or utility knife
- acrylic paint
- paint brushes
- paint trays
- smocks

What to Do
Toads are wonderful creatures to attract into our yards – they're harmless and cute. They can be gently held; they eat harmful insects. One thing toads need is a place to get out of the hot sun. A flowerpot can be used to create a shady spot for the toads.

To prepare, carefully cut a two to three inch, U-shaped notch in the rim of each pot. Now have the children paint the pots. Use acrylic paints to ensure that the paint will survive the weather. When the children are finished, bring the pots outside and turn them rim-side down in an area that will remain undisturbed. Put a rock on top of the pots to ensure that they will not turn over. With a little luck, a toad will soon visit the shady shelters.

Snack

ENJOYING "PACKAGE INCLUDED" FOODS

What You Need
- a variety of fresh fruits: bananas, pears, apples, oranges, clementines, etc.
- knife
- surface for cutting
- a package of animal crackers
- paper towels

What to Do
Show the children the package of animal crackers. Ask the children why they think the crackers are in the package. (to keep them clean, to keep them fresh, to keep them from making a mess, to keep them from breaking) Show the children the fruit. Do the fruits have packages? (yes, peels!) Ask which nature packages we eat. (apple skin and pear skin) Ask which nature packages we do not eat. (orange and banana peels)

Enjoy a snack of fruit and animal crackers, then dispose of the packaging correctly (in the garbage or the compost). You may want to create a compost jar from the leftover cracker wrappers and fruit peels (see the activity "Compost Jar" on page 289).

Independent Play Idea
Make the contents of the junk sorters (see activity "That's Not Junk!")
as well as a few other craft materials, such as glue, crayons, and paper,
available to the children during independent play time. You will be
amazed at the ways they play and create with the unusual items they
find in the boxes.

Book Ideas

CHILDREN'S FICTION

The Earth and I, by Frank Asch, Harcourt, 1994 – a boy explores how and why the earth is his friend.

Just a Dream, by Chris Van Allsburg, Houghton Mifflin, 1990 – a strikingly beautiful and haunting story about what the future might hold.

The Lorax, by Dr. Suess, Random, 1971 – Dr. Suess tackles the problem of saving trees.

Miss Rumphius, by Barbara Cooney, Puffin Books, 1982 – a lovely and inspirational story about an adventurous girl/woman who strives to "make the world a better place."

Mother Earth, by Nancy Luenn, Simon & Schuster, 1995 – a visually stunning book about mother nature and the earth.

Mowing, by Jessie Haas, Greenwillow, 1994 – a young girl watches for animals in the grass as her grandfather mows a field.

This Is Our Earth, by Laura Lee Benson, Charlesbridge, 1994 – a two-level book that celebrates the marvelous diversity of life in North America and beyond.

Wanda's Roses, by Pat Brisson, Boyds Mills Press, 1994 – a heart warming story of hope, faith, and community, as well as an introduction to plant stewardship.

CHILDREN'S NONFICTION

Each Living Thing, by Joanne Ryder, Scholastic, 2000 – a beautiful and simple book, offering an awareness of all creatures and advising children to "take care of them."

From Sand to Glass, by Gerry Ellis, Scholastic, 1995 – a photo-essay book describing the process of transforming sand into glass.

From Tree to Paper, by Wendy Davis, Scholastic, 1995 – a photo-essay book describing the many steps in the process of producing paper.

RESOURCE BOOKS FOR ADULTS AND CHILDREN

Best Kids Garden Book, by Lance Walheim, Sunset, 1992 – gives detailed instructions on gardening with flowers, vegetables, and herbs, includes a section on tools, compost, and measuring the rain.

Recycle: a Handbook for Kids, by Gail Gibbons, Little, Brown, 1992 – explains how the materials we recycle are processed into new products.

Worms Eat Our Garbage, by Mary Appelhof, Mary Frances Fenton, and Barbara Loss Harris, Flower Press, 1993 – a resource full of classroom activities for a better environment.

NATURE AND US

We have been learning that nature is part of our lives in many different ways, including in our special places and in the materials that we use every day. To care for our special places, we have been learning how to use resources responsibly.

Continue the Learning at Home

Take a walk and bring along a container for collecting small, beautiful items from nature (rocks, leaves, sticks, etc.). Don't forget to follow the collecting rules of the park or trail that you are using. Share your finds with each other and exclaim over their beauty. Decide which items you wish to keep and which to return to nature before going home.

More Fun at Home

Take a picture of your child in one of her favorite outdoor places (or find a picture you have already taken). Create a paper frame for the picture and on the frame write the many ways she cares for this special place (picks up trash, don't pick flowers, and so-on).

Appendix A

Equipping the Classroom for Small Wonders Nature Studies

Although most of the activities included in the Small Wonders program require simple, easy-to-find materials, a few additional books and supplies may enhance your nature studies. In addition, it may be useful to collect or construct a few supplies ahead of time.

HANDY ITEMS TO COLLECT AHEAD OF TIME

The items listed below are used in several activities and may be useful to collect ahead of time.

- **Milk cartons and/or jugs:** Rinse and keep on hand for creating bird feeders and other crafts.
- **Egg cartons:** Can be used for crafts and to store collections of small objects.
- **Magazines/calendars:** A great source of color photographs for illustrating lessons and art projects.
- **Toilet paper and paper towel tubes:** Good to have on hand for craft needs.
- **Plastic containers from items such as yogurt and deli salad:** Variety of sizes for collections and to help organize materials.

MATERIALS TO MAKE AND USE IN A VARIETY OF LESSONS

The materials below are simple to make and are used in many different lessons.

Puppet stage: If you do not already have a puppet stage in your classroom, a simple one can be constructed using a sheet of corrugated cardboard folded in thirds (so that it can stand independently) or a tri-fold cardboard or foam-core presentation board (available at many office supply stores).

Clipboards: Create simple writing surfaces by cutting old cardboard boxes into 9x12 inch rectangles and adding binder clips to the top. To avoid losing pencils during outdoor explorations, tape a string to the pencil and tie it to the binder clip.

Containers for collecting insects: Clean plastic peanut butter or mayonnaise jars work well for collecting insects. Secure a piece of nylon or screening to the top with a rubber band if insects are to be observed for more than a few minutes.

Collection bags: It is nice to provide children with containers they can wear as they collect outdoors. These can be created from something as simple as a gallon-sized zip-top freezer bag. Use duct tape and wide ribbon to attach a shoulder strap to the bag so that the children can wear it as they collect.

Blindfolds: Comfortable blindfolds may be created by cutting two-inch wide strips of fleece and tying the strips around the children's heads. An alternative that the children can easily slip on by themselves can be made by sewing an elastic band to a rectangle of thick felt.

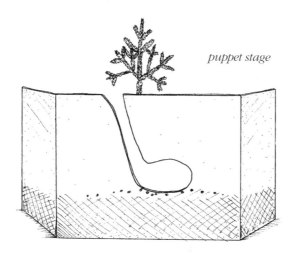

puppet stage

SUPPLIERS OF NATURE RELATED TEACHING SUPPLIES

As your children begin to get involved with the nature study program, you may want to expand your supply of nature study materials with a few purchased supplies. Insect collecting nets and sweep nets, plastic critter containers, and simple binoculars can really enhance your children's field studies. In addition, magnifying lenses, bug boxes, and cloth puppets make great additions to the available classroom supplies. The following is a list of a few suppliers we've found helpful through the years:

Acorn Naturalists
www.acornnaturalists.com
(800) 422-8886
Acorn has an extensive variety of resources for the trail and classroom – from books and puppets, to owl pellets and bug boxes.

BioQuip
www.bioquip.com
(310) 324-0620
BioQuip has books, nets, plant presses, and other hard-to-find resources for science discoveries.

Frey Scientific
www.freyscientific.com
(800) 225-FREY
Frey has an extensive selection of science resources for the classroom.

Lakeshore Learning Materials
www.lakeshorelearning.com
(800) 428-4414
Lakeshore has a wide array of classroom educational materials appropriate for young children.

Nature Watch
www.nature-watch.com
(800) 228-5816
Nature Watch has posters, games, skull replicas, animal skins, rock sets, track stamps.

SUGGESTED RESOURCES

The resources listed below represent just a few of the excellent reference materials available on natural history and environmental education topics.

General Field Guides

Eyewitness Guides (Dorling Kindersley) – Eyewitness produces a number of field guides on a range of topics. Some guides have companion videos as well.

Golden Guides (Golden Press) – These small, inexpensive field guides provide background and information for identifying and learning about a variety of animal species and habitats.

Peterson First Field Guides (Houghton Mifflin) – These introductory field guides address the most common species of insects, mammals, birds, trees, and other natural history topics by theme.

Peterson Field Guides (Houghton Mifflin) – These are comprehensive field guides that cover a range of topics from birds to mammals to reptiles.

Beyond Identification

Discover Nature (Stackpole Books) – This series covers a range of topics and suggest projects for curious naturalists.

Nature Smart: A Family Guide to Nature, by Stan Tekiela and Karen Shanberg (Adventure Publications) – A good, basic guide packed with general facts about groups of animals and information on common species.

Stokes Nature Guides (Little, Brown) – These nature guides provide abundant background information on topics including insect behavior, bird behavior, and animal tracking.

Sibley Guides (National Audubon Society) – These guides provide in-depth bird identification and natural history information.

Teaching Resources

Hands-On Nature: Information and Activities for Exploring the Environment with Children, by Jenepher Lingelbach and Lisa Purcell, eds. (Vermont Institute of Natural Science) – *Hands-On Nature* provides a wealth of information and activities for exploring nature with elementary-aged children.

Mudworks: Creative Clay, Dough, and Modeling Experiences, by Maryann Kohl (Bright Ring Publishing) – Kohl offers a wide variety of clay and dough recipes as well as modeling activities.

Sharing Nature with Children: 20th Anniversary Edition, by Joseph Bharat Cornell (Dawn Publications) – This edition contains many nature awareness activities that are appropriate for young children.

Four Seasons Movement, Jean Warren and Kathleen Kubley eds. (School Specialty) – Finger plays cover a number of seasonal themes.

101 Science Poems & Songs for Young Learners, by Meish Goldish (Scholastic) – Goldish provides science-themed poems, rhymes, and finger plays for young children.

500 Five Minute Games, by Jackie Silberg (Gryphon House) – Silberg offers a rich array of finger plays and short games for young children.

Great Explorations in Math and Science (GEMS) (Lawrence Hall of Science, Berkeley California) – This series of science curriculum guides is thematically organized (for example, animal defenses, eggs). Their "peaches" series includes activities appropriate for young children.

Little Hands (Williamson Publishing) – This series of books covers a range of topics, including activities in science and nature.

Children's Periodicals

Wild Animal Baby (The National Wildlife Federation) – Contains stories, activities, and finger plays for children ages 12 months to 4 years.

Your Big Backyard (The National Wildlife Federation) – Contains natural history information, stories, and activities written for children ages 3 to 7.

Zoobooks (Wildlife Education Ltd.) – While the text in *Zoobooks* is geared more toward older children, young children enjoy the photographs and illustrations they find in *Zoobooks* magazines.

Appendix B

Small Wonders Activities and Early Childhood Learning Standards

A variety of organizations, including the National Association for the Education of Young Children (NAEYC), as well as individual states, have developed standards that are intended to guide early childhood education. *Small Wonders* addresses many of these standards. The nature-based units incorporate multidisciplinary education and are structured so that each unit has at least one activity in each of the following areas:

- whole body
- group cooperation
- independent exploration
- child directed
- open-ended
- experimentation/inquiry science
- the imagination/role playing

The following is a list of content areas commonly found in standards documents. Underneath each content area is a list of the types of standards that various *Small Wonders* activities address. The skills you address in your program will depend on the standards document you are referencing, the activities that you choose, as well as the ages of the children in your care.

SCIENCE AND INQUIRY

Investigating the Environment

A variety of *Small Wonders* activities encourage children to

- use the five senses to explore and observe,
- ask questions about the natural world,
- explore and manipulate natural materials,
- use simple scientific tools (for example, a balance scale or magnifying lens) in their explorations,
- predict and or explore answers to questions posed,
- collect, describe, and record information,
- and engage in conversations about plants, animals, and other natural phenomena.

Scientific Concepts and Principles

A variety of *Small Wonders* activities support children as they learn about

- changes in their environment (day, night, seasonal change, etc.),
- the basic needs of life,
- life cycles,
- the properties of non-living materials (rock, soil, water),
- and the structure and property of matter (floating and sinking, dissolving, and melting).

A variety of *Small Wonders* activities provide children opportunities to

- discuss scientific concepts.

EARLY LITERACY DEVELOPMENT

A variety of *Small Wonders* activities provide children opportunities to

- record information using a variety of means,
- create stories,
- participate in read-alouds and book discussions,
- and create links between books to other curriculum areas.

LANGUAGE DEVELOPMENT

A variety of *Small Wonders* activities encourage children to

- compare and contrast objects with similarities and differences,
- describe objects in terms of their properties,
- independently provide explanations of phenomena,
- develop vocabulary through conversations, indoor and outdoor experiences, and read-alouds,
- and discuss their discoveries, reactions, and thoughts.

MATHEMATICS

A variety of *Small Wonders* activities encourage children to

- sort, compare, and classify objects,
- create displays of data (graphs, pictures, etc.),
- identify shapes,
- and experiment with a variety of tools to make measurements.

UNDERSTANDING OURSELVES, OUR COMMUNITIES, AND OUR WORLD

A variety of *Small Wonders* activities provide children opportunities to

- explore their local environment.

PHYSICAL DEVELOPMENT AND SKILLS

A variety of *Small Wonders* activities support children as they work to develop

- fine motor skills,
- and gross motor skills.

VISUAL AND CREATIVE ARTS

A variety of *Small Wonders* activities encourage children to

- explore different art tools and materials,
- engage in creative movement/dramatic play,
- and use and/or create a variety of props and materials in dramatic situations.

SOCIAL/DEVELOPMENTAL

A variety of *Small Wonders* activities provide children opportunities to

- engage in activities that involve group cooperation,
- engage in activities that are self-directed,
- and practice following directions.

Glossary

A **Abdomen** – For insects, the third segment of the body; for spiders, the second segment of the body. Contains the digestive and reproductive organs.

Adaptation – Structures or behaviors that help a plant or animal meet the demands of its environment.

Adhesion – The tendency of water to stick to or bond with surfaces.

Air sac (birds) – A bubble of air at the wide end of an egg.

Albumen – Egg white. The albumen provides nutrition and liquid to a developing embryo.

Altricial – A bird or mammal that hatches in a helpless and poorly developed state (blind and naked).

Amphibian – A cold-blooded animal characterized by moist skin and a life cycle that often involves both water and land.

Antennae – Paired sensory appendages located on top of the heads of some animals.

Anther – Anthers produce pollen in flowers. They are located on top of the stamen.

Anura – The group (order in the biological classification system) of amphibians that frogs belong to.

Arachnid – All spiders are scientifically classified in a subgroup of animals called arachnids. Arachnids are arthropods with jointed legs, exoskeletons, eight legs, and two body sections.

Arthropod – A group of invertebrate animals having exoskeletons and characterized by a segmented body and jointed legs. Insects, centipedes, crustaceans, and spiders are just a few examples of arthropods.

Axis (Earth) – An imaginary line running through the North and South poles around which the earth rotates.

Avian – Relating to birds.

B **Barb** (feather) – Parallel strands that attach on either side of the central feather shaft. Barbs create the flat surface of a feather.

Barbicel – A hook-like extension on the barbule of a feather that links the barbules together, creating a smooth flight surface.

Barbules (feather) – Thin, hair-like filaments that fringe the barbs of some types of feathers.

Bee bread – A combination of pollen and nectar.

Biodegradable – Made of material that can be decomposed and recycled into the environment by biological agents (such as bacteria).

Blade (birds) – The flat surface of a feather.

Bounders – Bounders place their front feet next to each other, and then leap forward so that their two back feet fall into the prints just vacated by the front feet. These long-bodied, "slinky"-like animals include weasels, otters, skunks, and mink.

Bridge (turtles) – The portion of a turtle shell that joins the carapace and plastron.

Bulb – Modified stem and leaf layers used for food storage or reproduction.

C **Cache** – The act of storing items in a hidden location; a hidden place where items are stored.

Cambium – The growth tissue in a tree, located just under the bark.

Camouflage – Elements of an animal's color, behavior, or morphology that help it blend in with its environment.

Canid – Belonging to the dog family.

Canines – A set of four pointed teeth that are found next to the incisors. Canines are used by flesh eating animals to grip and tear their food.

Cavity nest – A nest placed in a hole or hollowed area.

Carapace – The top of a turtle shell.

Carnivore – An animal that eats meat.

Casting – A pile of worm excrement.

Caterpillar – Larva of a butterfly or moth.

Cell (bees) – A single hexagonal compartment in a beehive.

Cephalothorax – Fused head and thorax.

Chalazae – Twisted, ropelike strands of protein that suspend an egg yolk in the center of the egg, protecting it from damage.

Chelicerae (spiders) – A spider's fangs.

Chemical weathering – The breakup of rock by chemical processes, such as the dissolution of rock by chemicals in the roots of lichen.

Chitin – Tough, flexible protein that forms the exoskeleton of insects, spiders, and other arthropods. Chitin is similar to the protein that forms human fingernails and hair.

Chrysalis – A hard case covering the pupa stage of an insect (often used in reference to butterflies).

Clitellum – A swollen band near the earthworm's head that is used in reproduction.

Cohesion (water) – The tendency of water to stick to itself.

Comb – A collection of cells within a beehive.

Cold-blooded – Animals that depend on their environment for heat.

Complete metamorphosis – A staged development of an insect involving an egg, larva, pupa, and adult. The immature form of the insect appears completely different than the parent.

Compost – The process of setting aside organic matter and allowing it to decay into material that can be used to enrich soil.

Compound eyes – In insects, eyes composed of multiple facets, or lenses. Each lens receives a small portion of the entire picture the grasshopper experiences.

Condensation – The conversion of water vapor to liquid or ice.

Condensation nucleus – a small particle around which condensation begins.

Cones – The reproductive organs of coniferous trees. These structures release and capture pollen and create seeds, performing a role performed by flowers in other types of plants

Conifer/coniferous – Trees with leaves shaped like needles or scales and that bear cones. Conifers are usually evergreen, holding their leaves throughout the year.

Corm – A modified plant stem used for reproduction or food storage.

Crepuscular – Animals that are most active at dawn and dusk.

Cross-pollination – Occurs when pollen from one flower fertilizes another flower of the same species.

Cryptic coloration – Coloration that helps an animal blend into its surroundings (many owls have cryptic coloration that helps them blend in with tree bark).

D **Deciduous** – Trees that have leaves that are broad and flat. Deciduous trees drop their leaves, usually once a year.

Decomposer – An organism that helps break down dead material.

Diurnal – Animals that are active primarily during daylight hours.

Dormancy – A period of plant or animal inactivity, or biological rest, that helps it survive periods of environmental stress, such as winter.

Down – Soft, fluffy feathers that lack barbules. Down is found on young birds or under the outer feathers of some species of adult birds.

Dragline (spiders) – An escape line that a spider creates out of silk and uses to drop away from its web to escape predators. Dragline silk is also used to construct the scaffold for a spider web.

Drone – A male bee.

E **Ear tuft** – A tuft of feathers located on the upper portion of some owl's heads, such as the great horned owl. (Ear tufts are not related to ears or used in hearing.)

Echolocation – Navigation by the emission of high-pitched sounds and reception and interpretation of their echoes.

Endosperm – The portion of a seed that nourishes the developing plant.

Erosion – The process of moving rock from one place to another.

Evaporation – The conversion of water from a liquid to a gaseous state.

Evolution/evolve – To change genetically over generations.

Exoskeleton – A hard covering that functions as an exterior skeleton, such as that of an insect's body.

Eye spot – A marking on an animal that looks like an eye and is intended to either distract a predator or to deceive it into thinking a small animal is large (many butterflies have eye spots on their wings).

F **Facial disk** – Circles of fine feathers around an owl's face. The facial disk helps funnel sound to the owl's ear openings.

Fecund – An animal that produces many offspring.

Felid – Belonging to the cat family.

Field bees – Worker bees in the second half of their lifespan that primarily locate and collect pollen and nectar.

Filament – In flowers, the structure that holds the anther.

Flower – A structure that holds the reproductive organs of some plants. A flower may contain male reproductive parts, female reproductive parts, or both.

Forewings – The first pair of wings on an insect's body, located closest to the insect's head.

Frost line – The point at which the ground below no longer freezes.

Fungi – Organisms (including mushrooms, molds, yeasts, and mildews) that reproduce with spores and sustain themselves by absorbing nutrients from organic material. Fungi are important decomposers and are neither plants nor animals.

 Galloper – Gallopers typically push off with their front feet, causing their bodies to become airborne for a moment before their back feet land around the outside and a little bit further forward than their front feet. The track pattern of a galloper will show hind footprints actually in front of the front footprints.

Geologist – A scientist who studies the earth and earth processes.

Geology – The study of the earth and earth processes, including the study of rocks.

Germinal spot – A white spot on an egg yolk containing the female genetic material.

Germinate – To begin to grow.

Gills – Structures fish and many amphibians use to breathe underwater.

Gizzard – A strong, muscular organ used to grind food. Found in birds and some invertebrates

Gravity – The force of attraction between two masses, or objects. The larger object exerts a greater force on the smaller objects.

Ground squirrel – Squirrels that live in earthen burrows. Ground squirrels include groundhogs and eastern chipmunks.

Grub – Beetle and other worm-like larvae.

 Habitat – The environment in which a plant grows or an animal lives.

Herbivore – An animal that eats only plants.

Hermaphrodite – An organism that has both male and female reproductive organs.

Herpetologist – A scientist who studies reptiles and amphibians.

Hibernation/hibernator – An animal whose body systems all but shut down during their winter's sleep. A hibernating animal's body temperature usually drops to just above freezing, while its heartbeat and respiration are greatly slowed (sometimes nearly undetectable). Hibernators include woodchucks (also known as groundhogs), jumping mice, and the little brown bat.

Hindwings – The second pair of wings on an insect's body, located closest to the abdomen.

Hive – The structure in which bees live, also used to refer to the bee colony itself.

Honey stomach – Sac within a honeybee used to store nectar.

Hopper – Hoppers typically push off with their front feet, causing their bodies to become airborne for a moment, before their back feet land around the outside and a little bit further forward than their front feet. The track pattern of a hopper will show hind footprints actually in front of the front footprints.

House bee – A worker bee in the first three weeks of its life. Jobs of a house bee include: cleaning old cells, producing royal jelly, feeding larvae, secreting wax to build and repair the hive, packing pollen and honey in cells, and guarding the entrance of the hive.

 Igneous rocks – Rocks formed from lava or magma that was once a liquid rock but solidified as it cooled at or near the earth's surface.

Incisors – Paired front teeth used for cutting and tearing food. In rodents, incisors grow throughout the animal's lifetime to combat abrasion from hard foods.

Incomplete metamorphosis – Three stage development of an insect: egg, nymph, adult. In incomplete metamorphosis, the nymph stage resembles the adult, also referred to as simple metamorphosis.

Insectivorous – Eats insects.

Invertebrate – An animal without a backbone.

Iris – The colored part of the eye. The iris contracts and expands to regulate the amount of light that entering the eye.

 Keratin – Tough, flexible material that forms fingernails and hair, feathers, and other animal parts.

 Larva – An immature stage of an animal that does not resemble the adult form.

Leaves – In plants, usually the principal surface of photosynthesis and transpiration.

Life span – The average time from birth to death that an animal species is expected to live.

Long-horned grasshopper – A group of grasshoppers that have antennae that are longer than the length of their bodies.

 Mammal – Warm-blooded animals that are covered with fur or hair and that feed their young milk.

Mandible (insects) – Mouth parts used to grab and take apart food

Mass – A quantity of matter.

Matter – A physical body that occupies space and has mass. Matter can exist as a solid, liquid, or gas.

Megabat – A group of primarily fruit-eating bats. Most have large eyes and depend on keen eyesight and their sense of smell, rather than echolocation, to locate food.

Metamorphic rocks – Igneous and sedimentary rocks (and even other metamorphic rocks) that were buried deep in the earth's crust and changed under heat and pressure before re-emerging at the earth's surface.

Metamorphosis – A series of developmental stages and changes by which an immature animal transforms into an adult. Metamorphosis involves a change in appearance and often a change in behavior as well.

Microbat – Group of bats, generally small in size, and primarily insect eaters. Microbats use echolocation to find food and are found on every continent but Antarctica.

Midden – A pile or grouping of material.

Migrate/Migration – Seasonal movement of animals in search of food, breeding areas, or warmer temperatures.

Molar – Flat, back teeth used for grinding.

Molt – Occurs when a growing insect sheds its exoskeleton, or outer skin. The skin underneath is somewhat stretchy and slightly larger than the old skin, and thus can accommodate the insect's growth.

Mutualism – A relationship between organisms in which both benefit.

Natural resource – A material that comes from nature and that people can change and/or use to make new things.

Needles – Small, slender leaves found on evergreen trees.

Nocturnal – Animals that are active at night.

Node – The attachment point of a leaf or bud on a stem.

Nonrenewable resource – A resource whose supply is limited: once used up, it cannot be recreated.

Nuclear fusion – A reaction in which two atoms combine into one, releasing tremendous amounts of energy.

Nymph – An immature form of an insect that undergoes incomplete metamorphosis. Nymphs resemble small versions of the adult insect, but lack wings.

Omnivore – An animal that eats both meat and plants.

Orbit – The path one celestial object takes around another.

Order – One of the taxonomic levels used to group organisms.

Ovary – In plants, the basal portion of the pistil, which contains the ovules and often ripens to form the fruit of the plant.

Ovipositor – An organ of a female insects' abdomen used to deposit eggs.

Ovule (plants) – A tiny structure that turns into a seed after fertilization.

Oxygen – An atmospheric gas essential for plant and animal respiration (plants produce oxygen by day, and use oxygen at night to convert sugar into energy). Oxygen composes 21% of the atmosphere.

Owl pellet – A pellet of indigestible material (such as fur and bones) regurgitated by an owl several hours after a meal.

Palps – Appendages near the mouth that are used by invertebrates to manipulate food, as sensory extensions, or in locomotion.

Paratoid gland – A poison gland on a toad.

Pedipalps – The second pair of appendages located near the mouths of spiders. Pedipalps are used to manipulate food and to sense the environment.

Perennial – A plant that grows year after year.

Pheromones – A chemical emitted by an animal (often insects) and used to communicate between members of the same species. Pheromones may also be used to affect the development of individuals within a species as well.

Photosynthesis – The process by which a plant uses carbon dioxide and sunlight to produce energy and oxygen.

Physical weathering – The breakup of rock by physical processes, such as a plant root wedging into a crack.

Pips – Apple seeds.

Pistil – The female reproductive organ of a flower (consists of a stigma, style, and ovary).

Plastron – The bottom of a turtle shell.

Pollen – Fine powder containing the male gametes of flowers, found on the anther in flowers.

Pollen basket – A structure used to collect and transport pollen. The pollen basket is located on the back leg of a honeybee.

Pollen brush – Stiff hairs on the honeybee's legs used to comb pollen off the body.

Pollen Tube – Grows after a pollen grain lands on a flower's stigma. The pollen tube grows from the pollen grain down the style allowing the pollen to fertilize the ovules contained within the pistil's ovaries.

Polliwog – A hatchling frog.

Precocial – Baby birds that are well developed upon hatching and can soon fly and fend for themselves.

Predation – The act of a predator hunting, killing, and eating another animal.

Predator – An animal that hunts and eats other animals.

Preen – Smoothing and cleaning feathers with the beak/bill.

Prey – Animals that are eaten by predators.

Proboscis (insects) – A thin, tubular mouthpart some species of insects use for **feeding.**

Pupa/pupate – The third stage of complete metamorphosis in insects, in which the larvae transform into adults, usually within a cocoon or hardened case. The pupal stage usually involves a great internal reorganization of the insect.

Q **Queen bee** – The dominant female in the hive. She represents the only fertile female and does all the egg laying.

R **Renewable resource** – A resource that replaces itself unless overuse, contamination, or other condition interferes with its regeneration. Wind, water, and solar energy are often also considered renewable resources, as they can be used to create power without using nonrenewable resources.

Reptile – Animals that are cold-blooded, use lungs to breathe, have dry, scaly skin, and (virtually all) lay eggs (usually with leathery shells).

Revolve – To circle around a central point, such as the sun.

Rhizome – A stem that grows horizontally.

Rodent – Family of mammals distinguished by their paired upper and lower front teeth that grow throughout the animal's lifetime to combat abrasion from hard foods.

Roost (birds) – A resting place.

Rootstock – A rooted portion of a plant used in plant propagation.

Rotate (planets) – To spin around an axis.

Royal jelly – A glandular secretion produced by worker bees.

S **Scales** (conifers) – Small, overlapping leaves in some coniferous species that resemble the scales of a reptile or fish (found, for example, on red and white cedar).

Scion – A budding twig used in grafting trees.

Scutes – The divisions, or scales, on top of a turtle's shell.

Sedimentary rock – Rocks formed from physical or chemical particles that have been cemented together (for example, sandstone and salt).

Seedling – A young plant growing from a seed.

Setae – Bristle-like hairs found on earthworms.

Shaft (bird) – The central hollow tube that gives a feather its rigidity.

Short-horned grasshopper – A group of grasshoppers that have antennae shorter than the length of their bodies.

Silk (spiders) – A fiber-like protein produced by spiders. Spiders can produce many types of silk, according to its potential use.

Simple eyes – Organs that sense light and dark, but that cannot see images.

Smelt – To melt or fuse ore to extract metals.

Solutes – A substance that has been dissolved in a solution.

Solvent – A liquid that is capable of dissolving other substances.

Snowpack – An accumulation of snow.

Species – A group of animals capable of interbreeding. For example wood frogs are a species of frog. They are uniquely identifiable and can breed with each other, producing viable young.

Spiderlings – Tiny baby spiders.

Spinnerets – Appendages on a spider's abdomen that helps them produce silk.

Spiracles (insect or spider) – Breathing holes in the exoskeleton.

Spore – Small, usually single-celled, reproductive structure used by some plants such as ferns.

Stamen – The male reproductive organ on a flower, consists of an anther and a filament.

Stigma – A sticky platform located at the top of a flower's pistil (female reproductive organ), receives pollen from pollinators or wind.

Stomata – Small pores in the leaf blade or stem that open and close to regulate gas exchange and water loss as the leaf photosynthesizes.

Stridulation – A sound produced when an insect rubs two body parts (such as wings) together.

Style (flower) – Portion of the pistil that connects the stigma to the ovaries.

Sublimation – The conversion of water from the solid to gaseous state.

Subnivean – A layer of space between the snowpack and the frozen ground that develops throughout the winter.

T **Tadpole** – A hatchling frog.

Terrapin – Any species of turtle that is used for food.

Thorax (insects) – The second section of the body. The legs and wings attach to the thorax, and the thorax contains the muscles that power the legs and wings.

Torpor – Dormancy or hibernation.

Tortoise – A turtle that lives on land.

Track pattern – The sequence of an animal's tracks. Serves as an indicator of the animal's gait (walking, galloping, etc.).

Transpiration – Occurs when plants give off water vapor through their pores.

Transpire – The release of vapor through tiny holes in a plant's leaf or stem.

Tree squirrels – Squirrels that focus their lives around trees. Tree squirrels include gray squirrels, red squirrels, and southern and northern flying squirrels

Trotters – Animals that move by placing their hind feet into the prints made by their front feet (left hind foot falling into the depression made by the left front foot). The result is a nearly straight line of tracks.

Trunk – The enlarged, central, wooden stem of a tree.

Tuber – A stem modified for underground food storage or propagation.

Tympanum – In frogs, an exterior ear drum.

U **Ultrasound** – High-pitched sounds, inaudible to humans.

Underwings – The hind wings of an insect located closest to the insect's abdomen.

Ungulate – Mammals with hoofed feet.

V **Veins** (trees) – Structures that transport water and nutrients from the roots to the leaf and distribute the sugars and starches produced by photosynthesis to various areas of the tree, including the roots.

Venom – Poisonous secretion that is usually injected into the target animal by a bite or a sting.

W **Waddlers** – Waddlers leave a trail of big and little tracks as they move forward, with their larger hind feet planted next to their smaller front feet in a motion similar to how a human baby crawls. Waddlers are chubby animals – raccoons and porcupines, for example.

Walkers – Animals that move by placing their hind feet into the prints made by their front feet (left hind foot falling into the depression made by the left front foot). The result is a nearly straight line of tracks.

Wanderers – Spiders that do not weave webs.

Water cycle – The process of moving water around the atmosphere and earth's surface through evaporation, condensation, and precipitation.

Wax glands – Glands on the bee's abdomen that produce wax.

Web weavers – Spiders that weave webs.

Worker bee – Sterile female bee that performs the majority of tasks in the bee colony, including gathering nectar and pollen, making honey, feeding young, and tending the queen.

Y **Yolk** – The yolk of an egg provides nutrition in the final stages of chick development.

Index

Notes

Notes

Notes

Notes

Notes

Notes